9/13/18

TINKER

to

EVERS

to

CHANCE

TINKER
to
EVERS
to
CHANCE

The Chicago Cubs

and the Dawn of

Modern America

DAVID RAPP

THE UNIVERSITY OF CHICAGO PRESS CHICAGO & LONDON

The University of Chicago Press, Chicago 60637
The University of Chicago Press, Ltd., London
Published 2018
Printed in the United States of America

27 26   25 24 23 22 21 20 19 18   1 2 3 4 5

ISBN-13: 978-0-226-41504-8 (cloth)
ISBN-13: 978-0-226-41518-5 (e-book)
DOI: https://doi.org/10.7208/chicago/[9780226415185].001.0001

Frontispiece photo (*left to right*): Joe Tinker, Johnny Evers, and
Frank Chance. (National Baseball Hall of Fame and Museum,
Cooperstown, NY.)

Epigraph poem: "That Double Play Again," by F. P. Adams, as it first
appeared in the *New York Evening Mail*, July 12, 1910. (Microfilm
image courtesy of Jack Bales.)

Library of Congress Cataloging-in-Publication Data

Names: Rapp, David, 1951– author.
Title: Tinker to Evers to Chance : the Chicago Cubs and the dawn of
    modern America / David Rapp.
Description: Chicago ; London : The University of Chicago Press,
    2018. | Includes bibliographical references and index.
Identifiers: LCCN 2017041630 | ISBN 9780226415048 (cloth : alk.
    paper) | ISBN 9780226415185 (e-book)
Subjects: LCSH: Chicago Cubs (Baseball team)—History. | Evers,
    Johnny. | Tinker, Joe, 1880–1948. | Chance, Frank L. (Frank
    Leroy), 1877–1924. | Baseball—History.
Classification: LCC GV875.C6 R36 2018 | DDC 796.357/640977311—dc23
LC record available at https://lccn.loc.gov/2017041630

♾ This paper meets the requirements of ANSI/NISO Z39.48-1992
(Permanence of Paper).

To my father,
ROBERT M. RAPP
(1925–2011)

That Double Play Again.

These are the saddest of possible words:
  "Tinker to Evers to Chance."
Trio of bear cubs, and fleeter than birds,
  Tinker and Evers and Chance.
Ruthlessly pricking our gonfalon bubble,
Making a Giant hit into a double—
Words that are heavy with nothing but trouble:
  "Tinker to Evers to Chance."

CONTENTS

PREFACE

"Baseball's Sad Lexicon"

On the afternoon of July 12, 1910, in the midst of another fevered pennant race between the Chicago Cubs and the New York Giants, a young scribbler for the *New York Evening Mail* had a brainstorm, which he quickly turned into a nifty piece of light verse. It began with these simple lines:

> These are the saddest of possible words:
> "Tinker to Evers to Chance."

Little did he know that his odd little couplet, with three more to follow, would soon become the manifesto for an epic American saga.

The writer, Franklin Pierce Adams, had just wrapped up his column "All in Good Humor," in which he routinely mixed stray bits of insider gossip with wisecracks and clever rhymes, including many submitted by his readers. Having shipped off his copy to the composing room, F.P. was about to head uptown to take in a baseball game when an urgent phone call stopped him. The copy he had just turned in was eight lines short!

Not to worry, Adams reassured his presstime-weary typesetters. Eight more lines coming up.

A man of "biting, brilliant wit," F. P. Adams would one day claim a charter seat at the Algonquin Round Table, where he matched bon mots daily with the likes of Dorothy Parker, Robert Benchley, and other quick-thinking aphorists. Adams would remain a member of the Manhattan literati and celebrity circuit until his death in 1960. The highbrow pundit had one plebeian eccentricity, however: he was a rabid baseball fan—and, as a transplant from Chicago, he remained ever faithful to his Cubs.

F.P. had no doubt seen the morning reports on a game played the day before, between the Cubs and their perennial rival Giants, at Chicago's West Side Grounds. The Cubs were on their way to another National League pennant, and they had frustrated the New Yorkers once again, this time by a score of 4–2.

A key point in the match turned out to be a smart defensive play in the top of the eighth inning—a rally-killing double play, from shortstop to second to first. From deep in the box score, next to the notation for double plays, jumped out the providential words:

Tinker to Evers to Chance

Adams quickly improvised a snatch of doggerel worthy of the Algonquin crowd, mocking the despair that his New York cronies felt whenever a ground ball landed within range of Chicago's slick infield combo: shortstop Joe Tinker, second baseman Johnny Evers, and first baseman Frank Chance.

"That Double Play Again," later retitled "Baseball's Sad Lexicon," was an immediate, nationwide sensation. Adams's good friend and poetic protégé, Grantland Rice, reprinted it in Nashville's *Tennessean*, as did many other sports editors. Would-be rhymesters among them followed Rice's lead and attached their own hasty stanzas in Adams's meter and cadence. They sent their rebuttals to F.P. via telegraph, and he dutifully printed them in the *Mail* with his own variations. This merry-go-round kept up for weeks, a 1910 version of "viral" social media.

Adams's inspired use of the word "gonfalon"—a medieval Italian term for a banner or flag with pointed streamers—anchors his obscure evocation of "pennant fever." In eight quick lines and one unforgettable refrain, he manages to capture a piece of the American psyche. As the *New York Evening Mail*'s managing editor Theophilus England Niles said to Grantland Rice at the time, "Frank may write a better piece of verse, but this is the one he'll be remembered for."

A century later, "Lexicon" remains the second most famous poem about baseball, after "Casey at the Bat." But unlike "Casey," a nineteenth-century shaggy-dog story about a fictional slugger's inglorious strike-out, Adams's terse ditty used a different kind of irony to celebrate three living ballplayers and their sport's newfound status as the "national pastime."

All manner of mass entertainment, from vaudeville houses and movie nickelodeons to college football games and big league baseball, had emerged in the first decade of the century, offering the surging number of city dwellers myriad ways to counter the stress and fears of urban life. Their escapes into theaters and sporting arenas were both entertaining and socially uplifting. But it was baseball, most of all, that provided thousands of men and women from all stations in life a rallying point for their burgeoning civic pride and social identity.

Something began to happen during this decade that America had not seen before. Baseball games started drawing twenty thousand to thirty thousand fans, even on weekday afternoons—double, triple, and quadruple the usual attendance of the previous decade. The new passion spilled out of the rickety ballparks into streets, saloons, and middle-class parlors. No radio existed yet to broadcast games, but ubiquitous newspapers discovered they could sell hundreds of extra copies by printing partial, middle-inning scores in their afternoon editions. Other outlets of popular culture of the day followed suit. To-day's seventh-inning-stretch anthem, "Take Me Out to the Ballgame," first appeared on Tin Pan Alley in 1908 in sheet-music form. Its little-known verse sets up the now universally recognized chorus, introducing a winsome tale of a young "Katie Casey," who "had the fever and had it bad," and who tells her suitor there's only one place she wants to go on their afternoon date.

Men and women, young and old, caught up in "baseball fever," wanted to take in a ball game.

As a youth-inspired leisure movement, baseball mania gave Americans the means and the permission to peel off an older generation's preoccupation with duty, piety, and "self-improvement." Such Victorian-era notions had governed society over much of the previous century. Crosscutting political and business pressures also emerged at this hour to fuel other forms of cultural awakening, including the Progressive reform movement and the rise of its nominal leader, President Theodore Roosevelt. The rough-and-tumble city of Chicago quickly became the epicenter of this awakening, the Chicago Cubs baseball club its crowd-pleasing exemplar.

From 1906 through 1910, the Cubs of Tinker, Evers, and Chance established an assembly line of victories, a veritable baseball machine, and as Adams's poem suggests, the singsong sequence of their names became synonymous with the twentieth-century notion of smooth and ruthless efficiency. They won 530 regular-season games over five consecutive seasons—a major league record to this day. The Cubs laid claim to World Series trophies in 1907 and 1908, in addition to their four National League pennants. The word most often heard to describe the Chicago Cubs' dynasty in those days was "invincible." The team's five years of baseball brilliance only gained in mythic stature during the century and more of frustration that dogged the franchise thereafter.

By the mid-twentieth century, the phrase "Tinker to Evers to Chance" became an American idiom as expressive—and as ubiquitous—as "slam dunk" is today, conveying much the same meaning. The trio didn't start out that way, of course. Joe Tinker, Johnny Evers, and Frank Chance were an unlikely assemblage of clashing personalities, layered and complicated family histories, and inexpressible ambitions. Each grew up during the late 1880s and 1890s in different regions of the nation, and each learned to play baseball according to the customs and expectations of his local culture: Evers in the Irish American hothouse of Troy, New York; Tinker in the urban parklands of Kansas City, Missouri; Chance in the rich fields of California's Central Valley.

They came together in Chicago in 1903 under the patient tutelage of a baseball mastermind named Frank Selee, a native New Englander and the manager of Chicago's National League team, which went by a variety of names. Newspaper reporters chuckled at the boyish looks and inexperience of Selee's motley crew and dubbed them his "Cubbies." But Selee soon fashioned the kids into a cohesive unit that could compete against the powerhouse ball clubs of the day: John McGraw's Giants, Honus Wagner's Pittsburgh Pirates, and Ty Cobb's Detroit Tigers. The Cubs of Tinker, Evers, and Chance would soon dominate them all with exasperating regularity.

This book is about a long-forgotten baseball team and the social transformation in America that their unrivaled success seemed to typify. The Cubs of this era, from 1906 to 1910, serve as a parable of their times and as a foretaste of ours. The stories of these early baseball stars shed unexpected light not only on the evolution of baseball, on the hungers of its players and fans all across America, but also on the broader convulsions of a confident new industrial society.

Their stories also tell us something about the passions and enthusiasm that team sports now engender in American ballparks, stadiums, barrooms, and TV rooms. One of the great cultural stories of the 2010s is the rise of the rebuilt Chicago Cubs—again a team of overachieving youngsters who finally found a way to overcome a century's worth of disappointment and alleged curses to win the 2016 World Series. Underscoring the Cubs' uplifting victory, and making it a cultural touchstone all across America, were the many moving stories of lifelong Cub fans who had waited so long and suffered so patiently in the desert. Such die-hard Cub fans, like me, and great players, like Ernie Banks, waited many long years for this moment, somehow remaining optimistic and ever hopeful. We are no longer a forlorn lot, no longer to be pitied or ridiculed.

The story of "Tinker to Evers to Chance" is also a tale of how baseball came to capture its followers and hold them in such staunch allegiance at the turn of the past century. For the fact is, baseball wasn't always the national pastime; it was on the verge of degenerate collapse just before these three men arrived in Chicago. Their stories, individually and together, show how baseball and America changed alongside each other, merging reality and myth to form a unique American folktale. Their day in the sun is when baseball became baseball as we know it, and when America came into its own as well. In retrospect, it seemed inevitable, almost easy. Just like that: *Tinker to Evers to Chance!*

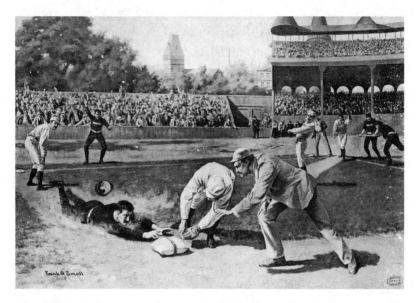

Mike "King" Kelly, baseball's first matinee idol, inspired the cheer "Slide, Kelly, Slide," which became the title of a Tin Pan Alley ditty and a painting hung in many barrooms. (Courtesy of the McGreevey Collection, Boston Public Library.)

BASEBALL'S GOLDEN ERA
AND DARK AGE

He was the ideal baseball athlete. About six feet tall, and his anatomy was moved by an electric engine, guided by an eagle brain, that would see a point in the game and execute it with a lightning move that no one possessed but the late lamented Kelly. TED SULLIVAN, *Humorous Stories of the Ball Field*, 1903

In his long-ago heyday of the 1880s, everyone called him the "King of Baseball." And it was true: Michael Joseph Kelly was the most brilliant ball player of his era. Brighter stars have emerged over the past century and a half, from Babe Ruth to Willie Mays to Mike Trout, relegating Kelly's legend to the deeper recesses of baseball memory. But the lad could play the game with the best of them. And he knew how to put on a show.

Baseball bards still slap their knees about the day Kelly made a leaping, circus catch—both arms reaching high above the right-field fence—to steal a potential game-winning home run. "Three out," the umpire barked as a beaming Kelly emerged from the gloaming. "Game called because of darkness," the ump declared. Trotting back to the bench, the Celtic imp gave his teammates a sly grin as he opened his empty palms. "It went a mile over me head!"

King Kel's proud and erect bearing, charismatic good looks, and rascal charm found a perfect daily outlet on the "diamond field," which he turned into his personal stage. And as baseball fanatics would someday do for Babe Ruth, himself a peerless crowd pleaser, the public followed King Kelly's every move, especially on the base paths. Chants erupted from the grandstand the moment he rounded a base and made a beeline for the next bag: "Slide, Kelly, Slide!" the crowds yelled, creating one of the slang phrases of the era—it later became the title of a Tin Pan Alley ditty and a popular painting that hung on barroom walls.

As his antics multiplied, Kelly acquired a national following. His likeness appeared on posters and in early baseball cards. He was the game's—quite possibly the nation's—first matinee idol. Kelly liked to think of himself as Ernest Thayer's model for "Casey at the Bat"—not so, but some vaudeville houses featured orations of it by King Kel. "Babe Ruth's popularity is a small thing compared to the worship that America lavished upon the King," came the sober assessment of Byron Bancroft "Ban" Johnson, a sportswriter-turned-baseball entrepreneur who witnessed the play of both legends. "How the country adored Mike Kelly!"

A Boston bookseller entreated Kelly to write baseball's first autobiography. *Play Ball* was published in 1888, and in it, with a ghostwriter's help, the King gave voice to an idea that would become a cornerstone of baseball's future popularity: "If I could afford it, I would allow all the small boys, of high or low degree, to witness the ball games free of charge."

Young boys were the lifeblood of the game, Kelly declared. They followed the box scores every day, knew player histories and statistics, and talked baseball constantly to their fathers, mothers, sisters, and cousins. "They make veritable gods of their favorite players at home," which in turn brought people out to the ballpark. "The small boys are a tower of strength to the game of baseball."

Kelly's overt bow to childhood and adolescence was a novel sentiment that didn't conform to nineteenth-century social custom. American children in the first decades after the Civil War still worked from dawn to dusk on family farms or as menial laborers in factories and mills. In rural and urban settings alike, young people were expected to contribute to their families' income until they were old enough to head out on their own. Parents and school authorities were slow to accept the idea that childhood was a distinct period of human maturation, that boys and girls needed ways to develop their bodies and explore their fantasies—that they needed *to play.*

Many adults frowned on child's play, viewing it as a form of idleness or, worse, a product of the "devil's workshop." Parents of this era had grown up in antebellum America, when a strict, puritanical strain of religious belief piled its moral weight on work and repentance. The notion that playing games might build Christian character was anathema to the inheritors of the Calvinist tradition in America. As one Unitarian minister was said to have recalled: "To play at cricket was a sin, in the eyes of the fathers, as much as to dance or to play on an ungodly instrument."

King Kelly's assertion that professional baseball owed its success to a boyhood passion for the game was all but lost on this generation of adults.

Yet times were changing, thanks to a long period of peace and prosperity that followed the Civil War. The trends of industrialization, migration from countryside to city, rising incomes, and shrinking family sizes altered the relationships of adults to children, opening doors to new forms of childhood expression. In the last decades of the nineteenth century, notes historian David I. Macleod, progressive reformers put forward a variety of plans to promote child welfare.

Boys and girls in the 1880s and 1890s had more freedom than their parents had had at midcentury. While child labor laws to restrict the employment of kids in factories and mills were still decades away, more and more families were beginning to enjoy a middle-class lifestyle in which children not only could avoid work but also could lead sheltered and relatively carefree lives. They could be left in school during the day and allowed to roam on weekends and in the summer months. And as kids do when left to their own devices, they invented games to play and then played them endlessly.

Their favorites, featured in numerous books of games of this era, included black tom, red rover, the ever-popular tag, and also run, sheep, run. An 1883 publication, *Games and Songs of American Children*, listed "base-ball" as a rudimentary form of a game "that has become the 'national sport' of America." A book from 1887, *The Tribune Book of Open-Air Sports*, described the game of "rounders," a precursor to baseball, also called "sockey" in some sections of the country. Yet another book, *In Door and Out* (1882), spends a good deal of space on the game of "shinny," played with a "stout leather-covered ball . . . and sticks, shaped like a Golf-stick, but not so heavy at the turn."

These free-form games and many others worked their way into playgrounds, streets, and open fields all over America, invented, improvised, and modified by kids. These games would spawn a national sports craze.

The first organized forms of baseball emerged in New York and other East Coast cities before the Civil War, although these activities had developed mainly as a social diversion for young gentlemen. To late teens and young adults, the American game offered a faster, more athletic, and easier-to-follow pastime than British cricket. Baseball's popularity spread across the country—both north and south—as wartime troops took to filling the long hours between battles. Soldiers took the game home with them, and a National Association of Base Ball Players, founded just before the war, soon grew to four hundred amateur clubs, some as far away from the East Coast as San Francisco and New Orleans.

The rise of baseball was not an isolated occurrence in the leisure customs of nineteenth-century America. Americans were showing new interest in outdoor activities, from skating and sledding to rowing and lawn tennis. Many of these games were adapted from juvenile pastimes by adults. Baseball was one such appropriated amusement, according to historian David Lamoreaux: "Like these other sports, one of the game's obvious attractions was the opportunity it gave its early players—momentarily, at any rate—to relive their childhood."

Baseball kept growing in the early 1870s, mainly as a quasi-professional activity in urban social clubs and recreational leagues. The professional game attracted skilled players and eager spectators, which suggested a business opportunity, and so the National Association of Professional Ball Players formed in 1871 to capitalize on it. But this player-driven outfit could never sustain success in such a loosely regulated environment, where players moved from team to team as it suited them, and clubs rose and fell from season to season (and even in midseason), depending on their ability to field a winning squad and draw a crowd.

This erratic climate changed in 1876 with the formation of the National League of Professional Baseball Clubs, an owner-driven combine known today as the National League. The NLPBC introduced strict player-contract regulations and predictable, summer-long game schedules among its eight charter clubs. The league also developed a relatively sophisticated public relations machine that created a handful of A-list stars like King Kelly and his Chicago teammate Adrian "Cap" Anson, as well as a second tier of such home-team favorites as Dan Brouthers, Buck Ewing, Old Hoss Radbourn, Mickey Welsh, and Tim Keefe.

Paying young men to play baseball and charging an admission fee to watch them remained a questionable proposition in "respectable" society. The Victorian moralists who viewed idle play and leisure activity as an affront to the Protestant work ethic were even more offended by sports professionalism. They ranked the pro game at the same low order as political corruption, social immorality, and demon rum. "I believe the whole tone of the base ball as played today is demoralizing and should be rated with the second class theater," said a leader of the Young Men's Christian Association. Thanks to showmen like King Kelly, however, this was becoming a minority view in the 1880s, even within the YMCA, although some stigma remained.

As more and more Americans moved into towns or cities, the new shop clerks and office workers found companionship and recreation in social and athletic clubs, which effectively replaced the extended farm families they had left behind. Before long the leader of a club in Brooklyn could rhapsodize on the occasions when he and his mates "would forget business and everything else on Tuesday afternoons, go out on the green fields, don our ball suits, and go at it with a rush. At such times we were boys again."

THE GOLDEN ERA

One day in the mid-1880s, King Kelly's White Stockings were hosting the Detroit Wolverines at Chicago's Lake Front Park, and the two teams "were fighting hard for the championship that year," as Detroit pitcher

George "Stump" Weidman later recollected. The score was still tied going into the thirteenth inning, Weidman said, when Kelly kicked off a rally.

King Kel was the star catcher, outfielder, and jack-of-all-trades for the White Stockings, a charter franchise of the National League and its most successful club in the 1880s. Cap Anson called the shots from first base as player-manager, and impresario Albert Spalding took care of the business dealings. And even though the White Stockings' roster was stacked with some of the best players in the game, everyone in the club—including Anson and Spalding—readily acknowledged that Kelly filled the seats. He "was a whole-souled, genial fellow, with a host of friends," Anson said.

On this afternoon, Kelly was about to pull off one of his most audacious stunts, as told (and retold) over the intervening decades. Stump Weidman remembered it clear as day: Kelly had gotten to second base with teammate Ned Williamson on first, and the pair staged a quick double steal. But as lead-runner Kelly barreled safely into third base, a loud shriek pierced the din of the ball park. The King stood up gingerly, limping in pain and slowly wandering over toward second base, where Williamson now stood. "They began talking," Weidman remembered, watching from the pitcher's box while his infielders tossed the ball around to keep loose. "We paid no attention to them."

Play resumed, runners now on second and third, and Kelly still appeared to be in agony over on third base. But just as Weidman began his windup, Kel darted up the line toward home—then he came to a stop halfway, staring straight at Weidman in the pitcher's box. Stump couldn't believe his eyes. "For the life of me I couldn't imagine what sort of jingle Kelly was up to," he said.

Weidman ran toward Kelly, figuring to corner him in a run-down. But Kelly no longer showed any signs of injury as he bolted for home. The speed demon was now chugging down the line "full tilt" as Weidman fired the ball to catcher Charlie Bennett. Bang-bang came a collision of ball and ball players. The ball trickled onto the ground, but the catcher had at least managed to stop Kelly in his tracks before he could cross the plate. Weidman picked up the ball and reached out to tag the King. Danger averted.

What no one had noticed in the melee was *Williamson* now charging home in Kelly's wake. (Williamson later confessed he'd made a shortcut past third base by some fifteen feet while everyone, including the lone umpire, had their eyes fixed on the King.) "Just then," Weidman recounted, "I saw Williamson make a flying leap in to the air. He hurdled [over] . . . Bennett and Kelly lying on the ground." Williamson tumbled onto home plate untouched, scoring the winning run.

The frenzied hometown partisans exploded in a torrent of cheers and delight. They all knew who the star of this game was: the mastermind, King Kelly, who popped up from the ground, brushed himself off, and bowed to an adoring crowd.

The 1880s were the golden era of nineteenth-century baseball, when the game hitched its boisterous, lighthearted play—and still-evolving rulebook—to a new American appetite for watching people play games. (Ned Williamson's leapfrogging was legal at the time, though not for long.) Professional ball players were not just athletic contestants—they were performers, actors, tricksters, and sometimes conjurers. Like the primping poseur in "Casey at the Bat," every ball player from Kelly on down had the same objective: play to the crowd.

Players took their cues from club owners, who staged elaborate entertainments each weekday and Saturday afternoon—though rarely on Sundays, when many Sabbath-observing cities still outlawed ball games, along with vaudeville theater and the circus. Like their show-business counterparts, Chicago owner Spalding and his fellow magnates strived for spectacle. Owners even tried outfitting players in fancy silk costumes with colored patterns on their jerseys and stockings, a quixotic attempt to identify players by position on the field: first basemen wore scarlet with white vertical stripes; second basemen, orange with black vertical stripes; and so on.

No one combined the sport's showmanship with dazzling athletic skills better than Mike Kelly, the Irish American prodigy. The King upheld his regal act off the field—"a sight for the saints to verify"—carousing from pub to pub with his tall, shiny hat cocked, "his cane a-twirling as though he were the entire population, his Ascot held by a giant jewel, his patent leather shoes as sharply pointed as Italian dirks."

One thing muddies the appeal of this rogue's story today, however: he's mostly a product of our imaginations. Kelly's aura, as well as his astounding baseball feats, has been exaggerated over the years—if not wholly made up. He was a spectacular and accomplished player, to be sure. But shopworn anecdotes like the dusk-hour circus catch have no eyewitness sources. Stump Weidman's vivid depiction of his trick play at home plate was probably fiction—or at least has yet to be documented.

Yet these tall tales have taken on a life of their own, right up to the present. Even Weidman took pleasure in recounting the home-plate ruse in 1904, a decade after Kelly had passed from the scene. Weidman died one year later, and his rendering soon morphed into more fanciful versions. Kelly aficionados have appropriated the fable, changed some of its key details (they say Williamson slid between Kelly's legs to score the winning run), and handed it down as the quintessential example of early baseball heroics. But no one cites an eyewitness. Kelly's feats "seemed to come from the tales of Baron Munchhausen or Paul Bunyan," concedes one of the fable's modern raconteurs.

But baseball needed Kelly's lifeblood and his vaudeville air. At the turn of the twentieth century—the start of what's now called the "modern" era of organized baseball—a much more sinister image had taken hold of the game. Baseball had been a raw, untamed sport in Kelly's days, its character and playing styles changing as often as its ground rules. By the 1890s, players, managers, and owners had agreed on most of the rules of play, but they also had entered a much darker period, flirting on the edge of one form of disaster after another, behaving like adolescents lurching through hormonal growing pains. It didn't take long for more nefarious actors to change the game.

The playful tricks and "manly competition" that Kelly had made popular in the 1880s took on the pall of "dirty ball playing" in the subsequent decade. Friendly razzing between players and baseball "cranks," as patrons were called, mutated into crude, loud, and abusive language. Both players and spectators routinely engaged in testosterone-laden brawls on the field and in the stands. The game's joy and innocent good humor, as personified by Kelly and his crowd-pleasing pranks, had descended into fin de siècle depravity.

The fun had gone out of Kelly's life, too, as he soon drank himself into an early grave. By the time he died of pneumonia in 1894, just three weeks short of his thirty-seventh birthday, King Kel was a spent force, no longer loved or appreciated. Organized baseball seemed likewise headed for its own self-indulgent dissolution, with no redeemer in sight.

BASEBALL ENDANGERED

Baseball history aficionados rarely discuss the game's rise and fall from King Kelly's playful trickery to a more heartless form of competition in the last decade of the nineteenth century. If anything, they still lump the 1890s into baseball's "fun age of rule bending," a phrase that better describes the playing style of Kelly and his peers, not the overt thuggery that replaced it.

However, such reverie overlooks telling evidence that professional baseball was close to being discredited, possibly even spurned and tossed aside, by the emergent middle-class society of the 1890s. An increasingly urban society found other, more enjoyable ways to spend free time. Baseball may well have gone the way of "pedestrianism," bicycling, and other passing recreational fads of the Gay Nineties, or perhaps worse. It was in danger of being lumped in with other unsavory spectator sporting events of the day—horse racing, prizefighting, and cockfighting—as both "dirty" and corrupt.

How bad could baseball have been? The popular press repeatedly remarked upon the disagreeable brand of play in these years. "There was but one drawback to the creditable success of the entire championship campaigns of 1894, and that was the unwonted degree of 'hoodlumism' which disgraced the season," lamented Henry Chadwick in *Spalding's Official Baseball Guide of 1895*. Chadwick, an English transplant who became baseball's chronicler and its greatest advocate in the game's formative years, decried hoodlumism and the use of "blackguard" language, also known as billingsgate, all of which he bundled under the term "dirty ball."

The most notorious hoodlums of the era, by all accounts, were

John McGraw of the Baltimore Orioles and Oliver "Patsy" Tebeau of the Cleveland Spiders. The diminutive McGraw earned his pejorative nickname, "Muggsy," on a daily basis even as the Orioles became a dominant team of the decade. Vituperative intimidation was his MO, whether dealing with opposing players or with umpires. He liked to drive his spiked shoes into an opponent's foot when crossing first base or sliding into a bag, likewise when arguing chin-to-chin with an ump. Playing third base, he would grab a base runner by the belt, or apply a stranglehold, to keep him from advancing toward home. McGraw believed his unbridled competitive fire should be emulated: "Because a man wants to win and plays the game for all there is in it, he is immediately put down as a rowdy, a leg-breaker and a spiker," he once griped.

Cleveland's player-manager Tebeau was a notorious umpire baiter, never missing an opportunity to contest a ruling on the field that went against him or his team. The press began referring to the widespread practice of "kicking," or incessant arguing, as Tebeauism. Its namesake offered no apologies. "A milk and water, goody-goody player can't wear a Cleveland uniform," he said.

By 1897, the game had only deepened Henry Chadwick's pessimism about its future. Still baseball's abiding conscience, Chadwick insisted that rowdyism in the game had reached a point at which it was jeopardizing "the good name of the professional base ball business at large." And his wasn't a lone voice.

In August 1897, *Sporting Life*, a national weekly newspaper out of Philadelphia, rounded up editorials from several big-city papers that also decried the violent state of the game. "If the men who have their money invested in professional base ball clubs throughout the country do not want to see their investments become worthless[,] it is high time they took steps to eliminate the billingsgate and bare knuckle features which are fast bringing the game into disrepute among all but a very few of its patrons," wrote the *Cleveland Leader*. "The public is getting tired," said the *Cincinnati Times-Star*, "of paying to see the clean, honest sport of several years ago, and then receiving as a return for their money long lessons in profanity and a few points in the manly art of self-defense." The *Pittsburgh Gazette Times* added: "At no time in the history of base ball has there been such disgraceful scenes on the diamond. . . . This, if anything, is going to cause the downfall of the favorite American sport."

The *New York Sun*, which had been among the first daily newspapers to cover baseball on a regular basis, joined the debate as well that summer. In a weekly series of editorials under the headline "Baseball Endangered," *Sun* editors took players and especially owners to task. "We warn those financially interested in baseball," they inveighed, "that the public's disgust at the rowdyism which the players have practiced with their permission is finding such widespread expression as to betoken a serious decline in the national game's popularity." The *Chicago Tribune* made a similar admonishment and predicted a fatal consequence: "Unless the relations between the managers [owners] and the public are changed, the game will soon become so unprofitable that it will have to be abandoned."

Yet beyond warning the owners to clean up their act and get tough with on-field behavior, no one had any suggestions for how the game might recover the public's good graces.

ROWDYISM, HOODLUMISM, AND BILLINGSGATE

As the newspaper editorialists of the 1890s bemoaned and lamented, dirty ball playing had moved by many degrees beyond the joking stunts that Kelly and his compatriots had liked to pull off a decade earlier. It was one thing to shortcut a base while the umpire was following the ball in the outfield—quite another to deliberately trip a runner in the base path, or grab him by the belt to keep him from advancing, or coldcock him, as McGraw and others were wont to do.

Such childish behavior, mean-spirited at its core when practiced by grown men, had become routine, all but expected of player and spectator alike. The cranks in the grandstand egged the players on, often joining in the fracases by starting fights of their own. "The 5,200 people at the ball park to-day saw a prizefight, an umpire rotten-egged and two good games all for one price of admission," the *New York Tribune* wisecracked in 1897.

But the grim truth was that people who followed the game closely reveled in its roughhouse style. They considered it "manly" and fitting. One Baltimore apologist worried that trying to curtail players' fighting spirit would weaken their drive and sap the game of its appeal: "You can bench McGraw and fire Tebeau out of the game for a month. You can and would keep many of the best players out of the game for a season. But that would just about ruin the game. You must have these very men, or you will not have spectators."

The *Washington Post* agreed. "The so-called hoodlumism on the diamond arose from zeal and enthusiasm rather than bad blood," said an item headlined "It's Only Exuberance." The writer concluded: "Go to, and la la with your hoodlumism. The wordy scraps of today are forgotten on the morrow."

Even more troubling to polite society, perhaps, was the foul language, or billingsgate, that Chadwick so deplored. Ballparks in those days were no bigger than today's minor league stadiums in, say, Erie, Pennsylvania, or Eugene, Oregon. Most of them held only five thousand or fewer spectators. In other words, every spectator at a big league game in the 1890s got an earful of just about everything said on the field, from the first pitch to the last out, especially if barked out around the close confines of home plate.

In one match in August 1895, New York's John "Dirty Jack" Doyle flew into a rage over an umpire's call and proceeded to horrify everyone within earshot, which is to say everyone in the ballpark. Doyle "used such vile language toward Umpire O'Day that the majority of the 800 ladies in the grand stand left the grounds," witnesses reported.

"Profanity belongs to the world at large, you know—a sort of universal language," rebutted another defender of the players, unwittingly making a case for those who found the banter to be obscene and offensive. "Baseball has a vernacular all its own, and what would be profanity in average society is as mild as milk in baseball."

When the target of invective turned toward the stands, the owners could no longer stand silent and pretend that their boys were just being boys. By 1897, the National League's imperious "magnates," as sportswriters liked to call team owners, were worried enough about sagging attendance to marshal their forces for drastic action. At a game that summer, a patron seated near the visitors' bench asked a player who would be pitching for his team that day. When he got no response, the spectator asked again: "The gentleman, his wife who sat with him, and others of both sexes, within hearing distance, were outraged upon hearing the player reply in a loud, brutal tone, 'Oh, go fuck yourself.'"

This remarkably explicit quotation served as the opening anecdote of an official memorandum issued by the magnates, in response to more than one hundred letters and telegrams of complaint from outraged fans. The owners vowed to impose stiff fines and suspensions for the "baseball crime" of profane language. The National League printed and distributed the memo to every team's clubhouse and possibly to every player. (An authenticated copy of the document came to light only in 2007.) The rest of the memo is even more astonishing in its catalog of vulgar expressions, detailing what would henceforth be proscribed on the field, on penalty of expulsion from the game:

> That such brutal language as "You cock-sucking son of a bitch!" "You prick-eating bastard!" "You cunt-lapping dog!" "Kiss my ass, you son of a bitch!" "A dog must have fucked your mother when she made you!" "I fucked your mother, your sister, your wife!" "I'll make you suck my ass!" "You cock-sucker!" and many other revolting terms are used by a limited number of players to intimidate umpires and opposing players, and are promiscuously used upon the ball field, is vouched for by the almost unanimous assertion of those invited to speak, and who are competent to speak from personal knowledge.

The new anti-billingsgate policy was the brainchild of John T. Brush, owner of the Cincinnati Reds (and a future stakeholder of the New York Giants). Brush goaded his fellow magnates into endorsing an over-the-top, twenty-one-point resolution on "villainously filthy language." His remedies had the predictably opposite effect: expulsion was too severe for what most baseball people viewed as standard behavior by macho young sportsmen.

Despite their concerns, league owners and officials virtually ignored the Brush resolution for the entire 1898 season. "No one dared to cast the first stone," as baseball historian David Voigt has observed.

The first case against on-field profanity didn't come forth until 1899, and then the "punishment" was little more than a stern verbal rebuke. The Brush rule, as Voigt puts it, remained a "dead letter and a monument to the petulance of baseball's feudal era."

Owners' blind petulance was one thing, but their outright bigotry and barefaced policy of racial exclusion quite another. Baseball by this time was being played and enjoyed by American kids of every demographic, ethnicity, and religion—white Anglos, German and Irish immigrants, African Americans, Native Americans. Organized baseball, in both major and minor leagues, had gradually opened to all white Americans whose parents grew up in the United States, regardless of economic background, and even allowed native Indians and Cubans into its ranks. However, the leagues early on erected an immovable barrier to one group: African Americans. Their half-century-long banishment from the game was effectively codified during this ill-starred decade.

The instigator of baseball's "color line" was none other than Adrian "Cap" Anson, King Kelly's teammate and captain of the White Stockings. Anson had begun playing professional baseball in the 1870s and quickly developed into one of the game's sharpest, most influential minds, as well its most domineering character. A huge man for his day at six-foot-two and two hundred pounds, Anson lorded over the White Stockings as player-manager for more than twenty-five years, leading them to six National League pennants in the 1880s and personally racking up more hits, runs scored, and runs batted in than any player in the franchise—ever.

What Cap wanted in these early days of organized baseball, he invariably got. Anson was an outspoken racial bigot, and while his views were hardly novel within white society of the time, his prominent position gave him outsize influence. The first target of Anson's prejudice was Moses Fleetwood Walker, one of just a few black men playing in the minor leagues in the 1880s. Anson in 1883 had refused to play an exhibition with Walker's team, the Toledo Blue Stockings, and although the Ohio team and city leaders came to Walker's defense, Anson eventually got his way. Other players and managers followed Anson's lead, and similar incidents occurred with regularity on other teams. By the early 1890s, no black players remained in the professional ranks.

National League magnates continued to honor Anson's color line through an unofficial "gentleman's agreement" that upheld baseball's overt racial segregation policy for another half century—broken only with Jackie Robinson's arrival in Brooklyn in 1947. Northern society in the 1890s was largely unmoved by Anson's early decree, which shunted some of the country's best athletes to the shadows and served mainly to deprive the game of many great players and vital competition.

Perhaps baseball magnates could have kept turning a blind eye to racism, rowdyism, hoodlumism, billingsgate, and all-round dirty play in the game they were putting on the field, figuring they were at least giving true baseball cranks the show they wanted. But the owners could not ignore the toll that baseball was taking at the turnstiles. Annual attendance from 1892 through 1900 continued to falter, year after year.

The two top-drawer teams of the decade, the Baltimore Orioles and the Boston Beaneaters, which between them won eight of the ten pennants, sustained a measure of fan interest for a few years, and their success served to carry the league. But even these clubs experienced stiff drop-offs in attendance during the 1898 and 1899 seasons. Their decline, on top of the sheer abandonment of fans in the moribund, or "dead rabbit," towns of Cleveland, St. Louis, Louisville, and Washington, DC, spelled disaster for the league's suspect business model.

The magnates at first tried to lay the blame on the banking Panic of 1893, which had spawned a nationwide recession lasting three long years. Then they fingered the Spanish-American War, which broke out in 1898—the first time that American boys had been sent into battle since the Civil War. Owners believed that newspapers were devoting more space and resources to coverage of the hostilities in Cuba and the Philippines, and less to baseball. But it was clear that something much more ominous for the sport was at work. "Had those worthies taken note of the 13 million increase in the nation's population over the decade," observed Voigt, "they would have realized that the league's attendance was lagging behind population growth."

SYNDICATE BASEBALL

As disgusting as the behavior on the field and in the stands had become, owners themselves seemed obtusely eager to drive the final nail in baseball's coffin. Since 1892, the National League had enjoyed a monopoly over baseball in the nation's largest cities. Yet the magnates weren't satisfied. They wanted to rid themselves of any business competition altogether, even among themselves.

Organized baseball had experienced real rivalries in the 1880s for players and for customers when other would-be major leagues tried to enter, and in one instance succeeded. The players themselves dared to launch their own circuit in 1890 in a bold but ill-fated attempt to take back control of their financial situations.

The one successful upstart major league, the American Association, had blossomed in the Midwest in the 1880s with beachheads in baseball-mad cities that the National League had either ignored or forsaken, including St. Louis, Cincinnati, Pittsburgh, and Louisville. (The AA also dared to compete head-on with NL franchises in New York and Philadelphia.) Its Barnum-like ringleader, a St. Louis beer-garden proprietor named Chris von der Ahe, knew next to nothing about baseball and was really looking for a way to sell more beer. But his maverick league, backed mainly by fellow saloon owners, brewers, and distillers, caught the haughty National League magnates off guard—helped along, no doubt, by fan-friendly innovations like twenty-five-cent ticket prices (half of the NL entrance fee), beer at the ballpark, and Sabbath-defying doubleheaders.

The "Beer and Whiskey Circuit," as it became known, featured the playful, just-for-the-hell-of-it spirit that made King Kelly and his cohort so popular among fans and so frustrating to the NL's control freaks. For a few years, at least, the American Association helped make baseball a "people's game" and breathed life into immigrant-laden industrial cities.

But after engaging in a few well-aimed (and expensive) raids on NL rosters, the AA owners soon decided they would be better off making a pact with the NL devils. The two leagues signed the landmark National

Agreement in 1883, wherein the AA agreed to honor current NL contracts and codified a $2,000 maximum salary for all but the top-shelf performers. The AA also acceded to boilerplate language in player contracts that had enabled each NL owner to "reserve" exclusive negotiating rights to each of his players from year to year.

The reserve clause, which was to remain in effect for almost a century afterward, effectively took away all bargaining rights from the players and made their services subject to owners' contractual whims and manipulations. The salary cap just made the players mad, especially when it allowed an owner to unilaterally "sell" or trade a player contract to another team and pocket the cash for himself.

The players not only took umbrage at the owners' antilabor policies and tactics; the radicals among them revolted by forming a quasi union, the Brotherhood of Professional Base-Ball Players. Their attempts at collective bargaining made little headway, however, and the impasse led to the creation of the Players League in 1890. But the Players League was clearly underfinanced and unable to recruit well-heeled investors; it folded after only one year in operation. Within another year the AA, its prosperous teams unable to prop up its own dead-rabbit clubs, also fell of its own weight and disbanded after the 1891 season.

By 1892, National League owners controlled a veritable baseball "trust" that was untouchable in its major markets—and likewise uninhibited by such basic business principles as fair play and good faith. NL magnates began acting accordingly, egged on by Brush, the Cincinnati Scrooge, and New York's menacing and even more spiteful owner, Tammany Hall kingpin Andrew Freedman. By a combination of bald-faced collusion and willful obliviousness to the consequences, they turned the National League into a cartel. The NL owners allowed— even encouraged—one another to take minority stakes in each other's ball clubs. There was no rule against double ownership, and some owners took this as license to brazenly acquire two teams and then shunt the better players from the weaker club to the contender. This became known in the press and by the public by the epithet "syndicate baseball."

Under syndicate baseball, in 1899, for instance, the Baltimore Orioles clearly were destined for the second division in the standings while their sister club in Brooklyn, the Superbas, remained in the running for the championship. Management promptly shipped the Orioles' best players, including future Hall of Famer "Wee Willie" Keeler, off to Brooklyn.

The cynical manipulation of rosters reached its nadir that same year when Fred Robison of the Cleveland Spiders acquired the bankrupt St. Louis Browns from von der Ahe. Robison then raided his own Spiders of its few competent players in a vain attempt to help St. Louis wrest the championship from the Superbas. St. Louis's renamed "Perfectos" collapsed regardless, to no one's lasting regret, but the Spiders' sad fate would leave a blemish on organized baseball, one that lasts to this day.

The eviscerated Cleveland ball club was so bad in 1899 that it won only twenty games all season—still a major league record for wretchedness—leading to the predictable disaffection of its hometown fans. Cleveland drew 6,088 spectators that season, or fewer than a hundred people a home game. Robison and his Cleveland cronies couldn't deliver to visiting teams any palpable share of gate receipts, so other NL teams refused to make the trip to Cleveland. The Spiders had to play all their games in the second half of the season on the road; sportswriters referred to the sad-sack ball club as the "Wanderers."

A sport now ruled by roughneck players, bloodthirsty fans, and smug, conspiratorial owners—an unwitting conspiracy of dunces— teetered over the abyss at the turn of the twentieth century. Baseball as practiced in the National League had lost any pretense of being the "national pastime." The fun-loving King Kelly and the carefree game he had once personified were gone and nearly forgotten, replaced on the field by a sport devoid of good cheer or any real fun. The gulf between baseball as it was played in 1899 and its promising beginnings just a generation or two earlier would have seemed unfordable to the game's founders. No one saw a way back—and certainly no one thought that the seeds of the game's revival were already being planted in such far-flung burgs as Troy, Kansas City, and Fresno.

PART ONE

Boys to Men

We need only realise our parents, remember
our grandparents and know ourselves and our
history is complete.

GERTRUDE STEIN,
The Making of Americans

John J. Evers Jr., circa 1903. (New York Public Library.)

THE IRISH GAME

Johnny Evers in Troy

At 11:30 p.m. on the night before Labor Day, 1902, John J. Evers Jr. hopped aboard a southbound West Shore Railroad train, the Fast National Express to New York City, and waved good-bye to a swarm of local mates on the platform. He headed straight for the rear smoking car. Wearing his only suit, a freshly starched collar, and a new derby hat, the first he'd ever owned, the young man gripped a small valise in one hand and a clutch of black cigars in the other—enough smokes, he hoped, to stave off the hunger pangs and keep him awake through the all-night journey to Philadelphia.

He entered the parlor of soft chairs and fired up his first stogie. The billows joined a cloud of smoke hanging there from other "sports" in the car, most of them on their way back from a weekend at the Saratoga Race Course. His sharp, piercing eyes and lantern jaw usually stuck out in a crowd, but the thin frame and freckled face would not have impressed these traveling companions. If anyone noticed him, let's hope they forgave him if he seemed cocksure. Fact was, Little Jack Evers, ball player, was on his way to the big leagues.

The journey began in Albany, a short ferry ride across the Hudson River from his hometown of Troy, and about 135 miles upriver from the great metropolis of Manhattan. Evers had turned twenty-one only six weeks before, and this was his first trip outside of his home state. When he wasn't touring nearby towns as a shortstop for the Troy Trojans of the New York State League, he was still living with his parents and six brothers and sisters in a two-story row house on Third Street.

He had buried his adored and adoring father just the previous Sunday. The Irish Catholic funeral filled the sanctuary of the massive St. Joseph's Church across the street from their home. He now had to decide what to do with his life and whether baseball, the game he'd played with a passion since childhood, could provide enough of an income to allow him to marry and raise a family of his own. A bright student and hard worker—and, like his father, a stranger to no one—Jack Jr. was a sportsman of some renown in and around Troy. He had a following.

Even so, there was nothing in his 105-pound frame to suggest he was ready to join the fast company of major league baseball players, much less that he could one day stand out on a national stage. Nothing about him could lead anyone to believe that Jack Evers might become a baseball star—except, perhaps, for two basic facts: He was second-generation Irish American, and he grew up playing baseball on the sandlots of Troy.

These two baseball benchmarks made for a potent combination in the decades leading up to 1900. As the National League of Professional Baseball Clubs matured through a half century's evolution in rules, playing conditions, and social attitudes for and about the game, Irish-born immigrants and their offspring came to dominate the game like no other demographic. The waves of families escaping Ireland's potato famine of 1845–50 found in baseball a welcome outlet for their talents and enthusiasm. More than 1,100 players who rose to the top of the professional ranks between 1871 and 1920 were Irish born or Irish American, about a quarter of all players in that period. More still peppered the minor and semipro leagues across the country.

The Irish rise to the summit of American baseball has been compared to basketball in the late twentieth century, when African Americans emerged from Jim Crow segregation to become the dominant force in that sport. Just as every late twentieth-century basketball team featured more blacks than whites, every nineteenth-century baseball team had four or five Irish names in its starting nine. "Many people, in the same way that people today believe that blacks are born athletes, thought that the Irish were born baseball players," according to baseball historian Bill James.

If Irish American veins bled baseball, then the industrial city of Troy was their pumping heart. Troy produced twenty-seven major league ballplayers between 1871 and 1913, more than any other town in America outside of New York, Boston, and Chicago. Two Hall of Famers were born there and another five started their careers there. Most of them were of Irish descent: among them the great "King" Kelly, as well as William "Buck" Ewing, Roger Connors, and Dan Brouthers. Three of the sons of Troy who made it to the majors in this time were named Evers.

The Irish-Troy connection wasn't lost on the new skipper of the Chicago National League baseball club. The "Colts," as sportswriters had been calling the old White Stockings back then, were in Philadelphia that Labor Day weekend to play a doubleheader on the holiday. Their manager Frank G. Selee had been brought aboard just that year by an ambitious owner who was eager to restore the fortunes of a charter NL franchise. Those glory days were long gone, however. Since the late 1880s, the Colts had been reduced to a perennial bottom dweller in the standings, and Selee just wanted to make it through the last weeks of another long, losing campaign.

Selee desperately needed an infielder after his team captain Bobby Lowe went down with a bad knee. Selee didn't have anyone else in reserve and didn't have time to survey the bushes for new prospects. When old friend Lou Bacon, manager of the Troy Trojans, told him about a plucky young shortstop on his Class B league team, Selee didn't hesitate. The telegram to Evers said for him to get down there before the first game started the next day.

"Little Jack" Evers, as he was routinely called back then, took an expedited path to the big leagues that delivered him literally overnight to Philadelphia. His journey started in Troy, the "Collar City," where baseball was as much a part of the local fabric as Mass on Sunday morning and the Irish stew and soda bread served up for dinner. Troy had been home to one of the first major league teams in the 1870s, the fabled Haymakers. It was an early National League city in 1882 and the progenitor of the New York (now San Francisco) Giants.

By the 1890s, it took an outsider to point out the Trojans' baseball mania to them, since by that time the game had been integral to their everyday lives for a generation or two. "For a city of only 65,000 inhabitants, Troy shows more interest in base ball than many of the larger cities," observed a correspondent for the *New York Sun* in April 1891. "One hears very little else talked about here now." The NL Giants had lost to the minor league Trojans in a preseason exhibition match at the West Troy Baseball Grounds, where three thousand locals turned out to cheer on the hometown boys, not the marquee players from the big city. When the big leaguers dropped a second match to Troy's upstarts the next day, the *Sun* correspondent was even more impressed: "If ever a team owned a town the home team owns Troy."

John Evers Jr., who turned ten in that summer of 1891, was already a "child wonder" at the game of baseball, people said. His father, uncles, brothers, and cousins were all bat-wielding knights of South Troy, the Irish-immigrant enclave tucked just south of the downtown city center. "With every breath I drew around the house I gulped down a chunk of baseball," Johnny recalled years later. He was about to show the world what his DNA could deliver.

THREE GENERATIONS

Like many immigrant families in the mid-1800s, the Evers family of South Troy started their life in America from all but nothing. Johnny's grandfather Michael Evers had arrived in New York City on April 28, 1840, on the ship *Rochester* out of Liverpool. He was said to be twenty-one and a laborer, a term for anyone who had no particular skills or education. He told U.S. customs officials that he was from Athlone, in County Westmeath in the Irish Midlands, and that he could not read or write. Michael Evers had no schooling, no discernible assets, and no marketable work experience. All he had to offer was a strong young back and, perhaps, nimble hands and fingers.

What could have possessed him, along with so many other desperate Irish émigrés, to abandon family and homeland for the uncertain promise of life in the New World? Although descendants of these early seekers tend to romanticize the European immigrant experience, seeing in that crossing an eternal testament to the American ideal of opportunity and renewal, the decision to walk away from the old way of life could not have been easy.

Since 1815, Ireland had been occupied by the British, who went to extreme lengths to try to quell the island's nationalistic impulses: Parliament outlawed Catholicism and banned the Irish language; English landlords, who owned most of the arable land, raised rents with impunity and subdivided large tracts of farmland into smaller and smaller plots, on which the only sustainable crop was potatoes. Unemployment and destitution spread across the island. The population had quadrupled to eight million just as the old textile economy, Ireland's economic mainstay, fell into the tank after England began importing U.S. cotton. By the time of Michael Evers's departure, most of the young men heading for America were poor smallholders, farmers' sons, cottars, and laborers with few or no skills. The one thing Evers took with him was a vague but deeply felt foreboding of the "end of days."

Pre-famine Ireland, much like other religious and tradition-bound societies affected by rapid change, was "rife with prophesies of doom and millennial expectations of earthly salvation," according to historian Kerby A. Miller. Single young men like Michael had more than an impulse to escape; they harbored a growing rage to chart their own destiny, driven by a dread of the apocalypse and their abiding faith in God's imminent deliverance.

Michael Evers soon found his way to Troy, New York, perhaps lured by the promise of jobs digging the Erie Canal or at the many mills in the area. Within two years he had set up shop as a tailor on Congress Street. He married Mary Gaffigan, five years his junior, also born in Ireland and also illiterate. Their first child, Hanna Anne Marie, was born in March 1844, followed by their first son, John Joseph, in 1848.

LIFE IN SOUTH TROY

John J. Evers (Johnny's father) was a creature of South Troy and everything it came to represent to the Irish immigrant families who built a life there. For the next half century, three local institutions came to dominate and ultimately define John Sr.'s life and career. Above all was the Roman Catholic Church, which governed the family's spiritual and moral universe as well as its tightly knit social galaxy. Second was the local iron molders union and, by extension, Democratic Party politics, which together gave John Sr. both a means to rise in the world and a way to make his mark in it. Third was baseball; after the Civil War, as John Sr. entered manhood, the sport found an avid following in Troy, where it became a passion of the Evers clan.

St. Joseph's Church and its watchful bell tower still looms high above the trees in the center of South Troy. The massive structure is a majestic presence in a neighborhood of modest row houses, clearly built to inspire awe in God and the immutable Church of Rome. The brick edifice was designed in the Gothic style, its sanctuary built to seat two thousand parishioners.

The local diocese established the church in 1847 to serve the wave of Irish émigrés. St. Joseph's $100,000 price tag—as much as $750 million today—covered such accoutrements as a marble altar, mahogany pews, and now-priceless Tiffany stained-glass windows, fashioned after the paintings of Titian and Rubens. John Sr. grew up inside the church, attended Mass and received the sacraments of communion and confession, witnessed christenings, marriages, and funerals, and participated in the many church-sponsored social functions that helped newcomers feel at home. St. Patrick's Day brought parades, special Masses, and plenty of friendly celebration and drinking, according to local historian Joan Lowe: "Those who were Irish speakers sometimes used their native tongue and played tunes on the Irish flute."

Evers joined a number of the church societies and allied volunteer organizations, including the singing group Young Men's Sodality, the Byron Literary Association, the Catholic Benevolent Association, and the Osgood Steamer Association, a local fire brigade. He was schooled

by the Christian Brothers Academy and learned the trade of iron mold-
ing. (St. Joseph's has always been known locally as the "iron workers'
church."). He established the wide network of friends and associates
that, by the time of his death in 1902, made him one of the best-known
and most liked men in the city.

While life inside the church nurtured and protected young Irish Americans like John Evers, tension between the Irish enclave of South Troy
and the Anglo-Protestant business magnates and shop owners on the
north side always hung over the city. The more the Irish Americans
felt the disdain of their Waspish neighbors, the more they withdrew
into their enclave and fumed. "It's South Troy against the world," was a
common chant heard in the Irish saloons and social clubs.

The roots of this tension preceded Michael Evers's arrival: On St.
Patrick's Day 1837, a riot broke out after local Protestants hung an
effigy "ridiculing the reverence of the Irish inhabitants for their patron saint." An incensed Irishman tried to bring it down before he was
driven away by the men and boys guarding it. The Irishman soon returned with a squadron of his mates. Stones were thrown, windows
broken, guns fired, people maimed, and stores burned. Recrimina-
tions on both sides lasted for years.

By the 1860s, the tension between Anglo and Celt found deeper expression in the contest between capital and labor. Troy by this time had
established itself as a global epicenter of the casting of iron stoves, with
eager buyers all over the world. "Llamas have carried them across the
Andes to the farther coast of South America, camels to the shores of
the Black Sea, and ships to Northern Europe, Turkey, China, Japan and
Australia," an 1891 history of the city boasted.

When competition from the American hinterland started cutting
into this lucrative business, foundry owners tried to cut corners along
with prices. That meant loosening the grip of guild artisans like iron
molders. Their hard-earned but also danger-filled skill for creating
the sand-packed molds for everything from stoves to church bells and
train wheels, then filling them with hot molten iron, was in danger
of being undermined by eager, less experienced, replacement "bucks."

As a result, the Iron Molders Union found itself on the forefront of the early national labor movement, acting as one of the first guild organizations to unite its shops against strikebreaking in one city using scabs from another. The national movement was inaugurated in Philadelphia, but Troy was home to Iron Molders International No. 2.

Troy was the eastern terminus of the 363-mile Erie Canal, which stretched all the way to Lake Erie. Troy became the water junction between the Great Lakes, Canadian forests, and New York City's harbor. The city was the ideal trading and manufacturing location in the mid-nineteenth century. It could receive lumber and Syracuse salt from the north, grain and salted meat from the western hinterlands, and all kinds of raw materials needed to fire, stoke, and maintain the iron-works and other factories that lined its miles of waterfront. Among the industrial workshops were those making "detachable" starched shirt collars and cuffs, invented by a Troy housewife who'd gotten tired of washing and ironing her husband's stained shirts.

The Collar City street grid was laid out in a rectangle about four miles long and a mile and a half wide, pinned between the river on the west and the Rensselaer Plateau on the east. With only the river's narrow floodplain to put up homes, shops, and factories, Troy's urban plan possessed some of the same cramped characteristics of early Manhattan Island. Its neighborhoods settled and grew in like manner: ethnic enclaves squeezed one against another from north to south.

Even though his father had made his way as a tailor, it made sense for John Evers Sr. to pursue the iron molders' trade. Along with such artisans as foundry men, pattern makers, and dressers, iron molders were highly skilled and respected. The job paid well in the good years, and the union offered something of a career path for anyone with an amiable disposition and modest political ambition. John started work for Fuller & Warren's Clinton Stove Works, maker of the famous "Stewart's Air-Tight" kitchen stoves, and he quickly became active in local Democratic politics, which, like many political machines emerging in industrial cities, nurtured tight connections to jobs and career advancement. Evers won an entry-level slot, election watcher, on a machine slate that had no Republican opposition in his ward, and he patiently served his formal apprentice years at the ironworks before becoming of member of the guild in 1874, at age twenty-six.

A short time later, Evers married Hellena Keating of Troy, and a few months after that John won appointment to the board of commissioners of the public school system. His fast rise displayed not only a natural ability to make friends but also an ability to work the well-oiled network of Irish cronies. A devout Roman Catholic, who would send all of his children to parochial schools, he climbed to the chairman's seat of the policy-making body of the city's sectarian school system.

Evers's network included two other rising stars in Troy's political hierarchy. Edward Dolan was elected alderman the year Evers was appointed to the school board. Dennis J. Whelan, a plumber who would later go into the sarsaparilla and "temperance drink" business, succeeded Dolan as alderman and within ten years became the second Irish mayor of Troy. The careers of Evers, Dolan, and Whelan would interweave and intersect for years, greased by a political machine created by the *first* Irish mayor of Troy: Edward Murphy Jr.

Murphy was a towering, gregarious, and bullying personality. He operated a brewery founded by his father, and from that perch played kingpin in both city and state politics for more than twenty years—first as mayor of Troy for four terms, then as chairman of the state's Democratic Party, and finally as a U.S. senator at the close of the century. Boss Murphy's fingerprints were on the Democratic presidential nominations of Samuel J. Tilden in 1876 and Grover Cleveland in 1892, although he later broke with each of them "on questions which involved the 'spoils system,'" according to the *New York Times*. Murphy was a shameless practitioner of political patronage—Dolan would eventually get the prized federal job of postmaster in Troy—and he could be a ruthless manipulator, routinely working one side against the other.

Murphy had won early gratitude among Troy's Anglo-Protestant community by tamping down a potential sectarian clash between Irish Protestants and Irish Catholics. He then leveraged that ability to harness Irish tempers (and votes) to win the confidence of WASP factory owners, society elites, and shopkeepers. He made good things happen for the entire city while enriching himself in the process. Under his watch Troy got paved streets, a water and sewer system, and some monumental public buildings. Though his political cynicism would eventually catch up to him, Murphy's largesse elevated his young, first-generation Irish American disciples to a status and lifestyle their parents couldn't have dreamed of.

In late 1875 John Evers and his new wife moved into a two-story row house at 437 Third Street. This central location joined John's two worlds—he and Hellena lived just four blocks east of the iron factories and half a block down from St. Joseph's. They could see the church's bell tower from their front stoop, the chimes orchestrating the rhythm of their daily life. Here the Everses spent the next twenty-seven years raising a traditional Irish "stem" family: the oldest son inherits, the girls live at home until married (in order of birth), and every child dutifully marries into another Irish family.

John and Hellena had three girls and six boys; first came two girls and oldest son Michael. Then, on June 21, 1881, Hellena gave birth to their second son, whom they made John Joseph's namesake. Like most Irish boys named John, he was called "Jack" by everyone except his father, who always called him by his Christian name.

As typically Irish as the Evers family still was, the world that Jack entered was forty-one light-years away from the Ireland Michael Evers had left behind. The city of Troy had grown into a prosperous industrial center thanks in no small part to the sweat and scars of its ethnic, working-class population, and many of those families took full advantage of American upward mobility. The public and parochial institutions of Troy had made it possible for John Sr. to get an education, learn a good-paying trade, and acquire respectability and influence. In the process, he earned social standing and secured a comfortable life for his wife and children.

Both John Sr. and his best mates, Dennis Whelan and Edward Dolan, would rise to positions of real power by the mid-1880s: Whelan as mayor, Dolan as postmaster, and Evers as president of the school board. They were touted as young Irish Americans at the "front rank" of Troy's business and political society. Evers eventually passed a civil service exam and Whelan persuaded the city council to give him a sinecure as assistant clerk of the Board of Water Commissioners, at a salary of $900 a year—equivalent, by some measures, to $250,000 in today's dollars.

In many respects, the life story of John J. Evers Sr. seemed a classic immigrant saga of achievement, acceptance, and assimilation, except that in South Troy, as in other Irish strongholds across the United States, there remained a powerful sense of ethnic identity and cultural pride. The Sons of Erin were not so easily absorbed into the Protestant American way of life. The more the WASP elites disdained the Irish, their religion, and their clannish ways, the more the Irish held on to their need for separation—or in their minds, independence.

As the Evers family story shows, Irish Americans had largely succeeded in their pursuit of the American dream, and yet they still felt like outsiders, waging perpetual war against their Anglo overlords. In that sense, their ultimate objective wasn't assimilation; it was conquest. "South Troy against the world!" remained their cry. What they lacked wasn't ambition, drive, or political clout, but the assurance that the conflicting "prophesies of doom and millennial expectations of earthly salvation" would resolve in their favor.

What the Evers clan and their South Troy compatriots needed at this stage was someone to come along and tell them they were, in fact, the good guys in the American saga.

THE GAELIC INVASION

The S.S. *Wisconsin* swung into its pier on the southern tip of Manhattan shortly before noon on Wednesday, September 25, 1888, under clear skies and light wind. The hybrid sail and steamship, one of the Guion line's weekly shuttles across the Atlantic, had been traveling for ten days out of Liverpool. It was typically full of emigrants from all corners of Europe, including the British Isles, the Netherlands, Germany, Russia, Scandinavia, and Poland. Among its many passengers were Jews, Mormons, and Salvationists.

Moments after docking, a phalanx of fifty "stalwart lads" bounded down the gangplank. The brash young men of "remarkably well-developed limbs" waved to a cheering crowd of expectant admirers and local politicians. The boisterous scene turned the heads of people crowded into the Castle Garden emigration depot.

The visitors were a troupe of elite athletes—runners, jumpers, throwers, and "hurlers"—hailing from every county in Ireland. Many were wielding big, blackthorn cudgels. "Their sticks commanded universal respect," reported a correspondent for the *New York Times*. "A big policeman eyed them with special interest and hid his own locust under his coat." The heavy sticks of carefully polished hardwood looked quite formidable, the reporter added, "but in the hands of the muscular athletes they were as switches."

Outfitted in smartly tailored tweed coats, corduroy knickerbockers, and multicolored leggings, the contingent dazzled the crowd amid hearty greetings and exuberant speeches in the Castle Garden rotunda. It soon became evident that these vigorous Irish lads weren't trying to escape from their homeland. Unlike most on board the *Wisconsin* that day, they had no intention of putting down roots in the New World. Rather, these star athletes—the handpicked shock troops of a self-styled "Gaelic Invasion"—had come to promote Irish sports, sponsored by the Gaelic Athletic Association. The GAA boasted a contentious and nationalist (some would say revolutionary) political agenda at home and an ambitious financial agenda abroad. The athletes were its cultural and political ambassadors.

Irish national revivalists had founded the GAA only four years earlier, hoping to stifle the spread of British sports on their home turf. They promoted the traditional Irish games of hurling, Gaelic football, and handball over the English pastimes of cricket, rugby, and soccer. Some Irish activities, hurling in particular, could be traced back three thousand years. The GAA codified the rules for those contests and set up a system of amateur competition with the idea of spreading a cultural reawakening in Ireland and in the Irish diaspora in North America, Australia, and Argentina.

This trip called for competition at hurling and track-and-field events in New York, Boston, Philadelphia, and other cities on the East Coast. The GAA hoped the gate receipts would raise as much as five thousand pounds to underwrite a revival of the ancient Tailteann games, a kind of Celtic Olympics, last held in AD 1169.

The athletes made a well-publicized stop at the West Troy Baseball Grounds on Saturday, October 13. They had placed advertisements in all of Troy's newspapers the day before, proclaiming that "Ireland's Gaelic Athletic Champions and World's Record Holders will give exhibitions in Running, Jumping, Weights, and Hammer-throwing. Also a Hurling Match in Irish Style."

What really caught the eye of Irish American spectators at these contests was hurling, a team sport played with bat and ball. The "Irish national game" looks like a cross between field hockey and lacrosse—"not unlike polo, minus the ponies," as the *Troy Telegram* put it. The Troy reporter greeted the Gaelic invaders as they reached Albany by train, and he could barely contain himself as he described the "magnificent specimens of muscular manhood" milling about the Union House hotel. The reporter shook hands with one of the squad leaders and reported experiencing then "what a grip of iron means." The exhibition of hurling warranted special mention: "a most ancient game . . . and also a most vigorous one, very similar to the American boys' game of 'shinny.'"

Irish American boys may actually have been more familiar with hurling—or shinny, as they had called it—than many back on the Emerald Isle. Hurling competitions had fallen out of favor there as cricket and English football (soccer) were promoted by the English. In the United States, references to hurling appeared in journals and newspapers throughout the second half of the nineteenth century. A picnic sponsored by the Clan na Gael association in New York in 1871 attracted representatives from Troy, Wilmington, and Philadelphia; Gaelic football and hurling were part of the festivities. "The object of these associations," explained a writer, "aims at the physical, social and intellectual elevation of the Irish in America. It promotes a love of literature and social life in its clubrooms[,] and in its gymnastic exercises it helps develop the Irish muscle." Another American writer estimated that forty-nine hurling clubs had formed in the United States by 1891.

Hurling is played with a wooden bat, usually made of hard ash. The bat is about the length of a man's arm, slightly curved at the end with a flattened paddle about the size of an open hand. Competitors wield these "hurleys" like scimitars to knock about and advance a seam-stitched ball. The ball, or *sliotar*, stuffed with cork and wool and covered with leather, looks and feels like a baseball, if slightly smaller and lighter.

Still called the "fastest game on grass," hurling may not seem to have obvious kinship with modern baseball, outside of the fact that both are played with a bat and ball. However, the athletic skills required to excel at hurling made it familiar to any kid who played baseball or any other form of "stickball" and vice versa. Hurling requires deft bat wielding to move the ball around the field—as did baseball in the so-called deadball era of the late nineteenth and early twentieth centuries. Hurley-wielding Irish teenagers can hit small targets as much as one hundred feet way, one after another, like sharpshooters knocking bottles off a fence.

Both hurlers and early baseball players also had to unflinchingly catch a rock-hard ball with a bare hand. Protective hand mitts weren't standard then. Gloves were gradually, but only grudgingly, introduced into the American game in the mid-1880s—even then, they were made of thin strips of leather, with no webbing between fingers and thumb. Their purpose was to protect the hand and fingers rather than to trap a ball. In the early days, baseball players, like their hurling counterparts, had to learn how use their cupped fingers rather than their palms to catch a ball, if only to protect against debilitating injury to the carpal hamate bone. Another fielding skill taught to hurlers at an early age is how to "catch" a fast-moving ball by letting it bounce off the chest, deadening its momentum. Nineteenth-century baseball accounts often refer to infielders "stopping" a ground ball before throwing to first base for the out, an indication that bare-handed defenders were willing to sacrifice other parts of their body to avoid injuring their hands.

Finally, hurling required using these batting and fielding skills under furious and chaotic game conditions. The ability to see a play develop as the ball comes off the bat and then react quickly enough to complete the play—or redirect it—was just as important in deadball era baseball. The "inside game" practiced and perfected by the likes of Johnny Evers and his fellow Irish American baseballers, such as John McGraw of the Baltimore Orioles, depended on quick thinking, practiced footwork, and the most efficient defensive positioning in the field. McGraw learned shinny from his father, who hated baseball.

Hurling has rarely been acknowledged as part of baseball's provenance, yet it seems quite likely that the hurling skill set and the battle-tested Irish culture combined to support the Irish American mastery of baseball in the mid- to late nineteenth century. One of the few baseball historians to make the connection is Jerold Casway in his biography of the great nineteenth-century slugger Ed Delahanty. Hurling and other bat-and-ball games were "part of an Irish kid's heritage," making baseball a natural extension of the games they grew up with, according to Casway. Irish kids like Delahanty "were enraptured with baseball as an individual stage for their identities and skills." The hurling connection to baseball is not just a modern, rearview-mirror suggestion. In 1902, a writer for the *Gael*, a New York magazine devoted to promoting Irish culture, thought baseball's debt to hurling should be self-evident: "All outdoor games played with a stick and ball have had their origin in the ancient game of hurling," the writer maintained. "The American national game of baseball had as its first parent a game systematically in vogue among the early Irish."

Athletic skills were one aspect of the Irish propensity for baseball. Ethnic and national identity proved to be even more significant. The GAA was determined to revive hurling all across Ireland, as well across America, as a way to promote a new national consciousness. The Gaelic Invaders hoped their Irish pride would echo throughout immigrant America, where Irish Americans—and Irish Catholics above all—were regularly belittled as a race with "strong backs but weak minds." "No Irish Need Apply," or NINA, was a slur etched on help-wanted posters nationwide.

To the Gaelic invaders, America was nevertheless a place where the Irish ethos had succeeded, and where a visiting group of Irishmen could showcase the best and most worthy exponents of that ethos. They promoted an athletic character that could compete with, even overcome, ethnic prejudice and put an Irish imprimatur on sporting culture in America.

Jack Evers was seven years old when the Gaelic athletes came to Troy. Several hundred people witnessed the exhibition contests, and the *Troy Telegram* reported afterward that "a hurling match was one of the best events of the day," no doubt the talk of the town for some time after.

LITTLE JACK EVERS

By the mid-1880s, the children of South Troy had the run of the city, or at least of their section of it. The community that enveloped Jack Evers in his young years provided him with security as well as a variety of outlets for unsupervised play. Holidays, in particular, brought entire families out to the local parks, where the city set aside picnic groves for clambakes and outdoor games. Some Victorian-era Protestants looked down their noses at these "popular amusements."

But the mill and collar workers were eager to be free of the claustrophobic factories and get outdoors. They abided by such customs as set out in an 1891 etiquette guide, wherein author Daphne Dale stipulated that a picnic meal should include group singing, musical instruments, and amusing stories. Picnics called for "games and romping—for the rigidest disciplinarian will romp when there is green grass underfoot."

The rest of the time most boys ran off on their own to play baseball or shinny on vacant lots or on the many slag hills beside the iron mills. The city streets were also commandeered for games, a situation that could endanger inattentive passersby. "To pedestrians," the *Troy Daily Times* had warned as early as 1870, shinny "is especially suggestive of broken shins or cracked heads." In Albany, the city council in 1884 adopted a statute that forbade "ballplaying and the playing of the game commonly known as and called shinny" in all but two small parks. Troy may well have followed suit; Evers, years later, told a sportswriter as they toured his hometown: "I used to play [ball] on that hilltop when I was a kid, and the cops used to chase us off."

Jack was hooked on baseball from the start. "During the summer evenings after working hours, baseball came before supper, and every available spot was the scene of some sort of a game," he recalled. "It was not an unusual sight in some of the fields to see the outfielders of one game within a few feet of the home plate and catcher in another."

Jack had any number of role models in his family and in the sports world to spur his passion. In the 1880s, his father and uncles played for the Haymakers, an independent semipro team; John Sr. commanded the pitcher's box. The Haymakers "became such a family organization that there was little room for outside talent," boasted Jack, whose first job for the Haymakers was batboy.

John Sr.'s younger brother Tom played for an early version of the Washington Nationals in 1884 in a short-lived "major" league called the Union Association. Tom was a left-handed second baseman, an oddity even in those days. But Tom was still high on everyone's watch list. "'Tom' Evers is too well known here to need much comment," said one Washington newspaper in a preview of the 1885 season. "Evers is one of the surest fly-catchers ever seen. He covers a great deal of ground, and is as agile and quick as a cat."

The Union Association folded before the season could begin, however, and Tom Evers was out of a job. He found work as a clerk in the War Department and stayed in Washington for the rest of his life, playing an occasional game for local amateur clubs. Tom Evers's reputation and glory days lived on for young Jack. They would visit each other on holidays and family occasions, and uncle and nephew remained close for years.

As strong and clannish as the Evers family was and would remain, there were other luminaries for a baseball-mad boy in Troy to admire in the late 1880s and 1890s. The National League was still the dominant force in organized baseball despite the extended rivalry of the American Association and here-and-gone upstarts like the Union Association and Players League. The undisputed star of the National League for much of that time was Troy's native son, "King" Kelly. Although Kelly's parents moved out of Troy when he was only five, every Irish American in the Collar City followed the King's career with a sense of pride and, no doubt, ownership.

Like his father before him, Jack went to the Christian Brothers Teachers School to learn reading, writing, and arithmetic from the Jesuit brothers. By the time Jack was fourteen years old, he was playing shortstop for the much more senior high school squad. "He was the only youngster on the team," according to a later account. "He was indeed precocious when it came to the art of fielding and hitting the horsehide." Jack also had a head for the intricacies of the inside game. "I not only wanted to see every play that was made, but, unconsciously, I wanted to study them," he explained in 1911. "I say unconsciously, for without thinking of what I was doing I would pick apart every play that was made and then ponder with myself whether the play was made right or whether it should have been played according to my ideas."

Jack graduated in 1898 at seventeen, then sought out a good-paying trade. He learned how to paint signs on windows and fences. He was just getting into it when he was stricken with "painters' colic"—a disease contracted from the poisons in the paints. He then found a job as a clerk for one of the local collar factories, in the ironing department, and apparently did a little boxing on the side. Still underage, he also worked as a "clerk" with his brother, who had opened the Evers Brothers Saloon next door to the family home.

The paychecks were spotty, leaving him with a lot of free time. One morning, while hanging out at a gym and watering hole, the Cheerup Athletic Club, Jack read a newspaper account of how the New York State League organized its summer schedule. It got him thinking, "Why wouldn't it be a good idea to have a league here in Troy made up of amateur clubs?"

Jack and his mates recruited others from across Troy to start teams, and Jack was soon elected president of the league. Jack served as "manager, captain, and financial backer" of his own baseball nine, the "Cheerups." He used his $4 weekly salary from the collar company to pay some of the young men. The idea was to put on a show good enough to attract a paid audience of parents and relatives and to give him a little extra income on the side. "Some of them I paid as much as fifty cents a game, but the average salary was a quarter." They played on Sundays since most of the players had day jobs.

As a business, the league drew paltry crowds. Still, in 1901 the Cheerups won the championship, and that winter the city's major and minor league players came home to form an exhibition team that challenged the Cheerups to a match. Jack played third base, shortstop, and pitcher against the assembled pros, "and somehow or other we won." Evers's success got the attention of Louis Bacon, the manager and owner of the Troy Trojans. Bacon had been prowling the parks and sandlots looking for prospects. When he saw how Jack led a group of youngsters over a team of professionals, he offered him a contract on the spot, but Jack turned it down. "I never thought very much of my ability as a player," he recalled.

He didn't stop hanging out in the bleachers, however. The following spring, when Troy was scheduled to play an exhibition against the touring black Cuban X-Giants, Jack bought a seat behind the Trojans' bench. During their warm-ups, he heard Bacon complain that his shortstop had yet to show up. Jack vividly recalled the moment years later. "Something happened to me—I could never describe it—I only know that I left my seat without a word to any one and vaulted over the rail to the players' bench." Jack marched up to Bacon and told him he was ready to play. Bacon looked over the skinny young man, not necessarily recognizing him as the prospect from the previous year. "Get in a suit, kid, I'll guess you'll have to do." The player whom Jack replaced that day never got his job back.

Bacon signed Evers to a contract for $60 a month, more than he'd ever earned, though probably less than others on the team. But as Jack approached his twenty-first birthday, he played well and started getting noticed outside of Troy. Everywhere the team played in the eight-team New York State League, sportswriters took note of him.

At first it was for his defense. "Evers had eight chances yesterday, and he accepted every one of them," noted the *Amsterdam Evening Recorder*. A week after that, the *Sporting News* reported: "Jack Evers, who is playing short, is conceded by the baseball writers in every city where he has appeared, to be the find of the season. He has made more than good." By June, the reporter of the *Schenectady Press* could barely contain himself: "'Little Evers grabbed up a number of difficult ones and planked them over to first in fine style." The *Evening Recorder* went whole hog: "Young Evers still keeps up his grand work at short for the Troy club, and his brilliant performances are conclusive proof that the kid is a natural ballplayer, and not an 'accident.'"

Even with those impressive fielding skills, no one anticipated Jack's standout performance at the plate. He was a consistent hitter—and that year, at least, a hitter with some power, a trait he would never become known for in Chicago. He led the league with ten home runs, nearly as many as he was to produce over eighteen seasons in the majors. Jack knew why: "There was a short right-field fence in Troy and on the other side was the river," the left-handed batter later recalled. "I made so many home runs over that fence that I was regarded as a sort of 'demon slugger.'" Bacon was happy with his new player and with the attendance that came along with Jack and other "Troy Boys" in the lineup. "The number of local players on the Troy team has its effect on the gate receipts," *Sporting Life* noted in June.

Jack was having the time of his life. He was feeling more confident in himself and in his ability as a professional ball player. He had his occupation listed in the *Troy City Directory* as just that: "ball player." It was about this time that the Troy newspapers started referring to him as "Johnny" rather than "Jack."

Johnny roomed at his parents' new house at 385 Third Street when he was in town. He would put on his uniform there and his street clothes over it before walking to the ballpark. By this time John Sr. was in poor health, "pretty much an invalid," but he would routinely accompany Johnny to the park and sit on a sunny hill overlooking the field. Then one day in August, the feisty, ever-proud patriarch informed his eldest son that he could no longer come to the games. "Why not?'" Johnny asked him. Turns out a heckler sitting near his dad had been "roasting" the shortstop on one of his rare bad days. "I was not in shape to take it up with him," John Sr. said. "I could not stand to hear him." In telling this story thirteen years later, the son's disappointment was still achingly real. "He never went to the ball park again," he said.

John Sr.'s health deteriorated rapidly after that, so much so that Johnny begged off the Trojans' next road trip to stay home and help care for him. After lingering a few more days, fifty-four-year-old John Joseph Evers Sr. died in his bed on Friday, August 21, with his large family surrounding him. "He had been a patient sufferer," the *Troy Record* reported in its obituary the next day. On Monday, newspapers took special note of the funeral. "St. Joseph's church was thronged to its utmost yesterday afternoon. . . . The funeral was one of the largest ever witnessed in the city," the *Record* stated. "The popularity of the man and the esteem in which he was held were not made evident alone by the many friends that gathered to pay their last respects, but by the great profusion of floral tributes in various beautiful designs." His pallbearers included Dennis J. Whelan, the former mayor; Edward Dolan, the former alderman and postmaster; Patrick Byron, the former fire chief; and William Coughlin, the former police chief.

Johnny took solace in the fact that he was with his father at the end. The Troy team had arrived home from the road trip an hour after John Sr.'s death. "If I had gone on that trip, I would have been away at the end," the son remembered, a mixture of love, disappointment, and anger still roiling inside him. "Often I looked for the 'fan' who had 'knocked' me and spoiled my father's little pleasure and sunshine, but failed to find him."

Johnny rejoined the Trojans for the last week of the season, but his heart wasn't in it. He was actually indifferent when Bacon told him about the opportunity with Chicago. Bacon had just sold a pitcher to the Colts' manager Frank Selee for $1,500 and offered Johnny as a "throw-in" for another $200. Always a New York Giants fan, Johnny had no feelings for Chicago or any desire to move to the "far" west. He was about to turn the offer down when Bacon suggested he talk to his mother and family members, still in mourning. The decision process that followed underscored the power of the clan. "After talking it over for some time *the family decided* that I might as well take a chance," he wrote, "and I made up my mind that I would go, more for the trip in order to see the big cities than for anything else."

He played his last game for the Trojans—his last game in the minor leagues—on the Sunday afternoon before Labor Day. He would tell the story many times over the years, his memory not always consistent, but newspapers in his days of glory seemed captivated by the origin story of this man from Troy, and they gave him many opportunities to relive the experience. In his most detailed account, which he penned himself in 1915, he recalled going to the Albany train station accompanied by "thirty or forty fellows" who would see him off on the overnight train. Knowing nothing of Pullman sleeper cars, he decided to hang out in the "Sullivan," a nickname traveling players long ago had given to smoking parlors, in honor of a bumpkin catcher who also didn't know that beds were available. "I did not get a wink of sleep," Evers said, "and I smoked until the smoke came out of my eyes."

By the time he had made his way to Philadelphia the next morning, Evers learned the difference between being a star player in a B league and a rookie in the bigs. He found Selee lounging in a hotel lobby and reported for duty. The manager sent him up to a room where he could catch a few winks, but as soon as Evers shut his eyes a bellboy knocked on the door and handed him a uniform. It had belonged to a mountain-sized player about ten sizes bigger than him, maybe more.

In those days, players dressed for the game at their hotel and then took a horse-drawn omnibus to the ballpark. When rookie Evers finally made it to the crowded bus, his new teammates refused to let him on board, ordering him to sit on top. He knew he looked ridiculous, "like a rail bird on a barn roof." But it only raised his Irish dander. "I made up my mind then and there to show [them]."

Hungry, exhausted, and fighting his way around the diamond in a uniform that billowed from shoulder to kneecap, Evers had a predictably lousy day, making four errors on four chances in two games. To add injury to insult, the opposing pitchers each hit him with a "purpose" pitch in his first times at bat. "This was an old trick of the veteran pitchers in those days, to 'bean' a youngster to scare him, or else drive one in his ribs," Evers said. "The lack of sleep and all the smoking had made my eye bad." Riding back to the hotel, again on top of the omnibus, he was tired and "none too cocky." He didn't bother to listen to the razzing from below. "I knew about what they were."

Yet something about Evers's play that day, as bad as it looked and as bad as it felt, must have impressed Selee, one of the shrewdest judges of talent in baseball. The next game, Selee put Evers in at second base and then took him with the team back to Chicago. In the twenty-four games left in the season, Evers committed only one error, playing most of the time at his new position. The *Chicago Tribune* was impressed. Evers "made a distinctively favorable impression in the games played here by his clean cut work at a position unfamiliar to him. The youngster's speed in completing the second half of double plays was one of the features of his work."

The *Tribune* closed its report with a brief appraisal: "Selee thinks Evers will be a valuable man."

Joe Tinker in 1900, when playing for the Colorado Grizzlies minor league team. (Courtesy of Jay Sanford.)

THE MIDWESTERN GAME
Joe Tinker in Kansas City

We cannot coerce a boy into being good, but we can surround him with moral influences. Physical training does this. Health of body must tend to promote a healthful mind and heart. **WILLIAM ANDERSON AND WILLIAM ANDERSON,** *A Manual of Physical Training for Boys and Girls*, 1914

The sun was warm and the prairie sky a brilliant blue on Decoration Day 1899, when it seemed that every man, woman, and child in Kansas City had poured out of their homes to attend one festivity or another. May 30 was the nation's solemn moment to place flowers on the graves of the war dead, and commemorations that year carried special meaning as veterans of the Spanish-American War had finally made it home from the Caribbean and the Pacific. Grateful citizens in western Missouri and eastern Kansas, like people across the country, welcomed the victors and honored those heroes who would never return—some as casualties of battle, many more as victims of yellow fever and other tropical diseases.

Decoration Day was also an occasion to celebrate, however, and thousands of Kansas City residents found ways to do so in public meeting places all over town. Ten thousand showed up at the downtown Convention Hall for "Anglo-Saxon Day," so designated by city fathers who were entertaining a visiting legation from the British government. Four thousand baseball fans took in a Western League doubleheader between the Kansas City Blues and the Buffalo Bisons. Many more filled a burgeoning network of public parks and picnic grounds, which the city had undertaken to build just a few years before—at a cost of millions—to introduce fresh air and greenery to what had long been a dreary urban landscape.

At the sprawling Fairmount Park, on the eastern outskirts of town, the United Christian Endeavor Societies convened that day for their annual picnic. More than five hundred young people from fifty chapters showed up to play games like a boys' running race, ladies' potato-sack race, and bicycle races for gentlemen. The "fair young women Endeavorers" laid out supper on the picnic grounds—typical fare would include cold boiled chicken and tongue sandwiches, spiced beef and sardines, fresh fruits and peach pickles, all washed down with tea, lemonade, and cider.

A brass band entertained with uplifting marches like "The Star-Spangled Banner" and the "Funston Quickstep," a tribute to a local Kansas hero. Prominent churchmen closed the daylong schedule with speeches titled "Our Country" and "True Patriotism." The final call to action by Dr. Hermon D. Jenkins, pastor of the Second Presbyterian Church, was entitled "The Twentieth Century," in which he encouraged his young charges to assume leadership roles in church and community.

Along with the food and games, the young men and women that day gave rapt attention to another entertainment: baseball. The Central High School team was squaring off against a group of teens called the "Endeavorers." The contest went into extra innings and riveted the entire crowd, to the exclusion—and eventual cancellation—of all other field-day contests. The high school nine finally emerged as 12–10 victors—a thrilling outcome, and probably a surprise to everyone, if only because the Endeavorers had at least one "ringer" in their lineup. Playing second base was a darkly handsome eighteen-year-old named Tinker.

Joe Tinker had made a name for himself playing ball in Kansas City's parks and sandlots, and he was already making small wages, if not exactly a living, as a semiprofessional ballplayer in Kansas farm towns like Parsons and Coffeyville. While Tinker had probably been there that day to fulfill a pledge as a member of the Young People's Society of Christian Endeavor, it was also a chance to show off for the hometown girls. The future vaudeville performer was a natural ham on any kind of stage. "He undressed you with a smile and cut you with a joke," said one writer a few years later, branding him the "jovial assassin."

Endeavor Society types tended to come from polite middle-class society, while Tinker came from an abjectly poor family. He was acutely self-conscious, and even angry about it. He was the only child of an unwed mother and the putative stepson of an itinerant butcher and restaurant cook. If he couldn't make it in baseball, Tinker's own job prospects seemed to be in the plasterer and paperhanger trades.

Most people who knew Tinker in Kansas City were probably unaware of his illegitimate birth. His mother, Elizabeth Williams, had been shunned in her adopted hometown of Muscotah, Kansas, upon the arrival of Joe in the summer of 1880; she had committed the unpardonable sin in the prairie Bible Belt. Elizabeth and infant Joe kept on the move in eastern Kansas until settling down in the middle of the decade with another wanderer, William W. Tinker. There is no record of a marriage, but a threesome under the name of Tinker lived across the river in one of the poorer sections of Kansas City, Missouri, from the time Joe was four years old.

By the age of fourteen, Joe Tinker had developed skills in baseball beyond those of other boys, even those many years older. And as a young adult in search of an independent, "modern" identity, he had found a supportive band of friends within the interdenominational Endeavor Society. Unlike a lot of church moral arbiters who equated play and exercise with the sin of idleness, the Endeavorers were one of a growing number of religious organizations that openly encouraged participation in physical activities and athletic competition. They saw such an active, outdoor lifestyle as a natural complement to spiritual "self-improvement," a way to offer both body and mind to the glory of God. Church reformers had a name for this new theology: muscular Christianity.

Equally important to young Tinker, the Endeavorers offered a path to social respectability, and even upward mobility. The society largely ignored Victorian class hierarchies in favor of ecumenical inclusiveness, and the Endeavorers had organized circles around the globe. It's quite likely that Tinker encountered his future wife, Ruby Rose Menown, at a social mixer like the picnic in Fairmount Park.

Ruby Rose was a "rich girl of a fine family," daughter of the late Francis P. "Frank" Menown, a wealthy merchant who ran a wholesale coffee and spice business downtown. Ruby Rose turned sixteen in May 1899, and Joe would not propose marriage until four years later, after he had sojourned across the west and established himself as a big league ballplayer in Chicago. But a Decoration Day outing under the auspices of the Endeavor Society was a natural way to bring this pair of social opposites together. It probably helped that Tinker had dressed for the occasion; as *The Sporting Life* would note upon their wedding, "she was first captivated by his fine appearance in a baseball uniform."

Baseball was more than a game for Joe Tinker, more than even a vocation. At this point in his young life, it looked like baseball could be his salvation.

OLD KANSAS CITY

The population of Kansas City, Missouri, had already topped 125,000 when the Tinkers settled there. Yet no one mistook it for anything but an overgrown cow town on the western edge of American civilization. It was an ugly town to boot, by all accounts, although that was about to change.

Kansas City became an unlikely starting point for the so-called city beautiful movement, which took hold in several metropolitan centers around the turn of the century. That would translate into parks and ball fields for everyone, even street urchins like Joe Tinker.

Early Kansas City fathers would not have predicted as much. In the decade before the Civil War, a motley and rambunctious collection of merchants, traders, and boatmen had arrived at the confluence of the Missouri and the Kansas Rivers, when steamboat travel was the most efficient way to transport farm supplies one way and agricultural products the other. They settled first along the bluffs on the Missouri's south banks. The ramshackle view, said one contemporary observer, consisted of "shady looking brick and frame warehouses, dry goods stores, groceries, hotels, saloons, restaurants, etc." The result was an assortment of rickety buildings that looked as if they were perched on stilts, peering down at the clay streets below.

By 1880, as railroads began spreading across the nation, Kansas City became a transportation and commercial hub for all points west, northwest, and southwest. But the city still was little more than a railhead for cattle drovers bringing in their herds for fattening and eventual transport to Chicago's slaughterhouses. The dirt and stench were profound. "The wooden sidewalks were treacherous, their defects not being discernible due to the layer of mud that covered them," recalled one memoirist about the summer of 1880.

As the city grew, merchants moved into a new downtown grid laid out in flatlands tucked under the Missouri's northward bend. They called their suburb West Bottoms. Stores were crammed together with railroad tracks, mills, packing plants, and a growing "community of dispossession," as one history of the city describes it. West Bottoms would soon earn the nickname "Hell's Half-Acre" from the newspapers, which supplied a steady diet of crime stories. Local historians give the original residents credit, however, for achieving some coherence as a neighborhood. Churches were active, community festivals kept people entertained (though they often turned violent), and for anyone brave enough to watch, there were regular baseball contests pitting the "Plug Uglies" against the "Nose Crackers."

A real estate boom in the early 1880s encouraged property owners to keep building on every square inch of land for maximum commercial value, and the population more than doubled in the process. Yet it was still an ugly city. Almost none of the city's eighty-nine miles of streets were paved in 1880, according to social historian Sherry Lamb Schirmer. Unlike most eastern cities and even some in the west, such as Memphis, which had installed sanitary drainage systems in the 1870s, fewer than a third of Kansas City houses were connected to sewer system by 1880, and they were inadequate in any event, while the rest relied on leaking vaults, cesspools, and gutters to dispose of wastes.

"Rains converted streets to quagmires and offal leached into sources for drinking water."

A few prescient reformers had made halting attempts to set aside some inner-city acreage for parks and recreation spaces. But the city's mercantile class resisted. Only after the real estate bubble burst in 1887 did city leaders acknowledge that Kansas City possessed no aesthetic appeal to outside moneymen or to westbound migrants seeking a decent place to work and raise a family.

It soon dawned on the growth advocates that they should make common cause with the aesthetes. The epiphany wasn't universally shared, by any means, but it visited enough important people to carry the day. "This community stopped for a breath, took a look at itself, and found something was lacking; something had been forgotten," observed a magazine writer in a 1906 assessment of Kansas City's stunning transformation. "It was without a foot of ground to be used as a public park. [It had] carefully overlooked the fact that parks, boulevards, playgrounds, are essential in the building of a city."

A theretofore laissez-faire local government led the way, spurred on by the crusading editor of the upstart Kansas City *Star*, William Rockhill Nelson, and the millionaire copper-mining magnate August Meyer, founder of the Kansas City Smelting and Refining Company. In 1892 Mayor Benjamin Holmes named Meyer president of the Park Board, and the board in turn hired a landscape architect to design a master plan for a boulevard and park system that would encompass the entire city.

The architect was George E. Kessler, a German-born protégé of Frederick Law Olmsted, mastermind of New York's Central Park and the grounds of the 1893 World's Columbian Exposition in Chicago. Like Olmsted, Kessler believed in working with natural terrain and native flora to create oases of green in the middle of urban browns and grays. The Park Board gave Kessler a mandate to create a "city within a park," where even those too poor to live in exclusive, tree-graced neighborhoods could escape the monotony of urban existence. Kessler and Meyer produced a working document that was unprecedented in scope and detail—a comprehensive analysis of topography, traffic patterns, population density, and growth. According to the historian William Wilson, "It was, in a word, planning."

Kessler and Meyer argued for their plan as critical to economic development, but economic growth wasn't the only reason to spruce up the city. Kessler and Meyer also argued on behalf of the city's poor: "How is the poor man's boy to grow into a cheerful, industrious and contented man, unless he can play where play alone is possible, that is, on the green turf and under the waving trees, and can take with him into manhood the recollections of an innocent, joyous boyhood."

Kessler's vision involved a system of wide, tree-lined boulevards connecting spacious parks and other "pleasure grounds," with statues, fountains, and greenery in every neighborhood. The boulevards were designed for the rich to promenade in their horse-drawn carriages, bicycles, and newfangled automobiles. The parks were for the poor, as picnic areas and playgrounds. Taken together, Kessler believed, his system would "arouse community spirit that would, in turn, stimulate the city's economic prowess and standard of living."

Within a decade, Kansas City built fifteen miles of "oiled and dustless" boulevards, including the two-and-a-half-mile Paseo, and 2,100 acres of parks spread among five park districts. Property values skyrocketed as a result, but something more important happened to the city's quality of life. "Children in no part of the city need play in the streets, for within easy distance there is a park, or square, where they may enjoy, under proper restrictions and supervision, the sports of which childhood and youth are fond," wrote one admiring reviewer.

Such was the new state of city life in Joe Tinker's teenage years, when his family never lived farther than a ten-minute walk from the spacious ball fields of the Paseo.

FROM MUSCOTAH TO KANSAS CITY

Joseph Bert Tinker, whose surname helped to personify a double play, began life as part of a tandem. His mother, Elizabeth Williams, gave birth to fraternal twins, a boy and a girl. The daughter died either at birth or in infancy; no record remains of her short life, and Joe never talked about her other than to acknowledge that he was aware of their brief coexistence.

Elizabeth Williams, born in 1856, had come west as a young child to Muscotah, Kansas, from Pennsylvania, with her parents, Joseph B. and Mary Williams, three older brothers, and a baby sister. Muscotah, a town of fewer than one thousand in Atchison County, was a farming center and depot on the Central Branch Railroad, about eighty miles west of Kansas City. Joseph Williams, a butcher by trade, and Mary, a housekeeper, subsequently produced two more children. Elizabeth moved out of the house at age nineteen and became live-in help for a prominent farm family in nearby Grasshopper Falls.

Elizabeth never revealed the father of her twins, conceived when she was about twenty-three. Some say he was an itinerant railroad worker, quite possibly of Italian descent, given Joe's olive complexion, sleepy Mediterranean eyes, prominent Roman nose, and dark black hair. (His mother's parents were Irish.)

Elizabeth named Joseph Bert after her father (and youngest brother) and raised him by herself during his infant years, but she got little to no support in censorious Muscotah. Resident Tom Wilson recalled for several interviewers some long-ago conversations he had with his grandmother Iva Cooper, who knew Elizabeth. "I can still hear her telling me, 'A lot of people gave Joe's mother a bad time because she had Joe out of wedlock, and that was the reason she moved away,'" Wilson said. Wilson's grandfather George Cooper, who delivered railroad merchandise to local businesses, told him Joe's father worked on railroad crews. Many of the men working crews in those days were Italian immigrants, and Muscotah was a frequent stop on their working itinerary. "One would have thought they were in Italy if they had passed through the railway station this Thursday," reported one local newspaper at the time. "A group of forty Italians were chattering in their native tongue."

How and where Elizabeth met William W. Tinker is unknown. Three years her junior, he was born in August 1859 in the Mississippi River hamlet of Oquawka, Illinois, to Heraclitus and Sara Tinker. He lived in

Oquawka at least until early 1880, where the census lists him as a clerk in a butcher shop. While there's no record of a formal marriage, William Tinker and Elizabeth Williams settled down on the eastern edge of Kansas City, Missouri. They listed their occupations as restaurant cook and dressmaker. In early 1900, they told census takers they had been married for sixteen years—that is, from when Joe was three or four years old.

Joe attended public schools and quickly developed a passion for baseball, which he played in sandlots and parks all over the city. "Lacking companionship at home he sought it in baseball," wrote sportswriter and future Tinker confidant F. C. Lane, "and from his earliest years he might be seen by the good citizens of Missouri, chasing rag balls among the tomato cans and ash heaps of vacant lots, and knocking out long flies into the neighboring back yards." In 1894, he joined a school team, the Footpads, and became the star infielder. Within two years he was recruited to join a young-adult City League team called the John Taylors, named after a prominent dry-goods merchant who paid for their equipment and uniforms.

In Kansas City, Tinker ran across his future Chicago teammate, Johnny Kling, who was five years older and played for Hagen's Tailors. Kling's club won the league championship, but Tinker distinguished himself to such an extent that Kling tried to poach him for a new team he was organizing called the Schmerzers, after its sponsor sporting-goods store. Kling "bought" Tinker for three silver dollars, and the Schmerzers went on to win the championship the next year. "The team was presented with fifty dollars," Tinker recalled with pride, "of which my share was two dollars and a half, the first money I ever earned playing ball."

Only eighteen, Joe already faced a crucial decision: keep working at a job he didn't like, or bet on his baseball skills. He had been attending manual training school and learning paperhanging—as an apprentice, his job was to apply the paste to the paper. But working his way up wasn't in the cards, at least not in his mind. "Paperhanging did not appeal to me," he said. He tried out other manual labor jobs, including mining calcimine, a whitewash for ceilings and walls. That suited him even less.

Baseball remained Tinker's first and only love, and on his days off he made a beeline for the ball field. He also made a pest of himself with the Western League's Kansas City Blues, which featured such future big leaguers as Jimmy Callahan. "I used to slip away from work and sneak over the fence, carry bats or do any odd jobs I could inside the ball park for the sake of seeing the games," he said. He had only one driving ambition. "I wanted to be a ball player."

THE ENDEAVORERS

Tinker joined the Society of Christian Endeavor sometime in his adolescence. Modeled somewhat on the Young Men's Christian Association, which had been founded in London in the mid-nineteenth century, the Christian Endeavor movement was the brainchild of Dr. Francis E. Clark, a Congregational minister in Portland, Maine. Clark wanted to revitalize Sunday school with a new kind of youth organization. One evening in February 1881, Clark put forward to a group of young parishioners a "constitution" for a social club. It required each member to commit to a regimen of prayer, daily Bible reading, and regular church attendance, and to devote his or her life to both religious and community activism. The teens were stunned, according to Clark. "A deathly stillness fell upon the meeting," he recalled. "These provisions were evidently more than the young people had bargained for. They had not been accustomed to take their religious duties so seriously." But Clark had not overestimated the spiritual yearning that can drive a teenager's search for identity and meaning. "One by one the young men and women affixed their names to the document," Clark recalled, "a few minutes were spent in conversation, a closing prayer was offered and a hymn sung, and the young people went out into the frosty night and into their homes with many a merry 'Goodnight' to each other, and the first society of Christian Endeavor was formed."

Clark created a template and the mission statement for what became an international ecumenical movement, but otherwise he claimed no authority over the society's offspring that mushroomed across the country. Within six years, more than seven thousand self-managed societies with half a million members had formed, including dozens of "circles" in Kansas City. The interdenominational nature of the organization also brought it adherents in Europe and even Asia, Africa, and South America. At the turn of the century the societies numbered sixty thousand worldwide. According to historian Sydney E. Ahlstrom, the Endeavorer collective not only had become a significant ecumenical force, "but had inspired emulation in almost every denomination not participating." Mainstream religion, he said, "had gained a new and effective means of nurture and extension, and youth had gained more distinct recognition."

A key element of Christian Endeavor participation was the explicit, signed statement of religious duty and fealty. All members pledged to attend monthly meetings and to rededicate themselves each time. That means that Joe Tinker's involvement with the Endeavorers' baseball team at its annual picnic would not have been a casual or even episodic appearance—he was no "ringer" in the mercenary sense. He was a very good player, to be sure, but to play in the Decoration Day game, he would have had to be a member in good standing of Christian Endeavor.

There are other indicators that Tinker fully subscribed to the Christian Endeavor tenets, at least at this stage of his life. Top among them is the Endeavorers' belief in the moral virtues of physical fitness and athletic competition. As an only child, Joe needed playmates; as a poor boy, he craved acceptance in respectable society. Baseball offered both, and the Endeavorers added the sense of higher calling.

In A Manual of Physical Training for Boys and Girls, published by the United Society of Christian Endeavor in 1914, a gymnastics instructor of forty years' tenure at Yale University postulated the principles by which physical fitness contributed to a godly life. "The object of life is a complete development of all the moral possibilities," he stated. "These possibilities are sevenfold. Man is capable of development physically, aesthetically, intellectually, socially, politically, morally, and religiously. The person who neglects one or more of these sides of his na-

ture is one-sided, and he who develops each one of these the nearest
to its utmost possibility of development comes closest to attaining the
object of life." A statement like this would find widespread favor in
America in the early twentieth century. It was still a controversial notion in the 1880s and early 1890s, however, when Joe Tinker was growing up.

Tinker's social mores were still governed by the American "gospel of
work," as historian Steven J. Overman has called it. This was a product
of Lutheran and Calvinist concepts of the calling, which imbued work
with religious significance. The Protestant disciples of the gospel of
work cited it as the force that tamed a continent and built a new nation. Even well into the nineteenth century, the emphasis on work and
self-control was useful preparation for dawn-to-dusk work in shops,
offices, and factories. But the Protestant work ethic took on a life of
its own, Overman contends. "The professional man or woman continued to labor unceasingly at 'getting a living' even after the living had
been got! Thus did work become less the path to salvation than its own
salvation." Both social and religious reformers saw worrisome signs
that an all work, no play compulsion was producing a haggard and
overwrought society. Compared with the "robust" citizens of England,
where cricket, rowing, and other sports were building strong bodies
and minds, Americans displayed "complete indifference" to their physical well-being.

Theodore Roosevelt, who had famously overcome a sickly childhood through exercise and outdoor adventure, saw another peril as
well—what he termed physical and cultural "emasculation" of the
American polity. In "The American Boy," an essay included in his 1901
book *The Strenuous Life*, Roosevelt insisted that a male citizen "won't
be much of a man unless he is a good deal of a boy. He must not be a
coward or a weakling, a bully, a shirk, or a prig. He must work hard and
play hard."

Late nineteenth-century religious reformers, led by advocates of
a newly emerging "Social Gospel," had already begun pushing for a
moral standard that emphasized social relevance, particularly as it

applied to industrial labor conditions in crowded cities. They set up charitable agencies for the urban poor, such as soup kitchens and homeless shelters, and pressed for limits on child labor. But the Social Gospellers, too, were struck by the increasing lack of men attending Sunday church services, and they began criticizing mainline Protestant denominations for ignoring what the critics called the "unmanliness" of modern-day religion. "There can be little usefulness, little intelligence, little moral character, little happiness without the right sort of body," wrote Josiah Strong, a Congregationalist minister and one of the founders of the Social Gospel movement.

The new "muscular Christianity" movement sought to get more boys and young men into the pews. Churches began preaching a moral message that put new emphasis on physical prowess. But they also appealed to the typical adolescent's craving for a higher calling. "Youths did not want simply to be 'amused' or tolerated; they wanted to be of 'service' and to have their 'soldier-like instincts' aroused on behalf of Christ's kingdom," historian Clifford Putney has written. The emerging young people's movement taught adolescents not only that the church belonged to them but also that it could be a primary agency for them to make an impact on the world they were about to inherit.

At the forefront of this uprising was the Young People's Society of Christian Endeavor. The organization's leaders attributed its success and rapid growth to a number of initiatives that were already standard in the secular world but still quite novel for a religious movement. They used committees to organize activities and created a sales pitch to recruit new members. They also used the signed membership "pledge" to maintain attendance and loyalty. But as one Methodist bishop observed in 1892, the real revelation of Christian Endeavor leaders was to treat teenagers not as children but as "straightforward, earnest, practical" individuals, deserving of respect. As a result, they mobilized an army of young men and women who championed a new set of values about work and play into the twentieth century.

Joe Tinker had not only a guiding philosophy to lead him into the world of professional sports; he had a guiding spirit to maintain his strength in the face of continual struggle, failure, and temptation.

ON THE ROAD

Opening Day in Denver in 1900 landed on Saturday, May 5. The always unpredictable spring weather delivered a clear sky. "She had never more plentifully beplumed herself with eiderish clouds, or more brilliantly bespangled herself with sunshine," beamed the *Denver Post* in its exuberant game account the next morning. "The air was warm, the occasionally impending showers withheld themselves, the softly budding trees bent their suppling branches gently with the languid breeze." And that was just the first paragraph.

"Denver loves baseball," the paper affirmed as its anonymous writer of purple prose went on to describe the parade of carriages and cars that started out at Fifteenth and Arapahoe Streets, following two horse-drawn omnibuses that ferried the hometown Grizzlies and the Omaha Omahogs to the ballpark. The crowd had grown to three thousand by 3 p.m., when Mayor Henry V. Johnson stepped out to the pitcher's box. A brass band greeted him with its rendition of the racist blackface tune "Mr. Johnson, Don't Get Gay." Owner George Tebeau gently steered the mayor toward home plate. "A ball was put into his hand. He held it as if it were a cut orange and he feared getting his fingers stained."

Johnson started into his windup and swung his arm, and everyone watched the ball fly some eight yards wide of the plate. "Ha! Ha! Ha! Hey, Mr. Johnson, you're wild!" the crowd shouted. But hizzoner "walked proudly off the field as if he felt that he had done something great—and so he had," the *Denver Post* writer allowed. "He had opened the baseball season."

Parading in the omnibus with his new teammates, and then warming up on the ball field, nineteen-year-old Joe Tinker no doubt shared the excitement even as he sensed the risks confronting him. He had just signed a contract with Tebeau for $75 a month, the most he had ever earned in his life. This was also the biggest crowd he had ever encountered. Jimmy Manning, the popular manager of the Kansas City Blues and a speedy infielder in his day, had seen Tinker play a slick third base and run the bases with flair in exhibition games the summer before. He recommended Tinker to a couple of scouts from Colorado, who gave him a tryout. "A very fast player has been claimed for the Denver club," the *Denver Post* announced in March.

Against his mother's wishes, and with no idea of when or if he would return, Joe packed a bag and headed west.

The pressure in Denver was probably too much for a kid on his first real proving ground. Colorado's love affair with baseball stretched back to the gold rush days of 1859. Practically every town in the state boasted a ball club. Baseball was played in mountain valleys and prairie fields, in farm towns and booming mining camps, by railroad workers, cowboys, and store clerks. "Wives, sweethearts, family and friends came out to cheer," said one history. The greatest team in the state was the 1882 Leadville Blues, a motley crew of high-caliber imports from the East Coast and Midwest, brought to Leadville specifically to revive the town's fortunes after the silver boom had busted.

By the 1890s, however, baseball was on the decline as newspapers started paying more attention to the new, raging fad of bicycling. Worse, Denver's teams, in particular, had put together a long string of losing seasons. "Ball cranks" at the turn of the century were so hungry for winning baseball that their eager anticipation of glory turned up the heat under Tebeau's young charges.

Tebeau, older brother of the notorious umpire kicker Patsy Tebeau, was not an easy man to play for. He was strict and unyielding both on the field and off. He insisted the entire team take rooms at Mrs. Wolfe's Boarding House on South Fourteenth Street downtown, then obliged Mrs. Wolfe to take roll call every morning. What's more, Tebeau decided he already had a serviceable third baseman, so he ordered Tinker to play second base during spring training. It might have seemed a good fit at the start. Tinker "showed up [at second] just as brilliantly as he did on the third corner," the *Denver Post* reported. "It will be only a question whether [he] can bat the ball, and if he is a hit his place is assured on the team somewhere."

But Tinker never got comfortable covering the right side of the infield. And his hitting wasn't good enough to compensate for his erratic fielding. As happens to many young players in their early years, Joe shone one day and stank the next. "Tinker is one of the most natural ball players on the team, but needs developing," judged the *Denver Post*'s longtime sports editor Otto Floto. "His errors are always made at a critical time and generally costly. This comes from being too anxious."

Denver's other paper, the *Rocky Mountain News*, was more forgiving, asking fans to let Tinker and his mate at shortstop take some time to reach their true potential. "All the youngsters need is some encouragement from the fans," pleaded a May 20 dispatch. "The tendency to be unpardonable in viewing the faults of Barnes and Tinker is not at all becoming and the flocks that patronize the game should not be so prolific in their abusing remarks when either makes a bad error or a stupid break."

A few weeks later, on June 11, a day after the *Post*'s Floto reported that Tinker "had his usual quota of errors" in the previous game, Tebeau cut him loose. "Tinker was a good boy, but too costly for the team," Floto concluded. Joe would put it even more bluntly when he reminisced on his start in baseball several years later: "I made of botch of it."

There he stood, unemployed and all alone in Denver, six weeks shy of his twentieth birthday and six hundred miles from home. He could probably return to Kansas City and the paperhanging trade, embarrassed by his failure even if welcomed back by family and friends. He would not be the first aspiring ballplayer to resign himself to that humbling fate, nor the last. Then again, he'd come this far on his own. Why stop?

Tinker got word that a new minor league had formed that spring in the wilds of Montana. The four-club circuit of Butte, Great Falls, Helena, and Anaconda had put together a schedule of eighty games each through the summer months, and they needed players. In fact, they were desperate for players.

Montana's entire population was less than 250,000 in 1901, about the same as Kansas City, and it was a tall order for the Montana State League to attract enough quality players to fill the rosters of four teams. The league was the handiwork of William H. Lucas, heir to a Wisconsin lumber business who had come west ten years earlier with grand ambitions for baseball in the Pacific Northwest. His Oregon and Washington business connections weren't so easy to convince, however, so Lucas had reduced his territorial foothold to western Montana. That was enough for his admission to the halls of organized baseball, which required him to adopt the current standards of the National Agreement and hire only players of good standing from sanctioned minor leagues.

Baseball was not new to the territory. In the 1870s, the Seventh Cavalry Regiment of the U.S. Army boasted a passel of athletic young men who loved nothing more than playing sports in their free time. One enlisted man in H Company, the secretary of his unit's athletic club, recorded purchases of boxing gloves, fencing equipment, checker boards, and "1½ dozen baseball bats" and "one dozen base balls." The club was named after H Company's captain, Frederick W. Benteen, a Civil War hero from Virginia. The Benteen nine dominated interregimental contests, right up to the Seventh Cavalry's ignominious demise in 1876 at the Battle of Little Big Horn, or Custer's Last Stand.

Community ball clubs had cropped up in just about every Montana town in the 1880s, and the competition was fierce and wildly popular. (Marysville's grandstand, erected in 1887 with a capacity of three thousand, remains the oldest ballpark in the state.) Local boosters made several stabs at forming a professional league in the 1890s, although the here-today, gone-tomorrow teams played according to the rough-and-ready rules of the times. Games often ended in fisticuffs or outright melees among players, umpires, and fans.

In their league, William Lucas and Helena team owner Frank Thayer vowed to recruit only "sober and gentlemanly star ball players." When Great Falls announced its roster in May, the local *Tribune* approved, reporting that every player "comes highly recommended, not only as a ball player, but as a sober, steady, reliable gentleman."

Perhaps the early morning roll calls at Mrs. Wolfe's Boarding House worked to Joe Tinker's favor; his good behavior, if not his fielding skills, got him a midseason tryout with the Great Falls Indians. And then after just one game with the club (at second base), his fortunes turned. The *Great Falls Tribune* immediately anointed him "the star" of the team and noted his part in a nifty (if not so poetic) double play, from

"Zearfoss to Tinker to McCloskey." The newspaper also let its readers in on another facet of this new kid's appeal; it gave him the nickname "Pretty."

Pretty Tinker didn't rest on his good looks, however. An Anaconda reporter watched its town's Calciners play a June 30 game against Tinker's Sun Dancers (that paper's moniker for Great Falls). Even while celebrating the home team's 12–3 victory, the story praised the visitors' hustling new second baseman: "Tinker . . . made a hit with the crowd by his clean playing and the manner in which he keeps busy all the time."

The good reviews kept coming throughout July. "Tinker played great ball, as the score shows," said a dispatch from Helena after a July 8 game in which Joe hit two triples and a single and threw out six runners at first base in a 13–8 victory. "Tinker was everywhere," said a story on July 13. "Tinker's home run did it," proclaimed a July 16 headline. Then two days later: "Tinker did the star fielding." Tinker celebrated his twentieth birthday on July 27, no doubt feeling pretty good about himself and his calling.

Even as Tinker's star was rising, however, the fortunes of the Great Falls team were going south fast. The club couldn't make its payroll, including Tinker's $90 monthly salary. Indeed, the club's bank account was $190 in the red. Yet by that time everyone in Montana knew about Tinker and coveted his lightning speed and fielding prowess. John McCloskey, the Great Falls manager and a former skipper of the St. Louis Cardinals, knew he had a valuable commodity. He traded Tinker to Frank Thayer's Helena club for a heavy-hitting (but soon forgotten) third baseman and persuaded Thayer to throw in a $200 cash bonus to sweeten the deal. Tinker took his bat and glove ninety miles south and checked into the Grand Central Hotel, ready to play the rest of the summer for the capital city's Senators.

The best part of the deal for Tinker was that Thayer needed someone to play third base, his favorite position. The switch to a new town and a new place in the lineup raised his entire game. His batting average, only .219 in Denver and not that much better in Great Falls, must have exploded in Helena, for he finished the season at .322 over a total of fifty-seven games. By the end of September, Helena was closing in on a pennant, fans and team owners were elated, and Tinker had earned another nickname. They now called him "The Two Hundred Dollar Beauty."

Only one problem interrupted this story, and it would prove to be another life changer. The Montana State League itself was going bust. Helena was the only team making ends meet, and the four-team circuit couldn't attract enough good players to put on a clean and competitive exhibition. The cellar-dwelling Butte Smoke Eaters were the butt of jokes. The Anaconda Calciners had little "actual knowledge" of their players' abilities, said the *Anaconda Standard*. More problematic, fist-icuffs had again become a regular feature of the games, which meant that Lucas, Thayer, and McCloskey could not maintain a semblance of the good sportsmanship they had advertised. "I see by the papers they have organized a state league," commented a *Helena Independent* reporter, adding caustically: "And if that don't end in bloodshed I miss my guess."

Lucas was already at work on a new scheme, reviving his original vision for a Pacific Northwest league. His Montana experiment had generated enough early enthusiasm to convince his business cronies in Portland and Seattle that baseball just might be a going concern in the more populous coastal cities. An old friend, former catcher Dan Dugdale, would run the Seattle franchise and help mobilize the league's financing. John McCloskey would run a Tacoma club. In Portland, the owners of two streetcar lines teamed up to build a new ballpark.

The Vaughn Street Park was at the far end of a long trolley ride from downtown, but that quite appealed to F. I. Fuller of the Portland Railway Company, which owned the land, and C. F. Swigert of the rival City & Suburban Railway Company. They rightly guessed that baseball would increase ridership on both streetcar lines while also making money at the gates.

Meanwhile, Helena owner Thayer still had control of Tinker's services, and he and Lucas knew they had a budding star and crowd pleaser in the making. They arranged to send Tinker's contract to Portland for an undisclosed sum. Tinker got a raise in the bargain; he'd be earning $125 a month when the circuit's first season opened the following spring.

With the roller-coaster 1900 season finally over, Tinker headed back to Kansas City in late October. He joined a group of top players from the Montana league on a tour of western and southern states, playing a series of exhibition games against local talent as they hopscotched their way back east. "Micky Roche is managing the team, and Joe Tinker, of Portland, has something to do with the selection of the players," reported the *Seattle Daily Times*. Tinker was quick to lock down third base for himself.

MAKING GOOD

The following season, when the pretty boy from Kansas and Missouri came of age, was Tinker's breakout year. Playing third base for the Portland Webfooters, Tinker produced a batting average of .290 over 106 games, including twenty-seven doubles, seven triples, and three home runs. He covered third base with youthful exuberance, if not total competence, making spectacular plays while also racking up 61 errors. The Webfooters led the league from Opening Day and finished with a 75–35 record, winning the pennant by sixteen games over the Tacoma Tigers. A season-ending doubleheader in Portland drew more than six thousand fans to Vaughn Street Park.

Lucas declared the Pacific Northwest League's 1901 campaign an unqualified success—financially for its stockholders and theatrically for its fans. "We have played the cleanest ball of any league in the United States," he said. "There have been no disgraceful scenes of rowdyism such has have characterized the game in many other cities."

What's more, Tacoma's John McCloskey was spreading word through his network back east about a fleet-footed infielder who could run the bases "like a deer" and appeared ready to play in the major leagues. Two National League teams showed immediate interest: the Cincinnati Red Legs and the Chicago Colts. Tinker's dealings with both teams during the winter months would show not only that he had matured as a ballplayer, ready to move into the fast company of the big leagues, but also that the moral compass he'd developed as a Christian Endeavorer still pointed true.

The Cincinnati club's crusty owner, John T. Brush, was particularly eager to grab Tinker for what he thought would be a bargain-basement exchange price: zero. He had assumed he could simply take Tinker away from Portland without compensating the minor league franchise that had legally "reserved" his contract for the following year. Brush's move was a direct violation of the agreement that both National and American League owners had made with the newly formed National Association of Professional Baseball Leagues, a consortium of regional leagues organized to protect its members from just this sort of player poaching. The pact was the beginning of a baseball pecking order of "major" and "minor" leagues that established the structure and ground rules of the game through most of the twentieth century.

Brush, who by that time held financial stakes in both Cincinnati and New York NL franchises, was a notorious practitioner of syndicate baseball, shamelessly "trading" players between his teams depending on which one needed help in the standings or at the gate. He was not well respected or liked, either. "Chicanery is the ozone which keeps his old frame from snapping," one critic said of Brush, "and dark-lantern methods the food which vitalizes his bodily tissues."

Tinker could have taken Brush's money and said good-bye to Portland, except for a sharp nudge to his conscience and a hardheaded calculation: he had no guarantee that he would "make good" in Cincinnati, as a caveat in the contract described it. Brush's offer hinged on Tinker making the team in spring training, where he would be one of thirty or so players competing for eighteen or nineteen roster spots. If he flopped, he'd have to pay a big fine to catch back on with Portland or any other minor league team, assuming any of them would accept such an apostate.

Brush applied more pressure, publicizing his offer to Tinker in the national press, then listing Tinker on the club's roster for the following season. He and manager Bid McPhee made it look like a done deal. But Tinker was having none of it.

"Tinker refuses to put his name to a contract until the Cincinnati management secures his release from the Portland club," the *Washington (DC) Evening Star* reported in November. *Sporting Life* suggested that Brush's personal offer letter to Tinker may have backfired. Tinker "does not like the tone of Brush's letter," its report stated. "The Cincinnati president talks as though he wants him to jump his reservation, and this, Tinker says, he will not do."

Tinker's spine stayed stiff as the public "negotiations" progressed, and it began to look as if magnate Brush had met his match in the twenty-one-year-old tenderfoot. Tinker was playing a pretty mean public relations game of his own. "If Brush wants me, he will have to secure my release from Portland. Then I will talk business with him," Tinker told reporters. "I have written Brush to that effect." A week later, Tinker was still holding fast and talking tough. "If they want me, they will surely be willing to pay a few hundred dollars to my former club."

The back-and-forth exchanges got nationwide attention. "One Loyal Ballplayer," ran an approving headline in the *Trenton (NJ) Evening Times*, marveling at the young man's sense of loyalty. "There are few players who stick up for their clubs when it comes to a matter of dollars and cents." The exchange certainly got the attention of James A. Hart, president of the Chicago National League team, still in the first phases of rebuilding the storied old White Stockings franchise. Hart was prospecting for players to stock Frank Selee's corral, and he was willing to do what Brush wasn't: Hart offered to pay Portland $600 if Tinker "made good" in Chicago the following season.

That December, both Portland and Tinker agreed to Hart's offer and Tinker was on his way east. He joined Selee's training camp in Champaign, Illinois, in March, one of ten infielders competing to make the team. It was rough going at the start, particularly with his meager hitting—he started the season as a "poor sticker," in Hart's words—but Tinker gradually won Selee's confidence. He got a roster slot for the rest of the summer, at what to him must have seemed like an ungodly salary of $1,500 for the season.

In May, the *Oregonian* reported that C. A. Whitemore, president of the Portland Baseball Club, had received a telegram from Hart, "in which it is stated that Joe Tinker has 'made good' in the Windy City. The Chicago people will pay Portland $600 for Tinker's release."

Selee was remaking the Chicago roster from the bottom up, and he liked what he saw in the infielder. His early assessment was quite generous coming from such a taciturn New Englander. "In Joe Tinker, I think I have a regular find," Selee told a reporter. "The boy has enthusiasm and ginger, and is the most natural ball player I have seen in many a day."

Frank LeRoy Chance, circa 1898 in Chicago. (Courtesy of Mark Braun, Old Timers' Baseball Association of Chicago.)

THE WESTERN GAME
Frank Chance in Fresno

Here perpetual summer is in the midst of unceasing winter; perennial spring and never failing autumn stand side by side, and towering snow clad mountains forever look down upon eternal verdure. **LANSFORD W. HASTINGS,** *The Emigrants' Guide to Oregon and California,* 1845

Forty years after Congress made it the thirty-first state of the Union, California was thriving. The nation was barely more than a century old itself in 1890, still filling in the massive gaps of its western frontier past the Rocky Mountains. But the Golden State, bathed in warmth and sunshine, abundant with fruit orchards, vegetable crops, vineyards, and cattle ranches, and teeming with a million and a half people, had grown to a point at which its economy was rich in oceangoing trade with Asia in one direction and rail commerce to the east in the other. Earnest farmers and ranchers—virtually all transplants from the east or their immediate offspring—worked the great Central Valley that stretches from Sacramento to Los Angeles. Adventurers, fortune hunters, real estate speculators, gamblers, and other sporting men filled cities and towns, eager to cash in on the next big ticket.

Railroads ran the length of the state and also spread eastward, across the mountains and prairies, through the commercial hubs of St. Louis and Chicago, all the way to New York, Washington, and Boston. Coast-to-coast telegraph lines cut the distance even more dramatically

as electric current made transcontinental communication almost in-
stantaneous. Yet Californians remained in virtual isolation, left to their
own devices for work, social interaction, and entertainment.

Practically untouched by the Civil War, which had taken 630,000
lives in the 1860s, "free-state" California had few scars to mend. Its
denizens developed their own, modern sensibility—a strange brew
of independence and recklessness, greed and avarice, social ambition
and civic insolence, undaunted courage and unbridled optimism. They
relished the idea of their society as both secular and spiritual—as an
American Mediterranean grounded in passion and sensual beauty,
and as a "City on a Hill" with mystical connotations, even if each aspect
of that culture remained a work in progress.

One of California's second-generation scions was Frank LeRoy
Chance, thirteen going on fourteen in the summer of 1890. Raised in
the Central Valley boomtown of Fresno, Frank was in many respects
a typical adolescent, still getting a feel for life while coming to terms
with a powerful family legacy. Yet he was expected to grow up fast. His
father and mother, William H. and Mary Russell Chance, were bona
fide pioneers, each coming across the country as children, by way of the
Oregon Trail. Paternal grandfather Dennis Chance and his clan were
among the first wave of farmer-settlers to brave the two-thousand-
mile expanse from Missouri to the Oregon Territory in 1846. Frank's
maternal ancestors Levi and Priscilla Russell made the trek in a post-
gold rush emigration wave in the mid-1850s. Frank's parents had
walked those two thousand miles in their bare feet.

William Chance and Mary Russell met in northern California and
married in 1870. Frank, their fourth child and third son, arrived on September 9, 1876, the twenty-sixth anniversary of California statehood.

Fresno was little more than a dusty farm outpost of a few hundred souls
when California entered the Union. Yet it would soon become the site
of many opportunities for the Chance family. By 1890 Fresno boasted
ten thousand people, with another twenty thousand in the surrounding county. Merchants, shopkeepers, bankers, office workers, bureau-
crats, and schoolteachers formed a thriving mercantile community in

the middle of a mother lode of agriculture and trade. Fresno enjoyed a propitious location, halfway between boisterous San Francisco and then-sleepy Los Angeles, which made it the ideal stopover on the four-hundred-mile rail line that connected northern and southern California. Before long Fresno served as hub to a network of feeder rail lines fanning out to farm towns across the valley.

For the Chance family and settlers like them, Fresno felt like El Dorado, "the golden one," a mythical destination believed by early Spanish conquistadors to hold fabulous wealth and good fortune. William Harvey Chance, for his part, embodied and led Fresno's can-do business culture. Known in and around town by his initials, W.H. had made a small fortune in the 1880s, starting out as a boy farmer-turned-rancher, then as merchant and railroad land speculator, and later as a banking and investment tycoon. One of his contemporaries and likely cronies was the infamous Elias J. "Lucky" Baldwin—hotelier, theater impresario, land baron, speculator, and shameless philanderer. Among Lucky Baldwin's more lucrative business ventures was Rancho Santa Anita in southern California, home to a large stable of world-class thoroughbreds.

By this time, W. H. Chance could afford almost anything he wanted. He was certainly ready to treat himself to some extended time off, to enjoy some perks of the good life. Or so he told his family and friends.

In the summer of 1890, W.H. announced that he was taking a pleasure trip back east, and as his boon companion, he had decided to take along his teenage son, Frank. Just before noon on Thursday, June 12, father and son waved good-bye to Mary and the rest of the family (including the two elder sons), jumping aboard the Pacific Express north to Oakland, where they transferred to the Central Pacific Rail Road. They chugged over the Sierra Nevada and across the desert to Promontory, Utah, the historic meeting point with the Union Pacific line, which in turn carried them through Wyoming, Nebraska, Kansas, Missouri, and Illinois. In Chicago, they hooked up with the New York Central System, tracing the lower rim of the Great Lakes through Indiana, Ohio, and the northwestern corner of Pennsylvania into New York State.

The trip took ten days at best back then, the average speed about thirty miles an hour, giving Frank plenty of time to take in a detailed rendition of the family's origin story—illustrated with real-life geographical landmarks. He also got an exclusive, front-row seat that allowed him to observe, and absorb, W.H.'s brimming confidence and quiet self-control.

Their destination was Saratoga Springs, an upstate New York spa resort famous for its thoroughbred race track and tony betting parlors. Here the Chance fellows would spend several weeks as railbirds, cheering (and wagering on) some of the finest horses of the era. They even got to put some money on Lucky Baldwin's West Coast darling, a four-year-old named Los Angeles. The comely mare would reward them in the climactic race of the season, the Excelsior Stakes, beating all odds and outrunning legendary Kingston, son of Spendthrift, a big black stallion with more than 130 victories to his name.

The extended trip gave Frank his first full taste of a sporting spirit that would intoxicate him for the rest of his life. Frank was already the youngest player on the first "kid" baseball team in Fresno. He would soon grow into the six-foot, 190-pound frame that made him a celebrated amateur heavyweight boxer. And throughout his adolescence there was hardly a sporting activity or contest that escaped his eager participation. Even the ponies stayed in his blood; in his later career as player-manager of the Chicago Cubs, his legendary strictness did not extend to keeping his players from exercising their competitive instincts at the track.

On the return trip, the Chance men once again enjoyed white-linen dining, round-the-clock porter service, and restful Pullman sleeping cars as they recrossed the frontier that W.H. had traversed as a boy. It was a far cry from then in comfort, style, and speed. That wagon trek had taken more than six months, at rarely more than ten miles a day, walking most of the way across prairies, deserts, and treacherous mountain passes. When the Chance party reached its destination, having sold, lost, or abandoned most of its worldly possessions on the trail, the family had to start from scratch in an unknown land.

Frank Chance never had to endure such a brutal ordeal during his privileged boyhood. But the repeated stories of his family's "westering" provided the foundation for Frank's own lifetime code of conduct. In his every endeavor, Frank embraced his family legend as if he had to live up to it.

THE WESTERING

Dennis Chance was a subsistence farmer in the northwestern corner of Missouri when the newly published journals of western explorer John C. Frémont began circulating in the eastern states. Frémont— the "Great Pathfinder," as he became known—had chronicled his efforts of 1842–44 to find and chart a route to California and the Oregon Territory. Frémont's vivid accounts of exotic landscapes, hostile and friendly Native Americans, majestic mountains, and serene coastal climes captured Americans' imaginations. His journals inspired a new sense of national identity, infusing an aspiration that would come to be called Manifest Destiny.

In the winter of 1845–46, Frémont's journals came into the hands of Missourian John McCurry Jones, whose wife, born Mary Anne Smith, was a sister of Dennis Chance's wife, Sarah Ann. Many years later, about 1915, Mary Anne Jones left a recollection of those days and the fever that spread through their family ranks. The Joneses' relatives and neighbors "began to talk of moving to the new country," she recalled, "and they brought the book to my husband to read, and he was carried away with the idea, too." She was not so easily persuaded. "I said, 'O, let us not go.' Our neighbors, some of them old men and women, . . . had large possessions and large families, but it made no difference. They must go." By the spring of 1846 "all were making ready to go to the new country, and we with them."

Other family connections reinforced the westering impulse. Dennis Chance's own sister, Julia Ann, was married to a man named Robert Gilliam. Gilliam's uncle Cornelius was one of the first pioneers to make the dangerous trek two years earlier, not only having staked out a land claim in Oregon's lush Willamette Valley but also being named a "colonel" in the local militia. Colonel Gilliam had sent back word that the northwestern territory was both fertile and welcoming to American settlers.

The colonel's enthusiasm was not tempered by the fact that Great Britain still maintained a long-standing, if tenuous, co-occupational treaty with the United States over the broad swath of territory that now encompasses the states of Oregon, Montana, Idaho, and Washington, plus the province of British Columbia. Britain's mercantile agent on the scene, the Hudson's Bay Company, was not about to cede valuable trading territory to American squatters. At that moment, no migrant had any guarantee that a homestead claim in Oregon would be honored by either the United States or Britain.

Like many struggling farmers, Dennis Chance was in constant search of opportunities that could not only support a family but also give him a sense of independence and security. That motivation had kept him on the move, continually pushing westward whenever he sensed a better deal ahead. Born in North Carolina in 1814 to a white settler and Cherokee mother, Chance had first migrated in the 1820s with his parents to Kentucky, where land was cheap and productive. As a young adult, Dennis set out on his own to west-central Missouri, where he married Sarah Ann Smith in 1838. The couple settled in Andrew County, upriver from St. Joseph, where their first child, William Harvey (Frank's future father), was born in April 1840.

Working a farm in the Missouri River bottomlands was hard, unpredictable, and dangerous. In 1844 came the Great Overflow, when more than eighteen inches of rain fell in May and June alone. "The downpours were of daily occurrence for weeks," reported a 1908 account. "Creeks became rivers, and rivers raging torrents." Making things worse, the floods caused a "General Sickness" that the locals called "the ague"—malaria, which yet had no known cure. The widespread suffering convinced many that a journey west was worth it, whatever the risk, "for the benefit of my health and to See if I could find a health[y] country to remove my family," as one pioneer put it. Recalled another: "Generally the first question which a Missourian asked about a country was whether there was any fever and ague."

For the Chances, Joneses, and Gilliams, the siren call was almost impossible to resist. A land of milk and honey—and free land—awaited them in the Far West, they believed. "We sold our home, and everything we could not take with us, and what we could not take with us or sell, we gave away and on the seventh day of May 1846, we joined the company for California," recalled Mary Ann Jones. The three families joined about 1,600 others who set out on the Oregon Trail that spring. William Chance had just turned six years old in April. His brother James was four.

The year 1846 was a momentous time—"The Year of Decision," as historian Bernard DeVoto put it in his classic study of the nation's push westward. President James K. Polk was playing a three-dimensional chess game inspired by Manifest Destiny, working a simultaneous diplomatic, legislative, and military stratagem to secure the Oregon Territory away from Britain, purchase (or conquer, if necessary) Alta California and New Mexico from a diffident Mexican government, and ensure that the United States could annex Texas and expand its borders westward along the Rio Grande. If Polk succeeded, which was no sure bet, the United States would soon become a continental nation, unimpeded from the Atlantic to the Pacific and extending from the forty-ninth parallel south to the Rio Grande. If Polk failed, North America would remain a patchwork of competing nations.

Nothing about the trip in 1846 was predictable or easy. "There were no bridges, no ferries and a stream too large to be forded was crossed by means of rafts, if there could be found timber along the banks to make rafts. If not, our wagon beds were used for flat boats," child traveler Mary Elizabeth Munkers Estes recalled. Like William Chance, Estes walked most of the distance, since the primitive, suspensionless wagons jarred the bones on the rutted, rocky paths. "We children had to go bare-footed (but that suited us), as our shoes of calf skin hardened, burned and shrunk until we could not get them on our feet, which chapped and crusted," recalled Elizabeth Lord, another child pioneer.

The first half of the journey went by without major incident. The trail along the south bank of the Platte River had been well marked, and the families worked together. Even the Rockies proved not daunting because previous explorers, publicized by Frémont, had discovered in southern Wyoming the only wide break in the mountain chain. The

South Pass allowed the emigrants to cross over a gentle incline up to 7,440 feet, which even ox-drawn wagons could manage. Not until they crossed the Continental Divide would the emigrants encounter what must have seemed like another planet. The Utah desert's dry, alkaline terrain was discomfiting and forbidding. "I have not said much about the dust, when in reality we suffered terribly from it," remembered Lord. "We traveled for days at a time through all those alkali districts, where the soil was cut up into the finest dust from t[w]o or three to five or six inches deep, where it rose in clouds. Our hands and faces were rough and sore, and everybody was burned as black as a white person can get."

Boys like William were given responsibilities of men twice their age. Enoch Garrison, age seven, was driving a team of oxen with a whip while standing on the tongue of his family's wagon. The wagon bumped over a rut and Enoch tumbled to the ground, unable to scramble free before both wagon wheels rolled over his tiny leg, "mashing down in a rut eight inches deep, mashing them into small pieces," recalled his older brother Henry. No one had experience in such gruesome medical matters, so they merely set the leg in a splint. Before long the boy complained about "feeling worms crawling" in his injured leg, and they realized that gangrene had set in. A two-hour operation to amputate followed, using primitive instruments and no anesthetic. Enoch Garrison did not survive the excruciating pain of the ordeal. "He saw his Mother standing by his side," Henry wrote. "He gave her his hand and said, Good by Mother I am going to Heaven."

Once a wagon train reached Fort Hall, the Hudson's Bay Company trading outpost in what is today eastern Idaho, travelers had a momentous decision to make: turn north on a well-tested path to Oregon, or stay on a vaguely charted southwesterly trail to California. Their fates rested on the call. By late June 1846, the pioneers would have known that the British government had ceded all claim to the Oregon Territory south of the forty-ninth parallel, its ministers cutting a deal with the Polk administration to pull back to Vancouver Island. That meant homesteaders who had set their sights on the Willamette Valley could expect to gain clear title to U.S. land claims—and, they correctly anticipated, freehold grants from Congress of as much as 360 acres per couple.

At the time, however, the only known route to Oregon City and the Pacific terminus of the Columbia River was to follow the Snake River north to where it flows into the Columbia, then trace that stream westward. Soon they would come upon The Dalles, the stony river gorge that effectively served as the end of the Oregon Trail. No wagons could pass beyond its steep cliffs, so emigrants had to build rafts and float downriver through dangerous swirls and currents.

While the Chances, Jones, and Gilliams were at Fort Hall, word came from a team of trail veterans, led by Jesse Applegate, that a southern route to the Willamette Valley had opened. The Applegate cutoff followed the California Trail along the Humboldt River before veering to the northwest. Applegate and his fellow trailblazer Levi Scott assured the exhausted travelers that their route would be easier and quicker, even though it was four hundred miles longer than the northern Dalles option.

Which trail Dennis Chance took isn't clear. He seems to have opted for the Applegate cutoff, since California seems to have been his and Sarah Ann's preferred destination. Another account suggests the Jones family, Sarah Ann's sister and husband, also followed the Humboldt River. They were in the same train as the ill-fated Donner party, according to this account, but managed to find the "old Dutch flat route" over the Sierra Nevada, crossing into California a mere one and a half days before the others. (The Donners, of course, were trapped by a sudden snowstorm and stuck in the mountains for weeks, to a horrific end.)

When the Chance clan finally arrived in northern California, the settler's life turned out to be no more stable or secure than the hardscrabble Missouri one they had left behind. Dennis pursued agriculture for a spell, then tried his luck at mining "for a few months" when the Gold Rush hit in 1849. He resettled in El Dorado County, making ends meet as a gardener in the gold rush camp of Growlersburg, named for the heavy, gold-laden quartz rocks that "growled" in the miners' pants pockets as they walked around town. Dennis eventually figured out there was more money in merchandise than in gold. The camp quickly grew into a proper village, Georgetown. Chance opened a hostelry, the Missouri House, with a partner, but for unknown reasons in less than two years his fortunes were "completely wrecked."

Dennis Chance died soon thereafter in 1852, at thirty-eight, leaving eldest son William, twelve years old, to fend for his widowed mother and four brothers.

A MAN OF WEALTH AND MEANS

William Chance no doubt gleaned from his father's experience that the real get-rich opportunity wasn't the mining of gold—most of the deposits had been found and exploited in the first year or two—but rather in providing goods and services to the miner economy. An enterprising man could earn still more by tapping into the potent agribusiness nexus of real estate and commerce that had already been developing.

William worked a series of agricultural jobs until 1862. Then at twenty-two he rented some land near Stockton, about fifty miles south of Sacramento in the north of the Central Valley, and began farming his own plots. Six years later he had saved enough money to buy property thirty miles farther south in Stanislaus County, where he maintained a farm near Modesto. There he met Mary Russell, like him a Missourian who could spin childhood tales about her family's Oregon Trail crossing. They married in September 1870 and began raising a family. Their fourth child, Frank LeRoy, was born six years later. The following year the extended Chance family, including Mary's parents and siblings, moved another hundred miles south to Fresno, where William had bought a large property and expanded his farming operations to a much greater scale, including cattle ranching.

Fresno at that time, according to a 1919 history of it, was little beyond a "barren plain with nothing to obstruct the visual horizon nearer than the Coast Range on the west and the Sierras foothills on the east side." A visitor in 1881 was even more unsparing, noting that the town was little more than "a handful of houses in a desert of sand." But unlike other nearby farm villages, Fresno possessed a ticket to the future.

The San Joaquin Railroad (later taken over by the Southern Pacific) in 1872 had located a depot there on its artery from the San Francisco Bay to Los Angeles. By 1880 the two-hundred-mile trip took less than four hours. Merchants of all stripes quickly filled streets around the depot. Besides the requisite hotels and saloons were a stove and tin shop, cigar and fruit stand, druggist, newspaper office, shoe store, a barber whose wife kept a notion shop, several law offices, and the Metropolitan Hall theater.

William Chance jumped at the opportunity to establish himself in this commercial hotbed. In November 1880, the *Fresno Morning Republican* began running front-page, two-column advertisements for the "new firm" on Mariposa Street near the depot. "Ready for business," the ad announced. "We keep constantly a well selected stock of GENERAL MERCHANDISE, and make a specialty of CHOICE GROCERIES. Our Prices are as Low as the Lowest!" Partners Thos. R. Brown and W. H. Chance were the proprietors.

What made dusty Fresno such a commercial hub, in addition to the railroad, was the ingenious introduction of water to the desert terrain. Three miles south of downtown was a four-thousand-acre agricultural project, enclosed by a fence and divided into twenty-acre lots. The Central California Colony featured a system of canals that delivered enough water from the San Joaquin River to support the cultivation of grapevines, orchards, vegetables, and dairy-cow pastures on every tract. For the average price of $900, with a $100 down payment and a five-year note (at no interest), a small farmer could purchase a tract with full water rights and expect to earn $5,000 a year from raisins or as much as $10,000 a year from prunes. The rapid success of the colony precipitated a wave of similar ones in the county. Fresno became known as a "cow town wonder."

The combination of railroad and water triggered a speculative real estate boom in the San Joaquin Valley that made the grocery business seem like small potatoes to W. H. Chance. In 1884 he led a group of twenty investors who surveyed a line for a narrow-gauge railroad from Fresno across the valley floor to the Sierra Nevada foothills. "The value of this enterprise to the people of Fresno and the county generally can hardly be overestimated," the *Fresno Morning Republican* reported in

May. Chance went on to make a small fortune as a land speculator scouting out routes for other railroad lines that would transport the agricultural bounty of the Central Valley to the Bay Area's rail hub and seaports. In the process, he became a role model in Fresno's business community. "The town was one great real estate brokerage community; every one was . . . a land seller," said local historian Paul Vandoor.

The Chances moved into a large, well-furnished home at 837 O Street, in a posh residential neighborhood that was considered "out in the country" at the time. W.H. became one of the largest stockholders in the First National Bank of Fresno, "one of the most substantial banking institutions in the state," serving as its director and vice president for many years. In January 1890, the *Fresno Weekly Republican* included him in a list of "People Very Well Off," based on his assessed personal property value of $18,000—not the richest man in town, but clearly a man of established wealth and means.

W. H. Chance was moving in a closely knit society of business tycoons who helped grease one another's inside deals and provide a statewide support network in the volatile West Coast economy. A ubiquitous presence in that network was Lucky Baldwin. Though there's no record of a direct association between them—Frank Chance would one day take his Cubs teammates to Baldwin's ranch—it's hard to imagine that W.H. wouldn't have worked with Baldwin on all sorts of business schemes, if only because of their shared interests in land speculation and thoroughbred horses.

Baldwin had come west in 1853, at twenty-five, from Racine, Wisconsin. Unlike the pioneer settlers of the Chance-Gilliam-Jones era, however, Baldwin embarked on the Oregon Trail as if it were a business venture. He outfitted four wagons and took along more than a score of horses. One of his wagons was loaded entirely with brandy and another with tobacco and tea. The brandy never made it to California, sold en route to Brigham Young's brother for a tidy profit. He sold the horses in Sacramento at a 400 percent markup.

Baldwin quickly bought a hotel in San Francisco for $5,000 and began making money in other motley investments. He became a force on the San Francisco Stock Exchange. In 1875, he turned his attention southward and purchased the Santa Anita Ranch outside of Los Angeles, where he shrewdly maneuvered his way into the ownership of an abundant sheep pasture called Rancho La Cienega. This he converted into a profitable dairy farm, ocean-side orchards and vineyards, and a thoroughbred stud operation.

By the summer of 1890, when the Chance father and son set off on their trip to Saratoga Springs, Lucky Baldwin dominated the West Coast horse-racing world. He would send his best runners east each spring to compete at the nation's top racetracks in Chicago and New York. This season, Lucky had sent a string of Santa Anita horses (including the mare Los Angeles) to Brooklyn. The Baldwin stable was expected to perform well that summer—"it was as strong a one as ever shipped east from the State," affirmed the San Francisco Call. But apart from the horse Los Angeles, who won high stakes races in both Chicago and New York, most of the Baldwin horses turned in generally disappointing performances. Lucky wanted to know why.

Did W. H. Chance go east as a secret agent of sorts, serving as eyes and ears for Lucky on the proxy management of the Santa Anita horses? The circumstances suggest as much. The Call reported on June 23 that Baldwin had sent his nephew George to Chicago's Washington Park to take oversight of the Santa Anita Stables' exports there. The younger Baldwin left California the same week that W.H. and Frank began their trip.

The reports back couldn't have been very favorable. By summer's end, Lucky hightailed it east to take "personal charge of his stable at Saratoga," the Call reported, because its "management was something dreadful to think of, and race after race was thrown away through incompetency and something much worse."

If W.H. was sniffing out corruption in Lucky's New York operation, his boy Frank provided convenient cover: a father and son moving casually about Saratoga Springs, befriending the "sports" and other regulars who populated the grandstand, pari-mutuel betting lines, and backstretch stables of the track. One of Frank's older brothers might have aroused suspicion.

Perhaps this experience enabled Frank to see that his father, a self-made man, had come to personify the California dream. William had come across the country in a wagon train and survived, had experienced the easy money and broken hopes of the gold rush, and had thrived through entrepreneurial risk taking. He also learned how to maneuver through the myriad cultures and personalities coming to California. "Whatever else California was, good or bad, it was charged with human hope," observed Kevin Starr in his seminal history of the state. "It was linked imaginatively with the most compelling of American myths, the pursuit of happiness."

BASEBALL FEVER

Frank Chance had, in a way, prepared himself for the journey to Saratoga Springs with his own introduction to athletic competition two years earlier. In the summer of 1888, W. H. Daniels was the head of circulation for Fresno's Democratic-leaning newspaper, the *Expositor*, when a ragtag group of boys and their "manager," a high school senior, came into his office on Fulton Street. Daniels and his boss, J. W. Ferguson, were in the midst of a bitter circulation war with the *Fresno Republican*, their arch political rival. The boys put forward a bold proposition that must have struck a nerve.

"Say, Mr. Daniels," said one of the lads, "don't yer believe Mister Ferguson will give us a uniform if we organize a baseball club and call it the Expositor?" Impressed, Daniels ushered the group into the publisher's office, where Ferguson didn't need much convincing. He had always encouraged "harmless and beneficial" sports among youth, and he readily agreed to underwrite this enterprising team. He told Daniels to take the boys down to the L. F. Winchell tailor shop and have each one measured. The team soon returned to the newsroom spiffed out in dark maroon shirts and knee-length breeches, accented by broad white belts and double-ringed caps. The name "EXPOSITOR" was embroidered in large white letters across each boy's chest. The uniforms were just bold enough to catch the notice of newspaper readers all over town.

Among the roster of Expositor players was its youngest member,

The *Fresno Expositor* newspaper sponsored the city's first youth baseball team in 1888, supplying equipment and uniforms. Twelve-year-old Frank Chance, reclining on the floor on the left, was its youngest player. (Courtesy of the Fresno Historical Society.)

Frank Chance, eleven. In a nearby photography studio, Frank and his teammates sat for a cabinet portrait, posed in front of a screen depicting a middle-class house and yard. The group's stern, if fresh-faced, expressions made for an earnest image of Victorian respectability, along with an unspoken message: we're ready to play ball. The Expositors quickly made a name for themselves and their sponsor. They beat another team 13–3 later that day, and immediately called out all challengers younger than sixteen. So began the first organized "kid" league in Fresno.

Chance and his compatriots had caught on to a wave of public enthusiasm for a uniquely American sport. Baseball was popping up in every farm town and village in the state. An earlier version of the game had been a regular pastime in midcentury gold rush camps, where prospectors wiled away their free time and frustrations on makeshift diamonds. As the game and its rules evolved, baseball found its way down into farm communities. By 1885, according to one report, rural Californians were "devoted to the game" and looked forward to their "accustomed amusement" on summer Sunday evenings; without baseball, life became "unbearably dull."

Baseball in California was something of a restorative antidote to the abject failure of so many veterans of the gold mines, according to agricultural historian David Vaught. Most Midwesterners who flooded across the country with infinite riches in their eyes were rudely disabused of their grandiose notions. But they never lost their competitive spirit. "Many of them, too ashamed to return home, turned to agriculture and rural life with the same intensity of expectation that brought them to California in the first place," wrote Vaught in *The Farmers' Game*. "Dread of admitting failure a second time infused them with a furious drive to succeed."

Frank Chance and the Expositors encountered this intensity in each opponent that summer. They regularly defeated teams from Visalia, Madera, Merced, and Tulare. Frank played pitcher, catcher, infield, and outfield, wherever his skills were needed, and he was "the star hitter of the outfit," as a friendly profile writer exulted years later.

W. H. Chance approved of Frank's baseball activities even while agreeing with Mary that he should focus on getting a good education and preparing himself for a career, preferably in banking. Whether that notion ever took hold in Frank's mind is unclear. Frank entered Fresno High School in the fall of 1890, just as he turned fourteen, and continued there for a couple of years. He met a girl, Illinois transplant Edythe Pancake, and began a romance that would last a lifetime.

Then a family tragedy changed his entire outlook on life.

In April 1892, W. H. Chance and his oldest son, Arthur, departed for San Francisco, on their way to Honolulu, "where they will stay the summer for the benefit of the former's health," reported the *Fresno Morning Republican*. W.H. was suffering from Bright's disease, a kidney ailment today known as nephritis, or an inflammation that impairs kidney functions. It's not clear why the family thought Hawaii was the place for W.H. to recuperate, but four months later the men returned to the mainland with W.H. in a worse state. "On the trip he began to sink rapidly," the *Morning Republican* reported on July 27, and upon arrival in San Francisco "he was removed to the hospital in a dying condition."

When word reached them by telegram, Mary and Frank rushed to San Francisco, accompanied by O. J. Woodward, president of the First National Bank. W.H. died the next day, at fifty-two. The funeral had to be held at the Seventh-Day Adventist church because it was the largest one in the city. "The services were more than usually impressive," the *Morning Republican* reported. The body lay in a black-cloth-covered casket in front of the pulpit. "Requiems were sung by the choir, and . . . Father Yager preached an elegant funeral sermon in which he paid high tribute to the many Christian and lovable qualities of the deceased. His remarks drew tears from the eyes of all present."

THE MAKING OF AN ATHLETE

More than ever, Mary Chance wanted Frank to continue his education. Frank told sportswriters several years later that he attended Washington College (in modern-day Fremont), 160 miles north of Fresno on San Francisco Bay. Washington College was actually a coeducational prep school of about 130 students who took classes in liberal arts and commercial training to ready them for university or the business world. Frank's older brothers had attended the school in its College of Commerce, where they could study anything from penmanship and mental arithmetic to commercial geography and international law. Frank appears to have enrolled for a couple of years at least (he was pictured as a member of the baseball team) before the institution closed its doors temporarily in 1894.

His heart couldn't have been in his studies. His passion for sports consumed most of his time and attention. In December 1893, he was playing football for the Fresno Amateur Athletic Club and pitching for the Fresno Republicans baseball team, which played in a statewide amateur league. In January 1894 the local paper reported that Chance had left for San Francisco, "where he will remain for some time." But just six weeks later he was back in Fresno playing left end for the football team. He also joined the National Guard during the spring, spending weekends in Stockton.

By April 1894, Frank was back playing baseball for Fresno as well, as they visited Visalia on a windy Sunday. Frank was at bat when a dust cloud blew across the infield as the pitcher delivered a high-inside pitch. Frank never saw it coming. The ball struck him on the side of his head, below the left ear. "He was knocked senseless by the blow," the *Fresno Morning Republican* reported. "His knees gave way and he fell to the ground as if dead."

Chance was rushed to a nearby hotel where two doctors labored over him for several hours before he finally revived, though barely. He was taken back to Fresno by train the next day, where he rested in bed under the care of his mother and a steady stream of worried teammates. It was another week before Frank could venture outdoors. The frightening episode was the first reported incidence of a career full of beanballs and body blows, which, taken together, many suspect as the cause of the severe headaches that plagued Chance later in life.

But the young Frank Chance, like most adolescent athletes, remained undaunted, resuming intense physical activities with a passion. He teamed with other National Guard corporals to organize a group they called the Big Six, which took on all comers in the drills and contests staged at the Stockton encampment. In August, Chance and another group of friends calling themselves Hobo's Rest, described as a "star aggregation of enjoyment seekers," took a four-week camping trip into the Yosemite Valley, including a two-week hike up the twelve-thousand-foot peaks of the Sierra Nevada range. They came back "hale and hearty."

In the fall came football and baseball again—and another head injury. Catching a game in Selma, Chance crossed signals with his pitcher and missed a fastball whistling straight toward his face. "The ball struck the mask squarely and broke one of the wires, which was driven into his forehead with considerable force," the *Fresno Weekly Republican* reported. It didn't stop the game, however, which Fresno won 9–5. "Chance has had several accidents during his ball playing, but they don't seem to have any effect on his enthusiasm for the game," deadpanned the *Weekly Republican*.

SEASONS OF CONTENT

Frank turned eighteen in September 1894, undecided about his future. Though acclaimed across the San Joaquin Valley for his baseball exploits, he wasn't at all sure that the sport was, or even could be, his vocation.

Truth was, organized baseball was a null slate in 1890s California. All the National League teams were located east of the Mississippi, and even regional baseball in the minor leagues had failed to take hold in the far west. The California League had operated in San Francisco and three other Bay Area cities since 1886, drawing throngs of ten thousand to twenty thousand for some contests. But the semipro circuit played only on weekends. Players got no salaries but rather a small share of gate receipts. It was almost impossible to attract and keep talented ballplayers.

Californians showed a ready appetite for weekend baseball, however. Sunday became a showcase day for every team in the California League, according to historian John E. Spalding. On many occasions, Oakland would host a morning game, followed by an afternoon contest in San Francisco, with many fans hopping aboard ferryboats to take in both. A new ballpark went up in Golden Gate Park, where well-heeled fans sat in commodious private boxes so they could take in the games at arm's length from the hoi polloi. Ladies' Day, inaugurated in May 1886, spawned a female fashion ritual: wearing a favorite team's colors on hats and gowns.

A wondrous feature of California baseball was the absence of winter. The balmy climate made it a year-round sport. Many fans might have tired of seeing the same four teams and the same fifty or so players every weekend. Yet it also meant that California offered big league players from the east an off-season place to play—and earn some pocket money—while giving league owners fresh attractions for their fan base.

Yet there remained inherent problems in the California League's rather ad hoc operating structure. The league essentially reconstituted itself every year, some towns dropping out with others opting in, and players shuttled among teams as each sought the best deal for the coming season. "Baseball here is in a constant state of turmoil," one baseball impresario told *Sporting Life* newspaper, adding that one manager told him that "it's an eye for an eye and a tooth for a tooth all the time."

The California League closed up shop at the end of the 1893 season, the victim of internal strife and the nationwide bank panic of that year. The league would not revive until 1898. But by then Frank was gone.

LEARNING THE MANLY ART

Despite the ups and downs of professional baseball, a fairly active amateur circuit gave players a venue and citizens something to cheer for. "The Fresno baseball team has sent an answer to the challenge of the Porterville boys, and the challenge is accepted," the *Morning Republican* reported in January 1896. The game was to be played in Porterville, seventy miles southeast of Fresno, and the eponymous Republicans were confident of winning, if only because they had a star pitcher, named Baker, and a man "behind the bat" who could both hit and run the bases. "Frank Chance ranks among the best catchers in the valley," the paper boasted.

Chance may have been a baseball star in the view of his teammates, fans, and chroniclers, but he was not convinced that baseball was his true love. The man who seemed impervious to physical punishment found an equal measure of enjoyment as an amateur boxer. He relished the more violent sport, which had also found widespread, if somewhat conflicted, popularity. Chance had appeared in an amateur boxing tournament at Fresno's Athletic Hall the week before the Porterville match. It was a fairly harmless exhibition of several weight classes; Frank, at heavyweight, dispatched his opponent in the first round. Chance spent the next two years pursuing both baseball and boxing activities, despite the negative societal reputation of professional fisticuffs in that day.

Boxing had only recently been evolving into a supposed "sweet science" of pugilism, which prized deft footwork, quick hands, and tactical thinking over brute strength and the ability to withstand incessant pummeling. But the introduction of gloves, plus new Marquess of Queensbury rules governing fair play, did little to make the sport acceptable in middle-class society. Prizefighting was illegal in most of the forty-four United States—in some places it was a felony subject to a ten-year jail sentence. Attempts to mask the blatant violence of the sport with euphemisms like "fistic argument" and the "manly" art of self-defense were largely seen for what they were. "Now I am determined that these 'knocking out' contests shall not be revived," vowed the New York superintendent of police in 1891. But even he allowed that so-called sparring exhibitions among amateurs might be permissible.

Amateur athletic clubs, like Chance's in Fresno, became the most popular venue for such exhibitions. They drew crowds in the hundreds or even thousands (club members only—wink, wink), and some of the top prizefighters of the day would show up to spar a few rounds with the local talent as a way to enhance their reputations and promote upcoming matches at other, more secretive locations. But enthusiasts went to great lengths to assure the public that amateur boxing had no relation to "a slugging match of race track style." An indignant member of the Fresno Athletic Club made the distinction this way: "The contestants are scientific boxers not hard punching 'pugs.' They are not boxing for money, and the question of superiority is decided by the neatest work not by the hardest punching."

Two of the most famous prizefighters of the era, heavyweight champ "Gentleman Jim" Corbett and perennial contender "Chrysanthemum Joe" Choynski, both hailed from San Francisco and maintained their own large followings on the West Coast. In May 1896, Choynski was the main attraction at Fresno's downtown Beaux Arts theater, the Barton Opera House, in a benefit for the Fresno Athletic Club's boxing instructor. Choynski first put on a demonstration of bag punching. "He is considered the best puncher of the bag in the world," the *Republican* said. A few other demonstrations by club members followed, plus "one of the best events of the evening"—a three-round sparring match between Choynski and Frank Chance. "Chance is Fresno's best boxer and he did nobly," reported the *Weekly Republican*, which nevertheless judged Frank no match for the "professional slogger." "Choynski taught him several things. Choynski has a cool bearing on the stage. He appears to preserve the best self confidence and never gets 'rattled.'"

Frank continued to box at the Fresno Athletic Club at night while playing baseball during the day. In April 1897, he was scheduled for a four-round bout with Tom Burns, the Los Angeles champion. A couple of months later, an accident in the gym almost—but not quite—prevented Frank from playing a much-anticipated ball game the next day against Santa Clara, one of the best teams in the region. "Frank Chance has broken a small bone in his left hand yesterday and the hand has swelled considerably. . . . The accident occurred while the Republicans' famous catcher was trying to knock a hole in the punching bag at the Athletic Club's gymnasium." Chance insisted on playing the game as if nothing had gone wrong.

It was during this time that Chance earned his lifelong nickname, "Husk," for he was tough as a cornhusk.

ROAD TO CHICAGO

Chance's boxing exploits earned him increasing attention, and even notoriety, in Fresno and elsewhere in California. But as he must have known, the idea of a professional career in the manly art was never a realistic prospect. (His mother would have surely drawn the line as well.) But how, then, could Chance make a living in a state that could not seem to maintain a professional baseball league? The only real opportunities for a California ballplayer lay in the east.

A former classmate at Washington College, Rod Waggoner, had found his way to little Sullivan, Illinois, in the east-central part of the state, within shouting distance of Decatur and Springfield. Waggoner managed the semipro baseball team, the Maroons, and he invited Frank to play catcher for the 1896 season. He offered a salary of $40 a month, hardly enough to live on. But Frank had another auspicious connection to Sullivan that helped clinch the deal: Nellie Eden, wife of his older brother Alonzo, was the granddaughter of a Sullivan hotelier, Joseph E. Eden. The family needed a night clerk at Eden House.

On May 19, nineteen-year-old Frank left Fresno on the morning train for his second trip back east. In Sullivan, Chance played catcher for Waggoner's squad during the day and manned the Eden House desk at night. He did well enough to get an offer to try out the following season in Hot Springs, Arkansas, a spa resort where Chicago's Al Spalding and Cap Anson had been taking the White Stockings for "spring training" since 1886. Frank headed home for the winter, thinking he might return east the following season.

Back in Fresno, Frank took up boxing again, but he also joined a reconstituted Fresno Republicans baseball team as its catcher, playing their first game in forty-five-degree January weather against Merced and winning 13–8. While the entire Fresno team did well that day despite "cold and disagreeable" temperatures, one player seemed to stand out on both offense and defense. "Frank Chance showed marked improvement in his playing since his trip east. Some of his individual plays startled the visitors," the *Morning Republican* reported.

Word of his fine play worked its way through the baseball grapevine to Chicago, where Anson was still on the hunt for a backup catcher. On April 1, the Fresno paper told readers that Chance had received an offer from Anson to play for his Colts that spring, "and he feels very much like accepting it." Friends and family tried to talk him out of it, appealing to his hometown allegiance. Perhaps they worried that this trip would be no summer lark but a real leap into a baseball career. They pulled every string they could. "Chance is a valuable member of the local team and besides is very popular, and the loss of him would be very much regretted," the *Republican* said.

Fresno Manager Russ Woldenberg was also contemplating his departure from the team, but he and Chance had made some kind of bond with each other, and they with Fresno. Woldenberg talked Chance out of leaving "for this season at least" and promised to stick it out with him. The Republicans went on that summer to play some of the best baseball ever seen in Fresno, competing on equal terms with teams in San Francisco, Oakland, and Sacramento, and getting invitations to play as far south as Los Angeles. Chance was named captain and one of its three business principals. "The boys all have confidence in 'Husk' and he never gets 'rattled,'" the *Morning Republican* said.

By October the Republicans were in a statewide amateur tournament staged by the *San Francisco Examiner*. The winner would go home with a large trophy and $1,000 in gold coins, in addition to the 30 percent cut in gate receipts the paper promised all team entrants. Fresno looked impressive early on, overwhelming the San Francisco Athletic Club, 11–0, in a Sunday-afternoon home game that drew so many fans that "those who came late were compelled to stand."

From both personal and career perspectives, Frank was in the best of all worlds. He was captain of a winning team and also hitting over .470 in the tournament, winning accolades in all corners. He had just received another "flattering" offer from Chicago to play catcher for Anson's Colts the following season. Other offers from Baltimore and New York were also in the works as a result of the telegrams that scouts were sending back east about this burly catcher who could both hit and steal bases.

Many baseball luminaries would later claim credit for "discovering" Frank Chance and sending him on his way to National League stardom. Chance himself credited Cal McVey, a star for Anson's Colts in 1897 who lived in San Francisco during the off-season. Another claimant was Bill Lange, also a Colts star and San Francisco native. He said he saw Chance while umpiring a game during the *Examiner* tournament and tipped off Chicago club president James A. Hart about Chance's exploits. Hart would later dispute both accounts and insist that Henry Harris, former owner of a San Francisco club in the *Examiner* tournament, first alerted Hart about Fresno's catcher, "a big, husky chap, over six feet tall and weighing about 190 pounds, who looked good." Even so, it's quite likely Hart would have already known something about Chance from Anson, who had tried to sign the youngster earlier that year.

Hart, eager to get some fresh talent, offered Chance a salary for 1898 of $1,000 a month. Other teams, notably Baltimore, were said to have offered as much as $300 more, but Frank figured that Chicago had the more pressing need for a catcher. He signed the contract with Hart and made ready to show up in West Baden, Indiana, the Colts' spring training camp that year.

Before Frank's last season in California came to a close, a group of thirty-six National League ballplayers came through Fresno to play one of a series of exhibition games. The players divided into two squads, the Baltimores and the All-Americans, and they invited some of the top locals, including Chance, to play. Managing the Baltimores was Frank Selee, skipper of the Boston Beaneaters, four-time NL champion. According to Selee, Chance was one of two players who were "the best [he] saw" during the entire trip.

It would be five more years before Frank Chance played for Frank Selee as a member of the Chicago Nationals in the summer of 1902, and another three and half seasons before Chance replaced the ailing Selee, in late 1905, as the club's field general. But the athletic skills, leadership traits, and almost death-defying ambition that "Husk" Chance developed over his twenty-one years in Fresno came east with him. Son of Oregon pioneers, fierce pugilist, and hardheaded beanball target, he seemed to know where he was going and what it took to get there.

Years later, the story goes, a green reporter asked him: "What one qualification, Mr. Chance, above all others, is responsible for your great success as a manager?"

The reporter probably missed the slight twinkle in his eye as Husk Chance answered: "My ability to lick any man on the ball club."

PART TWO

Chicago Century

Chicago. First in violence, deepest in dirt; loud,
lawless, unlovely, ill-smelling, irreverent, new;
an overgrown gawk of a village, the "tough"
among cities, a spectacle for the nation;—I give
Chicago no quarter and Chicago asks for none.

LINCOLN STEFFENS,
"Chicago: Half Free and Fighting On,"
October 1903

BASEBALL REVIVAL

1903–1905

Katie Casey was base ball mad,
Had the fever and had it bad;
Just to root for the home town crew,
Ev'ry sou—Katie blew.
JACK NORWORTH, "Take Me Out to the Ballgame," 1908

On the first day of spring 1903, inhabitants of Chicago had to hope against hope that an unusual warm spell was in fact a harbinger of a new season. For two unexpectedly balmy days, the coldest, longest, most lethal winter in memory appeared finally to be at an end. But the newsboys' high-pitched calls that morning would send more shivers through downtown streets, most of them still walled up by tall mounds of ice and snow. "Freezing Weather Due Here Today," the headlines cried. "Blizzards in West."

Yet another cold wave, moving across the northern prairies toward the Great Lakes, would push thermometers back down into the red by nightfall, a plunge of forty degrees in a matter of hours, forecasters said. Not what anyone wanted to hear when thousands of people had been freezing for months without access to fuel. Not what a city government already overwhelmed by demands for food, shelter, and coal had any capacity to manage. The city's population had doubled to two million in the decade since the World's Columbian Exposition of 1893 put it on the global map, and waves of migrants were streaming into the city from Ireland, Italy, Germany, Scandinavia, and Eastern Europe, as well as from depression-rocked rural America.

A coal miners' strike in Pennsylvania had lasted for six months the previous year and left many cities to the west without a stockpile of fuel for the winter. Chicago may have been hardest hit by the resulting "coal famine." Even streetcars were without heat, prompting health officials to advise the public to shun public transportation, "it being more conducive to health to walk than to ride in the cold cars." A Health Department report estimated that two hundred thousand people, or 10 percent of the population, were suffering from "grave" illnesses "caused by privation and exposure resulting from the coal famine." Hyperdefensive city officials vainly tried to redirect the blame to the strikers: "In the eyes of the department, those responsible for the coal famine are guilty of constructive homicide for every resulting death."

Deeper inside that morning's newspapers, however, lay reports of a more serene kind. Chicago's National League baseball team was conducting its "spring training" in the California resort town of Santa Monica. The image of young ballplayers frolicking on sun-drenched Pacific beaches must have seemed like a mirage on an untouchable horizon. And perhaps that's all it was. The caliber of this squad wasn't much to write home about.

Anyone who knew the recent history of the Chicago Nationals had no reason to think this season would bring any better fortune than the previous year. No new stars had been signed, no budding prospects had risen above the pack of greenhorns. "[The] club this year as compared with last season is fully 50 percent better," allowed a *Chicago Daily News* correspondent, already hedging his bet. The manager "expressed great satisfaction with the looks of his men," reported a noncommittal *Chicago Record Herald*. The *Sporting Life* weekly took note of the general drift and concluded that the Nationals "are a nice, willing set of boys, but seem rather weak with the war club."

And yet a writer in another Chicago paper proffered a much sunnier outlook. "This has been a great day for the Colts," beamed the anonymous dispatch in the *Chicago Inter Ocean*, using that paper's preferred nickname for the team. "To begin with, the weather was just ideal for ball playing. The day was warm, with just a light breeze blowing across the park to remind them of their proximity to the coast." The sentences were cheerful, confident, and no doubt naive, yet their forecast for Chicago and its frigid sports fans concealed an uncanny feminine intuition of better days to come.

Most Chicago baseball fans had few reasons to expect the summer to be one of joy and celebration. Their team had finished fifth in the eight-team league in 1902, another in a string of sixteen lackluster campaigns. No trophy had fallen into the team's clutches since 1886. It was going to be a challenge to recapture the public's interest in the bedraggled Colts or the sullied game of baseball itself. An even bigger leap was to win back the city's faith and allegiance.

James A. Hart, the club's owner and president, was keen to try. Hart had made the arrangements for the West Coast trip, his first spring training since taking sole financial control of the franchise the previous summer. His longtime boss and mentor, sporting goods magnate Albert G. Spalding, was now out of the picture. Hart had decided to make the expensive excursion to the far west—the longest train trip ever for a baseball team in that day—to help revive the players' spirits and jump-start the team's prospects. Perhaps he also wanted to show he was no longer Spalding's lackey but finally a baseball magnate of his own accord. Either way, Hart needed to raise the city's low expectations for this moribund franchise.

Frank G. Selee, Hart's field manager, came aboard the year before with a stellar reputation as a talent scout and turnaround artist. Hart gave Selee complete freedom to remake the roster. They assembled seventeen players in Santa Monica, a motley crew from all corners of the nation. Among them were several holdovers—including a slick infielder named Tinker from Kansas City, and a sturdy backup catcher named Chance from California, plus a more recent pickup from upstate New York whom everyone called Little Evers.

Selee had played this rebuilding role before, a dozen years previous, when he lifted the Boston Nationals from fifth to first in just one year. And he had a brainy, methodical way of going about the task. He collected these and other prospects like marbles, tossing away the rejects and, wherever possible, buffing up the hidden jewels. "You must be on the lookout for new material all the time," he said. At the end of the day, however, few seasoned baseball watchers expected any miracles from such a nondescript outfit. The restoration of Chicago's baseball fortunes was going to be a long, hard slog.

BASEBALL WAR

The Chicago Nationals of 1903 were mired in an identity crisis. No one could even agree on what to call them. The franchise had long ago abandoned its White Stockings nickname, even though that team had dominated the league through most of the 1880s. A subsequent rebuilding effort in the mid-1890s under Spalding and player-manager Cap Anson had spawned the nickname "Colts" from sportswriters amused by the players' youth and inexperience. Anson's Colts never amounted to much, however; they hadn't finished first, second, or show since 1892.

When an aging "Pop" Anson finally departed the diamond in 1898 after twenty-two years as the unrivaled father figure of Chicago baseball, some of the more sarcastic writers referred to the team he left behind as the Orphans, while others tried out the Remnants. The *Chicago Inter Ocean* clung to Selee's Colts. The *Chicago Daily News*, again seeing so many young faces, was the first and only paper to call them Cubs.

Making things worse for the Chicago Nationals, along with every other team in the league, was an upstart baseball organization calling itself the American League. Formerly the Western League, it had become one of the more successful "minor" circuits in the country in the 1890s. While it still comprised teams from Michigan, Minnesota, Iowa, Missouri, and neighboring states, its two hard-charging leaders, league President Ban Johnson and team owner Charles A. Comiskey, had national ambitions.

In 1900, Johnson and Comiskey had put the baseball establishment on notice with their aggressive moves. Comiskey—a Chicago native whose father, "Honest John" Comiskey, was alderman of the Seventh Ward—wasted no time in declaring his intention to move his St. Paul Apostles to his hometown, in direct competition with Hart's Nationals.

Hart, not surprisingly, was adamantly opposed to letting Comiskey invade his turf. He worried the city couldn't support two ball clubs and, more to the point, that Comiskey's local prominence would attract enough attention to eclipse his team. Hart threatened a serious legal battle, with other NL owners at his back.

Ban Johnson stepped in as peacemaker, inviting Hart and Comiskey to meet him on neutral turf in Cleveland for what turned into an all-night drinking session at the Hollander Hotel. It must have worked: Johnson persuaded Hart to back off his legal challenge as long as Comiskey agreed to locate his team on the South Side, below Thirty-Fifth Street, far from Hart's West Side Grounds. Once ensconced in his new ball park on Thirty-Ninth and Wentworth, however, Comiskey showed he was a public relations force to be reckoned with. He commandeered the old White Stockings moniker and shortened it to headline-friendly White Sox, then began signing top major league veterans. The Comiskey White Sox quickly developed winning ways, but more troubling to Hart, they also began winning the city's heart. In the summer of 1902, the Sox averaged more than twice as many paying spectators per game as the Orphans-Colts-Whatevers.

BAN JOHNSON MOVES IN

Ban Johnson had an equally aggressive vision for the entire American League. A Cincinnati sportswriter turned baseball impresario, Johnson looked the part of a corporate tycoon—tall and barrel-chested—and he acted like one, too. He brazenly moved two more teams into National League cities—Boston and Philadelphia—and laid claim to even more NL territory by setting up franchises in Baltimore and Washington. Then Johnson declared the AL a "major" league, ready to recruit and sign the game's elite players. When NL owners refused to recognize him, or even meet with him, Johnson declared war.

Johnson went right after the National League's brand of syndicate baseball, recognizing that this cynical approach to the game was alienating both fans and players. He prodded his team owners to flout the NL's restrictive player contracts, ignore the reserve clause, and outbid

Byron Bancroft "Ban" Johnson, a former sportswriter-turned-baseball impresario, founded the American League in 1900, challenging the National League's monopoly status with a new brand of "clean," family-friendly play. (National Baseball Hall of Fame and Museum, Cooperstown, NY.)

NL teams for their own best players. Many of those players were more than ready to jump ship. The derelict National League immediately began losing the battle for fan interest and civic loyalties. By December 1902, a rump group of NL owners sued for peace, with Hart and two others forming a committee to initiate truce talks. Other NL owners dithered, however, forcing repeated delays in a promised summit meeting with Johnson.

By the turn of the new year, knowledgeable observers were already putting their money on Johnson and his junior circuit over the feckless National Leaguers. Few doubted Johnson's ability or his leverage to decide the terms of any pact between the organizations. "The American League, young, vigorous, and managed by a lot of level headed hustlers, stands before the public as dictator of the national game," declared New York sports columnist Joseph Vila. The National League had not only lost its way, Vila said; it had forsaken its most loyal fans: "Mismanagement, cheap players, insults heaped upon notable cranks, riots on the diamond, wrangling over minor details, and general chaos have served to fill the public breast with anger and disgust."

The Hart group eventually met with Johnson in Cincinnati on January 10, 1903. As Vila predicted, the National League capitulated. The new National Agreement, or Peace Treaty, as the writers called it, created a National Commission to govern organized baseball, giving it final say over all league disputes, game rules, and player contracts. The National Commission would be composed of the presidents of the National and American League, plus a third person chosen by the two presidents to serve as chairman.

That person was August "Garry" Herrmann, owner of the NL Cincinnati Reds and a widely admired force behind the Peace Treaty. Over time, Herrmann would prove to be a consistent ally of Johnson in disputes between the leagues. The upshot was to make Ban Johnson the effective czar of baseball, a man his contemporaries called "the Theodore Roosevelt of the baseball world." Like Roosevelt, the protean Johnson could never wield absolute, unchecked power, but he used his bully pulpit to exercise an authority that no one could match, much less counter, over the next two decades. "Ban Johnson was to baseball affairs what Roosevelt was to national affairs—they each created a new and more progressive era," the *Sporting News* extolled years later.

The National Game now had a steady hand at the top of sixteen major league franchises spreading from Boston and New York to the "western" outposts of Chicago and St. Louis. Baseball was one of several forms of mass entertainment in America at the time, alongside diversions like college football and vaudeville, but it had yet to earn the title of national "pastime," embodying the American psyche, lifestyle, and civic spirit.

The city of Chicago epitomized both the passions and limits of the sport. By the end of the nineteenth century, baseball had been in Chicago's bloodstream for more than a generation. The fever spread beyond the White Stockings to scores of amateur and semipro clubs. For a brief period in the early 1870s, and then again in the late 1880s, Chicago saw a youth baseball craze, according to historian Robert Pruter. By the end of this period, the game was played not just on makeshift sandlots but also in well-kept city parks with teams organized under fraternal organizations, amateur clubs, and even factory owners.

To suggest that the game had captured the hearts of all Chicagoans would be a stretch, however. As Pruter's research shows, the teenage boys who gravitated to it were no angels of the diamond. "Games were marked by extreme verbal abuse and physical violence involving both players and spectators," Pruter observes, concluding that youth baseball was permeated with "disreputable idle young men, street urchins, and ruffians." To many of its participants, young and old, this was the way the game was supposed to be played. And to so many others in mainstream society, that was the problem with it.

MECCA OF THE MIDWEST

By 1903, Chicago had earned its reputation as a "wide open" city, with an urban culture that was intoxicating and vicious, aspirational and vainglorious, all-embracing and insular. Lincoln Steffens captured the many paradoxes of Chicago in *McClure's Magazine* that year: "Lying low beside a great lake of pure, cold water, the city has neither enough nor good enough water," Steffens detected, warming up his lather for a prolix, seesaw sequence of praise and condemnation:

> With the ingenuity and will to turn their sewer, the Chicago River, and make it run backwards and upwards out of the Lake, the city can not solve the smoke nuisance. With resources for a magnificent system of public

parking, it is too poor to pave and clean the streets. They can balance high buildings on rafts floating in mud, but they can't quench the stench of the stockyards. The enterprise which carried through a World's Fair to a world's triumph is satisfied with two thousand five hundred policemen for two million inhabitants and one hundred and ninety-six square miles of territory, a force so insufficient (and inefficient) that it cannot protect itself, to say nothing of the mobs, riotous strikers, and the rest of that lawlessness which disgraces Chicago. Though the city has an extra-legal system of controlling vice and crime, which is so effective that the Mayor has been able to stop any practices against which he has turned his face— the "panel game," the "hat game," "wine rooms," "safe blowing;"—though gambling is limited, regulated and fair, and prostitution orderly; though, in short—through the power of certain political and criminal leaders— the Mayor has been able to make Chicago, criminally speaking, "honest."

Steffens's essay "Chicago: Half Free and Fighting On" was later included in his book *The Shame of the Cities*. Steffens did give grudging approval to a concerted effort by one hundred leading Chicago businessmen, called the Municipal Voters' League, to root out graft in the City Council. The only problem with this noble and surprisingly successful effort, Steffens said, was they could not do the same for the city's corrupt administration, led by three-time mayor Carter Harrison II.

The city clearly couldn't keep up with the crush of new arrivals— after the Great Chicago Fire leveled the city in 1871, the population had steadily risen from 360,000 to 1.1 million by 1890, then to 2 million by 1905. The teeming masses included thousands of immigrants from the Old World. Joining them were rural Americans, black and white, escaping failing farms across the Midwest and Jim Crow oppression in the South, in search of whatever menial jobs they could find in the wake of the worst economic depression (1893–96) the nation had seen. The newcomers piled into poorly built and barely maintained tenement houses in the most cramped and dissolute sections of town. Jane Addams, the pioneer social worker and founder of Hull-House for destitute men and women, reported that the average density in just three poverty-stricken districts of Chicago would, if extended citywide, translate into a population of 23 million.

An honest government would have had difficulty meeting the demand for services as well as law and order in this era. A corrupt government, in a city growing so fast, had no chance. Throughout 1903, newspapers and muckraking magazines ran a series of exposés that revealed the extent of the cancer in City Hall: Jobs, city contracts, court decisions, licenses, elections, protection from prosecution—every function of government had its price. On the afternoon of December 30, the Iroquois Theater burned to the ground during a matinee performance of *Mr. Bluebeard*, with more than six hundred people trapped inside. It was the deadliest single-building fire in U.S. history—the result of unenforced fire and building codes.

CITY PRIMEVAL

Lacking so many of the basic necessities of life, Chicagoans turned to their own sources of support to find jobs, food, fuel, and companionship. More so than in any other city in America, the centerpiece of this entrepreneurial urban culture was the neighborhood saloon.

Ubiquitous—there were 7,600 "licensed" barrooms by the middle of the decade—but virtually unregulated, the saloon gave its working-class patrons more than a beer and a place to hang a hat. It gave them all kinds of sustenance. Royal Melendy, a sociologist and temperance reformer, visited all 163 saloons in the Seventeenth Ward and found that 111 of them offered free lunches, 147 had tables that could seat up to six people, and 139 were supplied with newspapers. Music, billiards, private meeting rooms, bowling alleys, handball courts, and showers were among the common amenities. Not least among these, Melendy delicately pointed out, were "the only toilet conveniences in large sections of the city." The saloon, Melendy concluded, "is an institution grown up among the people, not only in answer to their demands for its wares, but to their demand for certain necessities and conveniences, which it supplies, either alone or better than any other agency."

Chicago saloons reflected the city's permissive culture, especially compared to the highly regulated confines of Boston, where all forms of public behavior, "from praying aloud on the Charlesbank to whistling in a park," were subject to strict government oversight, according to historian Perry R. Duis. The Chicago saloon's openness and ubiquity also made saloon owners a political force that no self-preserving politician or government bureaucrat would trifle with. Saloon license fees alone made up 22 percent of Chicago's income in the first decade of the century.

Working both ends of this mutual benefit society were two rapscallions of the era, "Bathhouse John" Coughlin, and his alter ego, Michael "Hinky Dink" Kenna. They were longtime aldermen of the city's First Ward as well as saloon owners. Coughlin and Kenna controlled vice, police, and zoning in the central city for decades, but they also took care of their own and knew how to count votes. During the worst periods of the 1890s depression, Kenna fed eight thousand jobless men a week in his Workingman's Exchange saloon on South Clark Street.

Other commercial forces that would unite to shape Chicago's identity and culture in the twentieth century were only beginning to materialize in 1900. As historian Gunther Barth has argued, the thousands of new arrivals from wildly different backgrounds devised ways of getting by and getting along, putting urban institutions like daily newspapers, department stores, and vaudeville houses to work in structuring city life. From the half dozen daily papers and dozens more weeklies, Barth said, Chicagoans assembled "the pieces of an urban identity" as well as a common language. The department store gave women a place in city life and "made downtown the center of urban elegance." And the vaudeville house brought diverse people together under one roof, bridging the language divides with music and laughter, and giving rise to a common urban culture.

One especially effective vehicle for weaving the patchwork fabrics of diverse societies into whole cloth was, Barth said, ballparks. The highly regulated format of baseball and the remarkable skills of the athletes who played it combined to mesmerize people of every station and walk of life. Baseball provided a regular, almost daily respite from the city's stresses. "In the ball park," Barth observed, "men were exposed to the meaning of rules in the modern city and to that basic form of urban leisure, watching others do things."

In this way, baseball entrepreneurs like Ban Johnson and Charles

Comiskey—and eventually James Hart and Frank Selee—would play pivotal roles in the Progressive reform movement that was making small but increasingly popular inroads across the country in the early 1900s. Johnson and Comiskey had the business instincts to realize that baseball could capture a broad cross section of paying spectators and even instill a sense of civic-minded pride—so long as they put a respectable product on the field.

BASEBALL FOR EVERYONE

Johnson and Comiskey wanted to stage ball games that promoted fair play, honest competition, and respect for both the rules and the umpire's authority to enforce them. Their term of choice was "clean" baseball: the promise of a spectacle that all kinds of fans, including women and children, could watch and enjoy without fear of rowdy behavior on the field or in the stands. "We gave the people clean ball as well as fast ball," Johnson boasted years later. "I had the wit to see that baseball would never be the national game in the full sense of the word until men felt safe in taking their womenfolk to the parks."

As American League president, Johnson banned drunkenness, rowdyism, and profanity, suspended players at will, and even threatened owners and managers with the loss of their franchises. He demanded good conduct off the field as well, insisting that "ballplayers were public characters, and shamed the game when they shamed themselves." Johnson hired his own umpires and made them absolute dictators on the field, accountable only to him. Rowdyism and vile language drew instant and severe penalties from Johnson himself, and owners and managers were ordered to "drill it into their men that the game had passed beyond the beer-garden stage."

National League owners had little choice but to follow suit. Fortunately, they too had a new leader who wanted to turn things around. Former Pittsburgh Pirates owner Harry C. Pulliam, recently installed as league president, would prove a force for reform until his untimely death in 1909. Pulliam made it clear to his owners and managers that the old roughhouse style of play would no longer be tolerated. As the 1903 season opened, Pulliam sent out "explicit and mandatory" instructions to all managers and umpires on what he would do to "maintain deportment on the ball field each and every day through the entire season," *Sporting Life* reported. "There will be no rowdyism," Pulliam announced. "Any player who attempts it will eliminate himself, will efface himself."

Henry Chadwick, the sportswriter and longtime conscience of the game, felt an urgent need to weigh in as well at this momentous turning point. "The Kicking Evil," as he called it, must go back into its hole. "It is of vital importance to the future welfare of professional base ball, and especially of that of the National League, that these new regulations should be enforced to the letter."

But civic responsibility alone would not salvage the hapless Colts if they couldn't attract fans. James Hart and Frank Selee, with their team's very survival at stake, needed to turn the city's attention back to their West Side ball club.

THE SELEE TOUCH

Hart believed he had the right man in Frank Selee, one of the premier baseball minds in the country and a patient handler of young men. The two men had crossed paths many times as each worked his way up the ladder of organized baseball.

Frank Selee's renown has risen and fallen and risen again over the intervening decades. Relegated to oblivion throughout most of the twentieth century, he was inducted into the Baseball Hall of Fame in 1999 on a vote by the Veterans Committee. Yet even today, the self-effacing Selee remains little known to all but baseball history aficionados. In nineteenth-century baseball, however, Selee was universally lauded as a mastermind, particularly for his ability to spot talent and tap into his players' potential. "Frank Selee possessed a thorough knowledge of men, and especially of the ball player," recalled Ted Lewis, known in his day as the "Pitching Professor." Selee had rare ability to meld men

Manager Frank Selee had a reputation as an astute judge of baseball talent. He rebuilt the Chicago club from the ground up, starting with its now-famous infield trio. (Chicago Historical Society, Getty Images.)

into a "harmonious working body," and a gift for drawing out young players' skills, Lewis said. "For the latter, in fact, he had a veritable genius."

His contemporaries admired Selee as a master practitioner of the "scientific" or "inside" game, where speed, sacrifice bunts, hit-and-run plays, stolen bases, and defensive positioning were prized over all. Selee had only one equal: Ned Hanlon, manager of the Baltimore Orioles, though for "Foxy Ned" the inside game included foul play as well as fair. From 1890 through 1899, Selee's Beaneaters (the future Boston Braves), won five pennants and Hanlon's Orioles, three. But where the Orioles were known for their dirty baseball—bald-faced cheating, biting, cleat sharpening, and "kicking"—Selee's boys remained a relative model of grace and decorum. That Selee's teams managed to win games and avoid falling into the mud with Hanlon and others was a marvel even then. "The fact that the Bostons have always been noted for their gentlemanly deportment is due, in great measure to the example set by Selee," said one of baseball's first historians in 1897, adding that "the standing of his club during his incumbency is a tribute as well to his skill as a manager and his credit as a man."

T. H. Murnane, a Boston sportswriter and former major league player, placed Selee in the pantheon of the game's great managers. "Selee was forever working out some scheme and giving the players a private lecture, completing a signal code, and working out a campaign as if he were about to fight for a country's freedom," he wrote. Perhaps there was some subtle, manipulative psychology at work, Murnane seemed to say. "Selee was a *theorist*," he concluded.

Frank Gibson Selee was born on October 26, 1859, in Amherst, Massachusetts, the first of three children born to the Methodist reverend Nelson Pierce Selee and his wife, Dr. Annie Maria Case. Frank's mother had distinction as one of the first female physicians in New England, establishing a practice in the northern Boston suburb of Melrose, where the family had moved into a modest two-story house, a short walk from a park and nature trail at Crystal Lake. She became a leading practitioner of "homeopathic" treatments, a form of alternative medicine that thrived when medical science was still primitive and nonpharmaceutical treatments showed some success in treating infectious disease epidemics such as cholera, yellow fever, and typhoid. Perhaps inspired by his wife's work, Reverend Selee ultimately gave up the pulpit and became a manufacturer of "patent medicines."

Having grown up in a nonconformist New England household, Frank was bound to be a little different from other boys. Although a bookish child who watched and listened but rarely sought attention, Selee made friends easily and maintained them loyally. He joined the Benevolent and Protective Order of Elks, Lodge No. 1031, part of a large national fraternal association in which he would maintain strong connections all his life.

With some help from his friends, Selee learned to take risks. In 1884, when he was twenty-five and working in the Waltham Watch Factory, Selee contracted "baseball fever," as he called it. He persuaded some of his mates to form a baseball stock company with Selee as manager.

The group invested $1,000 together (about $25,000 today), to prepare a field, put up a fence, and erect some bleachers. Waltham proved to be a poor baseball market, however, which Selee attributed to its small size and a working-class population "composed of people who spend most of their time in labor." His business venture went nowhere, but his career in baseball had been launched, in a way.

He next found success with teams in the nearby towns of Lawrence and Haverhill, helped along by a lawyer friend—and Elks brother—named William H. Moody. Minor league baseball, then as now, was a business built on shifting sands. Selee figured he would have to leave New England to find a paying job in baseball, so he followed the advice of a friend to go west. He landed a position in 1887 as manager in faraway Oshkosh, Wisconsin, an upstate sawmill town and at the time second-largest city in the state.

Selee's baseball fever had met its match. The Oshkosh Indians belonged to the Northwestern League, a circuit of Wisconsin, Minnesota, and Iowa clubs, and their fans shared Selee's passion for baseball. "Oshkosh was one of the most loyal towns I ever saw," he recalled. "The patrons of the sport there would rather have had a win from Milwaukee than to have won the championship." Small wonder, then, that carpetbagger Selee didn't get run out of town within a month. The Milwaukee Brewers were owned and managed by Jim Hart, whose ball club proceeded to win fourteen straight games over Selee's Indians. The ever-analytical Selee refused to panic; the losses inspired him to get to the bottom of the team's real troubles. "While this was somewhat of a facer for me, still it was good experience, as it showed me where we were weak," he said.

Selee persuaded his owners to bring in some better players from the east, including a twenty-two-year-old named Tommy McCarthy who had some big league experience with the Philadelphia Nationals. McCarthy greeted his new fans by rapping out two triples, a double, and a single in his first game. Milwaukee never beat Oshkosh again that season, and Selee and McCarthy became local heroes by nosing out the Brewers for first place—on the last day of the season, by mere percentage points.

Then something strange occurred that could have ruptured the relationship between Selee and Hart from the start but may actually have sealed it for life. When Northwestern League owners convened in Chicago at season's end to formally declare a pennant winner, Hart tried to pull a fast one, arguing that a technicality in an Indians contract should disqualify one of Selee's midsummer wins. If Oshkosh forfeited the game, Milwaukee would top the standings. Selee's defenders produced evidence to the contrary, however, and Oshkosh took the crown.

To the amazement of the fans of Oshkosh, Selee never held a grudge against Hart. "Frank Selee is one of the cleanest and best baseball men I have known, and how in the world he ever came to associate himself with 'Jim' Hart is more than I can understand," commented one of the Oshkosh partners a few years later, when Hart hired Selee to manage in Chicago. To his credit, Hart didn't try to wash over the incident. "I have had a great deal of respect for [Selee's] abilities ever since, as he won the pennant . . . away from me that year," he told the Chicago press.

The Northwestern League folded later that winter, as it turned out, and the Oshkosh team with it. The Brewers jumped into the more established Western Association, and Selee found work there, too, assisting the owner-manager of the Omaha Omahogs with personnel issues. It took him two years this time, but Selee won a pennant there as well. In 1889, his second season, Selee became the on-field manager, and his knack for spotting talent and putting together a working unit on the field paid many dividends for his employers. "I had entire charge of the club that year and we won the championship with a club that cost about one-half as much as the one of the previous season," he boasted.

Selee's success got the attention of the Boston Nationals, where Hart had landed as manager for a year before moving completely into the business side of baseball with Al Spalding in Chicago. At Hart's instigation, Selee moved back to New England, and in his second year as Boston's manager he led the Beaneaters to the first of five pennants over an eight-year span.

Selee was happy to share the credit. "It was my good fortune to be surrounded by a lot of good, clean fellows who got along fine together," he remembered. It was an axiom he would keep for life. "To tell the truth I would not have any one on a team who was not congenial."

ENTER MRS. FRANK SELEE

By the time he showed up in Chicago in late 1901, Frank Selee was a balding man of forty-two, his pate only half covered by a comb-over. Ted Lewis, the Pitching Professor, described him as "a quiet little man, with the calm, placid countenance, the unobtrusive manner and the forehead—high and broad—which lent a strongly intellectual cast to the expression."

Given his slight build, Selee's huge walrus mustache seemed all the larger as it drooped down to his chin. That kind of face furniture had become an anachronism at the turn of the century, when most men adopted clean-shaven looks. But the effect in Selee was to focus everyone's attention on his piercing blue eyes. The brush often covered up his mouth, forcing players to strain to catch his few words. "The new manager is a man of retiring disposition, who impresses one as having little to say," the *Chicago Tribune* informed its readers upon Hart's announcement that he had secured Selee's services. "But when he does talk it is baseball sense, and only the superficial observer would say that he had not a strong reserve force."

Though widely respected by his peers and trusted by his players, Selee was no self-promoter. He wasn't averse to publicity—he did everything he could to promote the team, regularly giving interviews to newspaper reporters, making speeches at testimonials and banquets, and giving his players credit when they performed well. "Frank Selee manages to keep his team always before the public eye," said *Sporting Life* in 1904.

But neither Selee nor Hart had the local Chicago connections and the public charisma of their predecessors, Anson and Spalding. And they certainly couldn't match up against the hard-charging personality of Ban Johnson and carnival huckster Comiskey. Restoring the Chicago Nationals' image and status was never going to be an easy task for them.

What Hart didn't yet know was that he had gotten a twofer—a "Team Selee" that could breathe new life into both the ball club and its relations with the public. Selee had brought along a secret weapon of sorts,

WIFE OF THE COLTS' MANAGER
IS AN ENTHUSIASTIC FAN.

May Selee, wife of the Chicago manager, was an eye-catching, effervescent id to his squinty, deep-thinking ego. The *Chicago Tribune* profiled her on August 31, 1902, as an "enthusiastic fan." (Library of Congress.)

one that his Boston rooters never benefited from: his alluring, enigmatic, and entirely baseball-mad new wife, May. Mrs. Frank Selee, as she was customarily known, was a force in her own right, and in a very short time, she added an amiable touch to the burly game of baseball.

The *Chicago Tribune* ran a human-interest feature inside the sports section headlined "Wife of the Colts' Manager Is an Enthusiastic Fan." A portrait photograph of an attractive young woman appeared inside an illustrated oval frame, its border decorated with floral designs in much the same way as a feature on an opera singer or actress. The woman had bright, clear eyes and looked directly into the camera. Her wavy hair was parted down the middle and cut short across the ears, revealing a long, graceful neckline that framed a confident but demure smile. To the right was a smaller file photo of Frank's mustachioed face, a decidedly dour mug shot next to her sunny features. "While the manager of the Chicago National league club has been ingratiating himself in the hearts of the Chicago fans," began the text beneath, "Mrs. Selee has made many friends during her brief residence in Chicago."

The reader learned that Mrs. Selee, "who is many years her husband's junior," was born in Ireland but more recently hailed from St. Louis. She spoke with a slight brogue, "one of her many attractions." She was tall and commanded attention "with a sparkling, even roguish eye, and beautiful auburn hair." Unlike her unassuming husband, she was outgoing and also a musician. The unnamed *Chicago Tribune* writer was completely enamored: "One need only look at her to understand that she made short work of the good manager's heart."

But here was the most important thing about her for the reader of the sports pages: "Mrs. Selee is perhaps better versed in baseball matters than any woman in the country." This alluring ingénue was sufficiently conversant in the arts of pitching, hitting, and double plays to fill out her own scorecard. "She can report games and also has at her tongue's tip the history of all the league players."

As winter turned to spring, and as Selee's Colts made their way back from the California training excursion, *Sporting Life* reported that Mrs. Frank Selee had stopped off in St. Louis to visit some childhood friends. She volunteered in an interview that she had been serving as a correspondent for "several Chicago papers" while the team was in the far west, "so perhaps my opinion of my husband's team will be worth something." She proceeded to put the city of Chicago and the entire National League on notice: "We are going to be heard from," she said. "My husband likes his team's chances and so do I."

The *Inter Ocean* (*I-O*) never revealed the source of its spring training dispatches from the West Coast; Jack Tanner, the paper's regular baseball writer, was well known and would have been named if he had been there. Interestingly, the *Tribune*, a competitor, showed no compunction in running condensed versions of the *I-O* spring training reports, suggesting it had pitched in to help pay for the mysterious correspondent. It is easy to imagine who this ever-optimistic voice might have been: no jaded sportswriter but an unabashed cheerleader. "Those scribes who are at a loss for a name for Selee's team would still retain the old one of Colts had they seen them at practice this morning," the *I-O* correspondent had reported. "They were fresh looking, full of life, energy, and vigor, and working with vim enough to gladden the heart of the most exacting manager or fan."

TOAST OF CHICAGO

The former Bridget "May" Grant had been born on December 22, 1873, the seventh of twelve children of James Grant and Catherine Eagan of County Kilkenny, Ireland. She emigrated to America on her own on June 2, 1890, arriving in New York on the *City of Chester* with a group of other girls her age—probably servant girls, or "Bridgets," as they were dubbed back then. She eventually settled in St. Louis with relatives of her mother.

How or when she met Frank was a secret, although with her passion for baseball, she could well have been at the ballpark when Selee's Boston Beaneaters came to play the Cardinals. He was forty-two years old and she twenty-eight about the time they were married. The wedding was "quietly arranged," according to the *Tribune*, and the couple kept their union in confidence for several months, "so that now even their most intimate friends can hardly give the exact date of its occurrence."

From 1902 through the middle of 1905, Frank and May Selee were the toast of Chicago. They were a mismatched couple to some, perhaps, but their complementing personalities seemed to feed off each other. She was the eye-catching, effervescent id to his squinty, deep-thinking ego. She made a day at the ballpark seem like family fun even while he introduced "scientific" precepts to the field of play.

The journey was never easy. While Frank Selee was clearly up to the task of making the Colts a winner again, physical frailty dogged him almost from the beginning of his tenure at West Side Grounds. It didn't take long before he exhibited disturbing signs of a chronic physical weakness that living in dirt-, slime- and stench-ridden Chicago no doubt aggravated. Selee fell ill in October 1902 and was confined to bed at the Victoria Hotel for more than a week. He reportedly had a congested lung plus a throbbing pain on the skin next to his ribs—what medical practitioners called neuralgia. The hotel physician, Dr. Hammond, had feared pleurisy—an inflammation of the membrane of the lung—but he soon felt that "all danger is now passed." Yet something was seriously wrong, and traditional medicine seemed unable to provide a proper diagnosis.

Frank and May Selee decided to escape the frigid Chicago winter, spending two months at the new Faywood Hot Springs Hotel, a resort in southwestern New Mexico. Faywood was known for its geothermal mineral waters, said to cure gout, chronic pain, and other maladies. Selee, son of a homeopathic physician and patent medicine purveyor, badly needed a cure, for he had something far more lethal than a bad cold. The *Albuquerque Citizen* reported that he was recovering from typhoid fever, "which he had at Chicago."

RENOVATION PROJECT

A meandering train ride back to Chicago from Los Angeles in the spring of 1903 took the Colts through Tucson, Albuquerque, and El Paso, then up to Pueblo, Colorado Springs, and Denver, and finally over to Omaha and Des Moines. Selee and Hart had arranged exhibition games in each of these towns in exchange for a percentage of the gate receipts, which helped offset the cost of the trip. The contests gave the players some game experience before facing up against more formidable National League competition. It also gave local team owners an opportunity to draw a crowd eager to see big league faces they could otherwise know only in newspapers or on baseball cards.

But Hart and Selee had a larger agenda, too. The trip through the bushes gave Selee his only opportunity to scout prospects in the west. The hundreds of teams scattered across the country were the first stop for young players with talent. Yet these teams had no formal alliances with major league teams like they do today, when minor league "affiliates" provide a pipeline of ascending big leaguers. Nor did major league managers have scouting departments to track rising prospects. So Selee had to rely on a coast-to-coast network of fellow managers and former players to give him an inside track on the game's up-and-comers.

Johnny Evers came to Selee's attention this way in August 1902, courtesy of his old friend Lou Bacon, owner-manager of the Troy Trojans. Bacon had sent Evers to Selee on two conditions: if the kid didn't make the grade, send him back; if he did make the team, Selee would owe Bacon $200. It was a handshake deal typical of the times.

That $200 was still in play during the spring trip to California. Evers had had a good, productive September with the Colts and was offered a $1,350 annual contract with the team over the winter, effectively doubling his salary from the Trojans. But the offer was conditioned on his making Selee's squad in the spring. Troy's local hero almost turned it down, still unsure he was good enough to join the big leagues, and absolutely terrified he was going to be abandoned somewhere in the still-wild west.

At each stop on the way back east, Selee tried to persuade Evers to stay and play for the summer with the local team. At each stop Evers refused. "The battle between Selee and me . . . lasted across the Continent to Chicago," Evers recalled years later, still convinced that Selee had had no use for him. "He was trying to put me in the minors."

More likely, Selee was playing the personnel game as it had to be played in those days. Trying to cultivate allies and expand his network of sources, Selee was reciprocating in a well-established way: offering to loan a hustling but green youngster to a minor league manager who could provide the kid some needed seasoning before shipping him to the big city. "Next year you should be ready for our club," Selee said in Evers's account. "Your work in Troy won't do you any good. It won't give you the experience I want you to have."

Evers remained suspicious deep into his career that Selee had no other designs but to unload him. What's more, Evers continued to believe that his willingness to stand up to Selee and refuse to get off the train is what steeled him for the pressure of big league play: "After the battle I gave Selee on the way across the country, I felt equal and fit for anything, and determined to show him."

Then again, perhaps Selee, the master theorist, had Evers's number from the start, knowing just how to prod a feisty but pint-sized Irish American who always felt the need to prove himself.

Back in Chicago at last, Evers warmed the bench for the first few weeks of the 1903 season as a backup infielder. Then one Sunday, when the team was forced to take a one-day trip back to Chicago from Pittsburgh in the middle of a series (the Iron City had a law against playing on the Sabbath), Selee took only eleven players along to save on train fare—the starting nine plus backup pitcher "Pop" Williams and Little Evers.

A pregame injury to one of the starters forced Selee to shuffle his Sunday lineup, and Evers got the nod. "He sent me into the game with the hopeless air with which an automobilist puts on a tire that he has been carrying as extra but that he knows is very weak and won't run far," Evers lamented. All Evers remembered hearing from Selee was a mumbled "Go out to second and see what you can do."

All Johnny Evers did that day was hit two doubles and a single, driving in one run and scoring the other in a 3–2, eleven-inning loss to the Pirates—before a Chicago crowd of fifteen thousand. "Of the six hits slammed into safe territory a little light-haired individual, Evers by name, held three to his credit," the *Tribune* told its readers the next day. More revealing than his plate appearances was Evers's work at second base. He was part of a "fast" double play with Joe Tinker in the bottom of the ninth, which prevented a run and sent the game into extra innings.

Selee had found the right place on the field for this "bundle of nerves." The move to second base was a turning point for Evers, perhaps as momentous in his mind as the all-night train ride from Troy. This game clearly carried significance for him the rest of his life; by 1915, he was blithely telling everyone the Colts had won that day.

It wasn't long after that performance that Evers supplanted Bobby Lowe permanently at second base. Team captain Lowe had played for Selee in Boston, where he had been one of the game's elite players for twelve

productive years. But by 1903 he was thirty-seven years old with di-
minished skills, and he seemed to know it. Team captains in those days
were expected to serve as tactical advisers to the manager, so a couple
of times early in the season Lowe suggested that Selee have Evers pinch
hit for him. Lowe "hadn't been able to do much with [the pitcher] that
day, and he was man enough to admit it of his own accord," Evers recounted. "I don't think Selee would have made the change otherwise."
Evers vindicated both himself and Lowe by hitting a triple, and a few
games later repeated the feat, again pinch-hitting for Lowe.

Evers was soon getting more playing time at second base, and Lowe's
stay in Chicago was pretty much finished. He left the team before the
summer was out, catching on with other teams for a few more years
before retiring in 1907. He had a fan for life in Evers, however. "'Bobby'
Lowe was one of the best friends I had in baseball during my struggle to
stick," Evers said. "I want to say that I believe 'Bobby' Lowe had more to
do with me making good than any other man in baseball."

MUSICAL CHAIRS

The Selee system was beginning to show results. Whether subtly ma-
nipulating young men's ambition and competitive spirit, or deploying
veterans as mentors, or making the most of the elfin personality of his
pretty young wife, Selee's deft personnel touches were having positive
effects. One of Selee's keenest attributes, as Evers had discovered and
both Joe Tinker and Frank Chance had also learned, was identifying
a player's best position on the field, the place where he could demonstrate optimum performance and, more important, selfless contribution to team play.

Tinker had arrived at spring training in 1902 as a third baseman, one
of ten infielders Selee assembled in camp that year. Tinker wanted to
play third base, never forgetting his ill-fated switch to second in the
minor leagues. "I had always been a third baseman," he thought.

But Selee had other ideas. After watching him take grounders, Selee
suggested that Tinker move over to shortstop, which better suited his
speed, range, and arm. Tinker assumed then he'd never make the big

league squad. "I told him then that I might just as well return to Portland," Tinker said, but Selee wouldn't take the bait. "He looked me over and said: 'I know that you are going to make a good shortstop, and furthermore, you won't be returned to Portland.'"

May Selee had a different role in Selee's leadership ensemble. She attended all the games at the West Side Grounds and often accompanied the team on the road. She liked to tell the story of an occasion in early 1902 when she didn't go with the team, heading south to St. Louis while the team went east. Then one evening she walked unannounced into the Boston hotel where Selee was staying. "I just got lonesome and came to see you," she told him, "and if you don't want me I'll go right back." (She stayed.) May Selee also enjoyed bantering with the inexperienced players, most of whom were barely of legal age and easily taken by her charms.

Later that summer, when the Pittsburgh Pirates were on their way to a championship with one of the best records in baseball history, May Selee made a playful bet with Tinker, by then working every day at shortstop at the age of twenty-two. She wagered a dollar that the Colts couldn't win one game against the Pirates. Sure enough, when the Pirates came to town next, the Colts took a drubbing in the first game, 11–3. But the next day they rallied to win, 9–3, with Tinker handling four chances at short without an error, scoring a run, and driving in another. That night a large box appeared at Tinker's hotel room with $1 inside. "They're such good boys, and work so hard for Frank," May said with motherly pride, even though she was only twenty-nine herself.

There was one more critical move Selee needed to make in the second year of his rebuilding program. He had a hole at first base and a surplus at catcher.

Frank Chance was in his sixth year as the team's backup catcher. His lifelong fearlessness worked against him at this position, however. He had never played more than seventy-six games in a season partly because he was getting his fingers cracked from crowding the batter or suffering other injuries. He "fought the ball," as his fellow players put it. He was hurt five times in one game at New York, and a teammate found him later with a torn ear, a bruised arm, "and a finger stuck into a lemon."

Teammates looked up to the twenty-six-year-old Chance as much as anyone on the team. He was a large man for his day, over six feet tall with a playing weight of 190 pounds. He was an expert hitter but surprisingly also a quick base runner with the instincts of a thief. In 1901 and 1902 Chance stole twenty-seven and twenty-nine bases, respectively, while playing in fewer than half of the Colts' games. It was becoming clear, though, that Selee needed him in the lineup, at a position that would keep him on the field for the entire season. Hence: first base.

There was only one problem with this idea: Chance hated it, insisting that he was a catcher, first and last, even if it meant being relegated to a part-time role. Selee tried for weeks to persuade him, but Chance refused anything more than spot duty there. He even threatened to quit baseball instead. "I signed as a catcher," he said.

It didn't matter to Chance that the Colts already had a top-flight catcher in twenty-seven-year-old Johnny Kling, who in 1902 had a batting average of .289 with nineteen doubles, three triples, and fifty-nine runs batted in. Kling also had a whip arm and could throw out runners from a crouch. He was a better backstop than just about anyone in the league—some argue he's still one of the best catchers in baseball history. A "catcher who can throw, hit, handle pitchers, and direct the team work is the rarest of all players, and Kling is all of that," sportswriter Hugh Fullerton said.

No matter. Chance kept up a fight. "I'll stay [at first base] until you get someone else," was the most he would say. But Selee was equally persistent, if passive-aggressive. "Selee was just wise enough never to find anyone else," Evers recalled. Eventually the manager wore Chance down, his grudging agreement to stay at first base helped along, no doubt, by a raise in salary.

NEW GAME IN TOWN

Chance went on to play 121 games at first base that year with a team-leading batting average of .327 and a league-leading sixty-seven stolen bases. He was also on the receiving end of forty-nine double plays, most of them involving shortstop Tinker and second baseman Evers. A historic infield was in place, and it would stay that way for a remarkable ten seasons.

With the core infield completed, plus Kling behind the plate, in 1903 Selee's Colts started doing something unusual: they began to win ball games. By early June, they were 30–13. To everyone's surprise, Selee's Colts held a three-game lead in the early season pennant race.

Then the New York Giants came to town, and John McGraw's veteran unit showed the upstarts how hard it was going to be to contend for a championship. The New Yorkers took four straight games at West Side Grounds, most of them by lopsided margins. In front of the Colts' home crowd, McGraw's Giants rudely knocked Selee's boys out of first place, a perch they would never reach again that summer.

A few weeks later, after Captain Bobby Lowe had quietly cleared out his locker, the Philadelphia Phillies came to town for a four-game series. Selee gathered the Colts together in the center-field clubhouse for a rare team meeting. Rather than simply appoint a new captain, the manager announced, he was going to try something new: let the players elect their field leader.

Selee's democratic deference seemed entirely in character, but it was for show. He had a preferred candidate and told everyone so—third-baseman Jimmy Casey, a thirty-three-year-old, college-educated journeyman—the oldest player remaining on the otherwise unseasoned ball club. Casey had recently jumped back over to the National League after two years playing for the Detroit Americans. His teammates called him "Doc" because he spent his off-hours cramming for dentistry exams.

Players put forward two other candidates as well: Kling and Chance. Despite Selee's entreaties, the vote wasn't even close. According to Evers, Chance won eleven votes; Casey, four; and Kling, two. The players had spoken—loudly. "Selee was dumbfounded and for a time annoyed," Evers said.

By the end of first Tinker-to-Evers-to-Chance season in 1903, the Colts had won a total of eighty-two games against fifty-six losses—a pretty good ratio by any historical standard. But it was good enough only for third place that year in the National League, just a game and a half behind McGraw's Giants but a full eight games behind the Pirates.

A more telling statistic than Chicago's win-loss record that year was the attendance at West Side Grounds: more than 386,000 fans came out to see the Colts play in their seventy-three home games, an average of 5,500 a game, or almost 50 percent more than the year before.

The Pirates went on in October to face the Boston Americans in the first "World's Championship" between the National and American league champions, a stipulation of the Peace Treaty back in January. Boston won the series, five games to three, in a best-of-nine format. Also a product of the Peace Treaty were postseason series in the cities that were home to franchises in both leagues. In Chicago, the Colts and the White Sox played the first of their "City Series," possibly more significant to local fans then than the "world" series. Fan interest was so intense that most of the games had to be played in South Side Park, which could hold more people. They played fourteen games in the first two weeks of October, each winning seven.

TEAM BUILDING

Flush with cash and genuinely excited about his ball club's prospects, James Hart took the team back to California the following March, setting up camp at the Los Angeles ranch of none other than Elias Jackson "Lucky" Baldwin, the old friend of the Chance family who had just opened the nearby Santa Anita Race Track. Frank Chance thus played a kind of host to the team even while starting to exert his authority more firmly. He rarely countenanced late-night bar crawling or other off-hours revelry, except for wagering on ponies. "A little bet now and then results in moderate excitement [and] helps to stir up mental activity," he said.

On the way back east, the team stopped off in Colorado Springs for an exhibition game and a little horseback riding, led by expert horsewoman May Selee, during a sightseeing trip to Pikes Peak. May led her posse at a fast clip through the town of Manitou Springs—too fast, perhaps. They almost got pulled over by the local constabulary for "speeding" down Main Street. The sight of a dozen gangly ballplayers trying to hang on in their saddles while galloping through town made everyone laugh, not least the policeman. "Mrs. Selee easily avoided the minion of the law and galloped on, the rest of the party following, bounding about their mounts like monkeys riding ponies at a circus." "She was the only one of the party who knew anything about riding horseback," said one eyewitness. "Fortunately, the policeman decided not to arrest her. He could easily have knocked any one of the ballplayers out of the saddle."

The team was starting to come together, on the field and off. Frank Chance, taking on the lieutenant's role that Selee expected of his team captain, started exerting his influence on the makeup of the team. Joining them on the western swing this time was a pitcher acquired in a winter trade at Chance's instigation. The ungainly name of this future Hall of Famer was Mordecai Peter Centennial Brown; he had many nicknames, but he would go down in baseball history as "Three Finger."

Born on October 19, 1876, and raised in Nyesville, Indiana, population one hundred, Brown was named after his uncle, his father, and the hundredth birthday of the United States. Most people called him "Miner" because he had worked in central Indiana's coal country. When he was five years old, Mordecai had suffered a gruesome farm injury while helping his brother operate a feed chopper fitted with circular knives. His right hand slipped in among the moving blades, slicing his index finger below the second joint, mangling his middle finger, and damaging the nerves of his little finger. "Every finger was chopped to ribbons," he told a reporter years later, "but the doctor managed to sew them together, although you see he didn't do much of a job."

The local physician was a former Civil War surgeon who probably "fixed" the hand the way he'd been trained on the battlefield, amputating the index finger and splinting the others. The boy's hand, still in splints, was further blunted a few weeks later as he and his sister were playing with a pet rabbit, trying to get it to swim in a bathtub. Mordecai slipped and fell into the tub, smashing his right hand on the bottom

Mordecai "Three-Finger" Brown was the Cubs' ace pitcher during their years of dominance, despite (or because of) a childhood accident that mangled his throwing hand for life. (Bain Collection, Library of Congress.)

and breaking several more bones. "Don't tell dad," he insisted, fearing a tanning.

Brown was left with a fleshy stub next to his thumb that, by some combination of quantum physics and hours of throwing rocks at knotholes in a barn, made it possible for him to throw the strangest, most elusive curveballs anyone had ever seen.

HOPE ON THE HORIZON

As the team moved through the 1904 season, a new kind of optimism began to spread across Chicago. Selee's Colts were coming into their own, winning eight games in a row during one stretch in May, including a 3–2 victory at West Side Grounds over Christy Mathewson, the Giants' matinee-idol pitcher. Two days later, Miner Brown pitched a two-hitter against the Giants before an estimated twenty-six thousand fans. The years-long Colts-Giants rivalry was born during those summer games.

In New York in June, the Colts played the Giants before a purported 38,805 fans at the Polo Grounds, which would have made it the largest crowd in major league history up to that point (other estimates put attendance at half that). However many were there, Giants fans witnessed a long, disappointing game: The Colts' twenty-six-year-old right-hander Bob Wicker, squaring up against the Giants' other star pitcher, Joe "Iron Man" McGinnity, held McGraw's sluggers hitless for nine innings, finally giving up an infield single in the tenth. The game remained scoreless, however, until the twelfth inning, when Evers hit a bloop single into left field, scoring Chance from third base. Wicker then shut down New York in the bottom of the inning, sealing the Colts 1–0 victory.

The Chicago fans (a few of them New Yorkers, it seems) were so thrilled by the Colts' victory they carried Wicker off the field on their shoulders. The *Chicago Tribune* summed up the contest with more than a touch of civic pride and a rival's spite: "Gloom unutterable from a baseball standpoint was the bitter portion of the thousands of men, women, and children who, for twelve heart-breaking innings at the Polo grounds today, sat and writhed under the shadow of defeat, only to have Chicago thrust the iron of humiliation into its composite soul and twist it."

If that day in New York ordained the future, it could not carry the current season. Even though the Colts' ended their 1904 campaign with a record of 93–60, they came in a distant second to the McGraw Giants. New York won the pennant with a record 106 wins and only 47 losses. Yet McGraw and the Giants' new owner, Cincinnatian John T. Brush, thumbed their noses at Ban Johnson and refused to play in a World Series against the Boston Americans. Brush had always been against the National Agreement, and McGraw was still feuding with Johnson over what McGraw believed to be a broken promise to install him as manager of the New York Americans.

Chicago's strong run in September had pushed them past the Pirates and given the team its best finish since 1891. Fans had several more reasons to believe that bigger possibilities loomed. In July, Hart had signed Selee to a three-year contract extension for $10,000. Selee had been rumored to take over the Highlanders in New York, but "I like Chicago," he said. "The people stick with us, winning or losing, and I am going to stick." On the field, Tinker, Evers, Chance, and Doc Casey were ensconced in their positions and becoming known around the league as a brick wall of defense. Kling was a standout at catcher, and they had a solid rotation of pitchers led by Jake Weimer, winner of twenty games, and Mordecai Brown, who gave up fewer than two runs per game over twenty-six starts. Chicago fans were turning out in droves to watch them play; attendance at West Side Grounds pushed up another 15 percent to 439,000 that year.

The sporting press also took notice. Francis C. Richter, founder of the *Sporting Life* newspaper and editor of the annual *Reach's Guide*, gave Selee's Colts high praise in his year-end review: "The Chicago team, which astonished the base ball world in 1903 by its evolution from a second-division team into a pennant possibility, and which then finished a good third, last season kept up its form and reputation by remaining in the race from start to finish, and finishing a very good second."

The job wasn't finished, clearly. Going into the 1905 campaign, both Hart and Selee believed that one or two more good players would enable the team to finally contend for the pennant. They took the men to the West Coast again that spring, and Selee again set about collecting outfielder prospects. He gave ten men tryouts for the three positions and one backup he would ultimately keep on his roster.

Expectations were high. "If any team overhauls the Giants this year it will probably be Chicago," wrote Harry W. Ford for an *Inter Ocean* season preview headlined "Fans Glad the Baseball Opening Is Approaching." Then Ford summed up what many people in Chicago at the time believed to be true: "When the team gets working together, directed by Frank Selee's brains, it will be one of the hardest in the business to beat."

BASEBALL INSANITY
1906

There is still a reasonably large element of the population that cannot fully comprehend the madness of baseball fanaticism. . . . They do not stop to consider that the sufferer is doubtless happier with his madness than without it. *Chicago Tribune* editorial, 1906

On a quiet Saturday morning in the summer of 1906, in the heart of the city's financial district, motorcars began assembling at the corner of LaSalle and Jackson Streets. Before long more than two hundred runabouts, touring cars, and open-air tonneaus were lined up alongside the Board of Trade building. Soon, an army of young men piled aboard. Those who couldn't find a seat or perch on a running board clambered into tallyho coaches that held twenty to forty people each in bleacher-style seating boxes. This peculiar weekend congregation called itself the Board of Trade Rooters. As the engines roared to life, the blocks-long convoy thundered off to a baseball game.

The Rooters were a raucous bunch by nature, even outside of the frantic competition of the trading pits. The racket of their cars must have been deafening, the two- and four-cylinder engines revving and belching in a cacophony of street music. The all-male chorus pitched their voices high above that din as they barked out chants and popular rally songs through megaphones large and small. Their "leathern lungs and quick wit and scorching invective" would have startled to attention everyone along the way as the cavalcade proceeded west across the South Branch of the Chicago River, then through Greek, Italian, Ukrainian, and Jewish neighborhoods. Residents cheered them on from porches and sidewalks. The drivers were in no hurry, nor could they be, the streets being pocked with a riot of trolley tracks, railroad crossings, and chuckholes.

The two-and-a-half-mile excursion led them to the Cook County Hospital on Polk Street. After turning south onto Lincoln (today's Wolcott), they arrived at their destination: the main entrance to the West Side Grounds, home field of Chicago's National League baseball team. Here the Rooters were joined by thousands of fellow partisans streaming over from the Polk Street streetcar station, which provided connections to neighborhoods north, south, east, and west. All of them—young and old, male and female, native son and immigrant, white and black fans alike—had come together to bear witness to a grand occasion.

The fast-rising Chicago Nationals, led by player-manager Frank Chance and his companion infielders, Joe Tinker and Johnny Evers—and supplemented with top-flight ballplayers at every other position—were about to take on the reigning world-champion New York Giants. The National League pennant hung in the balance. The Giants, always hard to beat, would be out for blood, and yet everyone in the Windy City liked the hometown boys' chances.

The Rooters club was a relatively new organization—for the simple reason that baseball fans in Chicago hadn't had much to root about for twenty long seasons. Then again, nothing like these "fans" had existed before. Unlike the cranks, gamblers, and loutish saloon denizens who populated baseball parks in the 1890s, the Rooters were among the city's most ambitious young strivers: brokers, grain merchants, sales agents, and office clerks. Many had played baseball while growing up. Some no doubt excelled at it for amateur teams. All of them were eager to hitch their hopes to a pennant contender.

The Rooters' exuberant ringleader was Edward G. "Eddie" Heeman. A transplanted Cincinnatian, Heeman was a hail-fellow-well-met type who enjoyed the companionship of his fellow traders. A successful commission broker in cotton and grains, he had earned a reputation as a workaholic by spending fifteen- to eighteen-hour days at his occupation and as self-publisher of the tip sheet "Grain Trade Talks." At thirty-nine, Heeman showed little interest in other diversions popular among hard-charging capitalists in his day—no time for golf, billiards, theater, or so-called entertainments at drinking clubs. "Here is a young man whose greatest pleasure is to be working," according to an approving profile in a trade publication.

As earnest as he seemed, Eddie Heeman allowed for two playful indulgences. First, he was a fashion peacock, the "Beau Brummel of the exchange floor," as a newspaper writer described him. He arrived at the trading floor each day in new combinations of spats, brightly colored neckwear, and flamboyant waistcoats—"almost as many 'changes' as the king of England." Most of his pals in the pits cared little for personal appearance as long as they were clean-shaven and wore clean collars. Not Heeman: "When he is in his semi-frock he possesses all the appearances of an afternoon boulevardier."

Heeman's other permitted passion was baseball. Since moving to Chicago he'd gone head over heels for its two big league ball clubs: the White Sox (owned by his good friend Charles A. Comiskey) and the revamped team with many names: Colts, Cubs, Orphans, Spuds. In full-throated support of both clubs, Heeman had been a founding member and financial underwriter of the Rooters club, and he was now widely acknowledged as the "generalissimo extraordinary" of a growing legion of baseball fans.

MUGGSY ON A SPIT

The Rooters organized their demonstration on August 18 as a show of support for Chicago's new claim to baseball supremacy. This was a bold assertion when facing the Giants, whose manager, John "Muggsy" McGraw, and star pitchers, Christy Mathewson and Joe "Iron Man" McGinnity, were regarded as exemplars of baseball talent, brains, and tenacity.

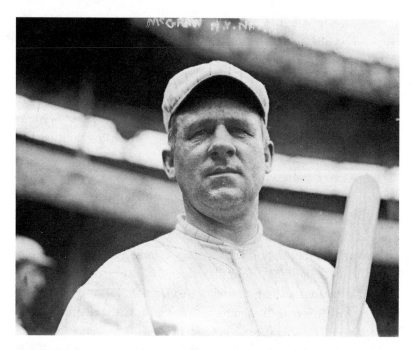

The New York Giants' longtime manager John McGraw earned the nickname "Muggsy" with his brand of baseball that featured dirty tricks and umpire baiting along with a Napoleonic style of generalship. (Bain Collection, Library of Congress.)

The Giants had won the pennant in 1904 and 1905, and had easily dispatched the Philadelphia Athletics in the 1905 World Series. McGraw and company were kings of the game. Even Chicagoans had to pay deference: "Apparently [McGraw's] Giants are in a class by themselves in the baseball world," the *Tribune* had conceded at the start of the season. By midseason, however, the Giants were scuffling, unexpectedly stuck in second place behind Chicago. When McGraw's troops pulled into town for this four-game series in August, they were determined to even things up. The Giants had, after all, trounced Chicago, three games to one, on their trip there in May.

That series had offered no hint of waning fortunes in New York. But in a June rematch at Manhattan's Polo Grounds, Chance's men turned the tables, themselves winning three out of four contests—the first two decisively, 6–0 and 11–3. There followed a humiliating massacre in which the runs kept racking up to a final score of Chicago 19, New York 0.

This was music to the ears of Eddie Heeman and his Rooters. They immediately began working on their welcoming plans for the Giants' next visit.

The rivalry between the Giants and the Cubs illustrated the intensifying competition that their cities felt for each other. Chicagoans struggled to overcome a collective inferiority complex, despite having rebuilt their city from scratch in the thirty-five years since the Great Chicago Fire of 1871, and even with fresh memories of the 1893 World's Columbian Exposition, the peerless international showcase of architecture and culture. In many locals' minds, though, Chicago was still a "second city" to the global polestar on Manhattan Island. After Chicago had annexed 125 square miles of former suburbs in the 1890s, New York was spurred to annex not only Brooklyn but also parts of Queens County, the Bronx, and Staten Island, maintaining its status as the largest city in America. Architects in both cities competed to see which could build the tallest or most impressive buildings. Board of Trade employees felt this competitive drive acutely. Chicago was the world's leader in commodities trading at a time when commerce in grains, livestock, and cotton were driving the entire U.S. economy. Yet the financial lords of Wall Street managed to retain their sense of entitlement, an imperious pose that rubbed off onto other aspects of urban culture, not least in sports and entertainment. Typically regal New York social events included Mrs. John Jacob Astor's lavish ball at Louis Sherry's handsome Fifth Avenue restaurant, where 450 guests dined on a nine-course midnight supper. Two weeks later, James Stillman installed an artificial waterfall in his dining room for a dinner dance. Rudolf Guggenheim stocked the Waldorf's Myrtle Room with nightingales borrowed from the zoo. The only thing missing in this exhibition of kingly self-regard was a winning baseball team.

The 1905 New York Giants remedied that problem by winning the National League pennant for the second year in a row, and then, after having refused to play their AL counterparts at the close of the 1904 season, deigning to play for the ultimate title in 1905, winning handily. When the 1906 season rolled around, the Giants immediately began flaunting their alpha-dog status by replacing the customary "NY" branding on their uniforms in favor of the words "World's Champions" across the chest. Both home and away jerseys featured the same proclamation.

But the Chicago Rooters had some ammunition for a sharp riposte. Warming up their vocal chords during the motorcade, reaching fever pitch at the ballpark, the boys devised a chant they would recite throughout the weekend—and for many years to come. It was a childish taunt, as crude as it was merciless: they merely counted out each run that Chicago had scored, without answer, in the June 7 annihilation of the Giants: "One . . . two . . . three . . . four!" they began, the volume rising with each digit. "Five . . . six . . . seven . . . eight . . . nine." The mantra soared as other fans joined in: "Ten . . . eleven . . . twelve . . . thirteen . . . fourteen . . . fifteen." The crowd kept yelling, ever louder yet more slowly, toward the punctuated climax: "Sixteen . . . seventeen . . . eighteen . . . nineteen!"

Then they'd do it again.

The crowd had swelled to nearly twenty thousand hours before the 3 p.m. start. Estimates put final attendance in the range of thirty thousand, believed to be the largest Saturday crowd in the history of the rickety West Side Grounds (whose actual seating capacity was fewer than ten thousand). Team officials had to fasten steel cables to posts behind home plate and extend them down the field toward the outfield corners. The makeshift barrier walled off space on the sidelines where a few thousand more fans could squeeze in.

Photographs show the packed grandstand and bleachers with patrons squatting on the field seven to eight deep in foul territory. The ballplayers would have had to step over and through these fans to get from the bench to the batter's box. Still more bodies stood behind ropes in deep center field.

One hundred and fifty cops—"a flying squadron of bluecoats"—were on hand to keep things under control. They had little reason to worry, for this was a good-spirited multitude. "No one offered to harm the New York players," noted one correspondent. "The crowd was sportsmanlike, and gave the New Yorkers a generous hand for everything they did."

The Rooters set the tone as they filled up dozens of grandstand boxes. They had painted their megaphones yellow and waved yellow "pennons," or flags, each inscribed with "Muggsy" in black letters. They also hoisted placards with a caricature of McGraw with a streak of yellow daubed across his face. This signified their contempt for the dirty tactics that he had always been known for—and made no effort to disavow—over his long career.

Yet the object of the Rooters' derision wasn't on the field that day to receive the catcalls. He had come to town with his team, but he could not dress for the game, as he was still under suspension by the league for "vicious" umpire baiting in the team's previous home series. But McGraw got the crowd's message; sportswriters spotted him in the stands, in street clothes huddled amid a claque of New York supporters.

A Rooters glee club soon moved into position, striking up hoarse renditions of popular songs and some new tunes contrived for the occasion. They were backed up by a motley band of musical instruments—piccolo, bassoon, violin, bass drum, and "bazzou," or mouth harp. The biggest applause came with the refrain, "So Long Muggsy," as well as the oft-repeated "Nineteen" chant. Just before the opening pitch the Rooters also cut loose nineteen yellow balloons, calling out the number as each one set sail. The noise level must have been excruciating. "From the time the bell rang to start the scrap until the finish," marveled one scribe, "there was a constantly swelling roar of rooting which drowned out of hearing and almost out of sight everything except the great battle itself."

The contest didn't disappoint. Both teams were riding hot streaks, Chicago racking up ten straight wins and the Giants eight. Chicago's best pitcher, Mordecai "Miner" Brown, started, as did the great Mathewson for New York. Cubs hitters roughed up Matty early with two runs on three hits in the bottom of the second. The Giants clawed their way back with single runs against Brown in the third and sixth innings, knotting the score at 2–2.

Then the real fun began. Leading off the bottom of the sixth, Frank

Chance sliced an outside pitch into the right field corner, where it bounded into the crowd behind the ropes—a ground rule double, by pregame agreement. Through the crowds of fans in front of the Chicago bench strode the self-assured figure of Harry Steinfeldt. He was Chicago's new third baseman, picked up in the winter, and he had quickly become the club's best hitter and a ready crowd pleaser. Steinfeldt had been an itinerant teenage entertainer in Texas before emerging as a ballplayer. He knew how to seize his moment on stage.

A fresh plug of tobacco bulging his cheek, the switch-hitting "Steinie" jumped on Mathewson's first pitch and roped a hard line drive deep into the right-center field gap. He rounded second and cruised into third base before the ball made it back from the outfield. Meanwhile Chance walked home easily, putting the Cubs in front, 3–2, as the crowd went wild. Next up: Joe Tinker, one of the team's weaker hitters, though he always seemed to have Mathewson's number. Tinker promptly rapped out his third single of the day, scoring Steinfeldt and sending the fans into "another paroxysm of glee." A sacrifice bunt, an infield single, and another bunt then loaded the bases. Center fielder Jimmy "Rabbit" Slagle delivered the knockout blow by pulling a single through the right side of the infield, chalking up two more runs.

By the time the inning was over, the "Giant Killers," as the *Inter-Ocean* took to calling the club, had put up four insurmountable runs. Brown's overpowering pitching and some slick defensive plays by Tinker and Evers made the 6–2 score hold up for a rousing Chicago victory.

"So long, Muggsy! How we hate to beat you so," crooned the Rooters' jubilant choir. McGraw and his Giants would have to wait a long time to avenge themselves.

Throughout the game, Chicago loyalists had been keeping an eye on a young man standing alongside a billboard in the outfield. His job was to post out-of-town scores fed to him by Western Union telegraph. Charlie Comiskey's White Sox were playing in New York City that day, against the Highlanders, also becoming known around the league as the Yankees, and the Sox had their own American League pennant hopes on the line. When the scoreboard first showed that the Sox were leading the Yanks by one run, the crowd let out a yell.

Then, just after Chance's squad had jumped ahead in its contest with the four-run rally in the sixth, the scoreboard boy hoisted a placard showing nine more runs for the Sox in their half of the ninth inning. That gave them a 10–0 lead, and the celebration at West Side Grounds was complete. "The roar which followed the Spuds' great rally was continued without abatement at the double victory for Chicago," the *Tribune* beamed.

The city of Chicago was on its way to becoming the new capital of baseball's rising kingdom. Like Eddie Heeman, the teeming metropolis of two million people was going downright daffy over baseball.

SELEE TAKES HIS LEAVE

The ball club that took the field against the Giants in August 1906 looked much like the up-and-coming team of the year before. Yet many things were quite different. Top among them: master theorist Frank Selee was no longer manager, and James A. Hart no longer principal owner. Frank Chance was calling the shots on the field as player-manager and, unusual for his day, offering his voice on matters of club policy as a minority stockholder.

Some things hadn't changed: Joe Tinker and Johnny Evers were ensconced at their keystone positions, and Mordecai Brown and Johnny Kling continued as one of the premier batteries in the league. Singly and together, Chance, Tinker, Evers, Brown, and Kling were Selee's legacies, as each man readily acknowledged. But by mid-1906, Frank and May Selee were no longer central to the city's baseball endeavors, having departed for Colorado in a desperate, and ultimately despairing, attempt to save Frank's life.

Selee's health had nagged him for years. The first sign of more serious concerns had appeared during spring training of 1905, when the Colts were traveling from Santa Monica to San Francisco for some exhibition games. Selee fell seriously ill, and it seemed likely the team would have to head east without him, if only to get "a week or so of perfect bedrest," according to his doctors. But he made the trip home.

Then Selee came down with what seemed to be an attack of "acute indigestion." He doubled over in such pain that he could no longer manage. "The team was crippled by the absence of his shrewd head and clever directions," reported *Sporting Life*. A new diagnosis made his real malady clear: appendicitis. But at this point Selee was so weak that his physician believed he could not withstand surgery. He was ordered to stay away from the team for several weeks, the doctor insisting that "absolute rest and freedom from the cares of the ball field are necessary to enable the manager to gain the vitality his needs for the operation."

Selee applied to Hart for an indefinite leave of absence, bowing to his physicians' recommendation that he seek out a better climate than the muggy shores of Chicago. The Selees made preparations to spend the summer in Colorado and New Mexico, but while sportswriters were already speculating that Frank's departure was permanent, he refused to give in completely. He continued to scout out pitching prospects by reading newspapers and telegrams in bed. Hart was as generous with his praise as with his leave granting. "You have the admiration and affection of not only your employers and your players, but of the entire baseball fraternity and of all the baseball loving public," he said in a letter to Selee.

Hart quickly named Frank Chance interim manager but otherwise gave no indication that anything else was amiss. In fact, as Selee would reveal later, Hart was the restless one, even before Selee's health became an issue.

After twenty-five years in organized baseball, most of it as an executive with the Chicago Nationals, James Abner Hart wanted out. Perhaps he was tired of battling the likes of John T. Brush and Alfred Steedman in smoke-filled board rooms. He may have tired of the constant competition with the White Sox for fans. Or, more likely, he had an inkling of the coming financial ruin of his main backer and co-owner, banker John R. Walsh. While Hart gave no public indication of the source of his dissatisfaction, early in 1905, while he and Selee were on the West Coast, the two men had had a conversation about the future of the franchise.

Selee had asked to meet Hart at the St. Francis Hotel in San Francisco to say that he wanted give up management of the team, "as I did not feel that I was able to take charge again that season." Hart, not in the best of health himself at the time, asked Selee to stay at the helm for little while longer. Then Hart confided that he was planning to sell the team; Selee could make him the first offer. Selee, who had a number of friends in high places, began looking for a backer. One prospect was Phil Auten, former co-owner of the Pittsburgh Pirates, who was keen to get back into baseball.

Once back in Chicago, Selee confirmed Hart's intentions. But on his walk downtown to telegraph Auten, he was "taken sick" and had to return home. He never fully recovered. The deal fell apart on that sidewalk; Selee would soon be convalescing in the high-desert air of Pueblo, Colorado.

It became clear that Selee was suffering from a variety of lung illnesses, including pleurisy, rheumatoid fever, and, worst, tuberculosis. He would bounce back long enough the following year to consider a founding stake in a minor league venture. But there was no way he could return to Chicago and the stress of the big leagues.

Selee was not a wealthy man and now had no regular income. To help him, Hart and other NL officials staged a series of tribute games for Selee at the end of the 1905 season. A crowd of five thousand showed up at West Side Grounds on September 28 for a game against Selee's old Boston Beaneaters. The guest list was a who's-who of baseball, including Pop Anson, NL President Harry C. Pulliam, and the grand old historian and conscience of the game, "Father" Henry Chadwick, whose encomium read: "Frank Selee has done so much work for clean base ball that his work will live long after him."

The gate receipts put $4,000 in the Selees' bank account, with more to come from other "testimonials" that month in ball parks around the country. Among the contributors was John McGraw. Even sportswriters agreed to pay their way into the games for his benefit. "If Selee has an enemy the latter has never made himself known," the *Tribune* warmly observed.

THE NEW GUARD

It was getting late on a damp April afternoon in 1906 when big Frank Chance lumbered up to the plate, his heavy, bottleneck bat resting on his shoulder. The Chicago Nationals were locked in a scoreless tie with the visiting Cincinnati Reds in the bottom of the ninth inning. Some 5,200 spectators had been waiting more than three hours during a rain-soaked pitchers' duel between Miner Brown and Jake Weimer, and they were anxious for a resolution.

In the luxury boxes up front, two well-heeled businessmen took in the scene. One of them had just arrived from Cincinnati; the other was a recent transplant from there. Both were dressed in dark three-piece suits, starched shirts, and bowler derbies, casting lordly eyes over the entire proceedings as if they owned the place.

Chance began his batter's-box ritual as darkness began creeping over the expansive grounds. He gently tapped the plate, then waved his war club high in the air with his right hand while tugging on his belt with the left. He placed the bat down, resting it between his legs, a signal to the waiting pitcher that this encounter could proceed only when Chance was ready for it. At last he pulled his cap down tighter and yanked at his trousers once more. He gripped the bat with both hands and looked up at the mound, his face a picture of stone-cold determination.

Weimer had no less sense of purpose—or motivation. The hurler known as "Tornado Jake" had been unceremoniously dumped by Chicago that winter after three stellar seasons. He'd been traded to Cincinnati for an out-of-shape, seemingly expendable infielder named Steinfeldt. Chicago had been marching its way up in the standings, thanks in no small part to Weimer's fine pitching for manager Selee. But Selee was gone, and Weimer had good reason to feel disrespected by Chance, who had insisted on the trade—against all advice—in one of his first moves as field general.

Chance would quickly sour Weimar's taste for revenge, however. For the second time that day, Husk got the jump on Tornado Jake and pulled a hard liner to left field, putting him safely on first. Chance then flashed a signal to the next batter, none other than "Fatty" Steinfeldt, to drop a sacrifice bunt, which he did to perfection, moving Chance into scoring position at second. Up to the plate walked Joe Tinker, hitless so far that day. The meeting turned into a long affair. "Jake wouldn't give Joe anything he liked, and Joe wouldn't hit anything he didn't like," observed an eyewitness at the press table behind home plate. A dozen foul balls later, Tinker finally wore out Weimer and drew the fourth ball.

With runners on first and second, one out, it was Johnny Evers's turn at bat. Chance had something else in mind, however. Barking out instructions from second base, he called for backup catcher Pat Moran to pinch hit. Chance must have wanted a right-handed bat in this situation, even though Moran was hitting about .100 at the time, compared to Evers's .300 average. It was a bold, risk-filled move, though it's hard to believe the rookie skipper anticipated what would happen next.

Moran gently tapped a routine grounder to third base, a tailor-made double-play ball that seemed destined to retire the side. But the Cubs were never that predictable. As Cincinnati's Jim Delahanty gobbled up the ball and whipped it to second, Tinker sprinted down the base path and hit the dirt with spikes high. His only objective was to block second baseman Miller Huggins, all five-foot-six-inches of him, from completing the throw to first. Their collision served its purpose. Huggins jumped up in protest and danced around umpire Bill Klem, demanding Moran be called out at first because of Tinker's interference at second.

Chance, meanwhile, never looked back. While Huggins ranted at Klem, Husk alertly rounded third base and tore for home. The big man was an exceptional runner in a league full of jackrabbits—he led the league with 57 stolen bases that season and went on to swipe 401 over his career. Huggins heard his teammates' alarm bells too late: a hurried throw to the plate sailed high and wide of the mark. Chance slid under the tag—scoring from second base on a dribbler to third. The amazed crowd rose to its feet as one. As far the sodden fans were concerned, the afternoon's lone run was "as good as a million."

Even more impressed were the two Cincinnati bigwigs in the front-row seats. One was a round little man named Charles Webb Murphy, a sports-editor-turned-press-agent for the New York Giants. Murphy hailed from Wilmington, Ohio, where he had played a little baseball as a teenager. He had always aspired to a frontline role on the big league stage, and he had recently realized that ambition, having paid James A. Hart a reported $105,000 for the team. C. W. Murphy was now president and putative owner of the Chicago Nationals—the newest "magnate" of the National League's oldest franchise.

There's no way Murphy had the cash he needed to buy the team outright; he was little more than a salaried flunky for the abstemious John T. Brush in New York. But Murphy was a "live wire" with a sense of showmanship, and he had always relished hobnobbing among baseball's high and mighty. He was also enough of a baseball man to appreciate what Hart and Selee had been building in Chicago over the past four seasons. Chicago was the "smartest team in the country," Murphy had noted. "I know that Mr. Chance and his men do things in ball games which surprised me—things that the public frequently does not observe." He called Chance and company the "foremost experts" of the inside game, a thinly disguised slap at John McGraw and his long claim to that title. "The [Chicago] men work with a 'cause and effect' calculation," Murphy said, "and little, if anything, is done without the hope of attaining some object."

Murphy's companion that day was Charles Phelps Taft, one of the most prominent businessmen in Cincinnati, if not the country, and owner of the *Cincinnati Times-Star*. He was the older brother of William Howard Taft, the secretary of war at the time. When Murphy got wind that Hart was putting the team up for sale, he had hurried to inform Taft, his former employer.

"I need a hundred thousand dollars," Murphy brazenly told him. "I'd like to borrow it from you." Taft agreed and accepted a 40 percent stake of the business in return. It was Taft's novel idea, based on his observation of Chance, his ingenuity, and his leadership skills on that soggy April afternoon, to bring Husk into their inner circle.

Taft called Chance into a private meeting at the team's offices in the Masonic Temple. "Any man with the brains to do what you did deserves more than a salary," Taft told him. "How would you like to buy 10 percent of the Cubs?" The stake cost Chance $10,000, which he paid for with a slip of paper on which he had written "I O U ten thousand dollars." Chance had already received a three-year contract to manage the team after Selee's departure had become certain. Now he won assurances from his bosses that he would have complete control over all baseball affairs, including personnel decisions and trades.

After consummating the deal with Hart after the 1905 season, Murphy had taken to the role of magnate at the league's winter meetings in New York. He regaled his new peers with an apocryphal and somewhat impertinent story of a freshman senator from Ohio whose election was widely regarded as a fluke. The pretender "had never shown the ability of a Gladstone or a Disraeli," Murphy said, but after a week in Washington he had arrived at a first and then a second impression of how it felt to be a senator. "The first day I employed most of my time wondering how I had really got there," he began. But then, "having listened attentively to the measures being introduced and the accompanying speeches, I began to wonder how the other fellows got there."

The NL magnates, far from being affronted, smiled and nodded in agreement. They had among them a man who seemed ready to stand up and defend their interests against their nemesis, American League strongman Ban Johnson.

IN THE MATTER OF EVERS V. TINKER

The year 1906 promised to be a breakout year for the Cubs. Even before the 1905 season had wound to a close, the Cubs were showing the league and the city what was in store for the future. In the second half of that season, with Chance managing, Chicago had won forty games and lost only twenty-one. Their ninety-two total wins for the year pulled them up to third place behind New York and Pittsburgh.

Twenty-four-year-old Evers and twenty-five-year-old Tinker formed a reliable bulwark in the middle infield. The flamboyant Tinker had led NL shortstops in double plays in 1905, with sixty-seven. The more workmanlike Evers was earning his nickname, the "Human Crab," not just for his sideways footwork but for his constant rants against umpires. ("My favorite umpire is a dead one," he liked to say.)

Shortstop Joe Tinker, *left*, and second baseman Johnny Evers covered the middle infield in tandem almost wordlessly. They had to, because the two firebrands carried on a nonspeaking, sometimes violent feud that lasted for decades. (National Baseball Hall of Fame and Museum, Cooperstown, NY.)

His nonstop carping often drove his teammates to distraction. Chance once confided to Tinker that he wished Evers played in the outfield so he couldn't hear him.

But Tinker was also tightly wound and just as competitive. He certainly wasn't going to take any grief from an Irish runt. "Perhaps Evers has been the more fiery, but Tinker never has been slow to retaliate in kind any time the occasion demanded it," noted longtime Chicago baseball writer George Rice.

Yet by all accounts the hot-blooded duo of Tinker and Evers were a marvel of cool efficiency in the field. They could operate in concert almost wordlessly, adjusting their positions with each batter and pitch, working by eye contact with catcher Johnny Kling on steals and pickoff plays, and of course executing a double play when called for. "Tinker and myself played through one entire season without once giving each other a signal even as to who would take the throw at second," Evers recounted. "We understood each other's movements so well that we did not need signals." It was a good thing for the Cubs that the two young men could play so well together, because they hated each other.

The game's most famous double-play duo carried on a notorious feud for decades. Their mutual vendetta ostensibly began in late 1905 but probably had its roots in their first encounter on Labor Day in 1902, when Little Evers was forced to ride to the ballpark in Philadelphia atop the omnibus in his quasi-clown suit. Tinker was one of those seated comfortably inside the bus that day, making fun of the freckled rube. A rookie himself only a few months earlier, Tinker was no doubt eager for the team to have a new target for its hazing—and quite ready to deliver a few gibes of his own. Irish American Evers surely resented all the more any insult delivered by someone with an Anglo-Saxon surname like Tinker. The Irish have long memories, it has been said, as well as a willful inability to forgive or to forget.

Three years to the month later, Evers may have found his moment for revenge. In September 1905, the Cubs had a couple of extra days before a series in St. Louis, and Chance had grudgingly agreed that the team would play a few exhibition games against Indiana minor league teams en route.

On September 13, the team stopped off in tiny Bedford, south of Indianapolis, hometown of Cubs pitcher Bob Wicker. A reception committee provided elegant carriages to transport the visitors from the hotel, where the players dressed for the game, to the ball field across town. Tinker and Evers were both late getting dressed, but Evers finally bounded downstairs in uniform and jumped into the only remaining hack. He "drove away in state," occupying the entire carriage as if to the manor born, Hugh Fullerton later told *Tribune* readers.

When Tinker finally came downstairs and discovered no rides left, he had to trudge over a mile of dusty road to the game. He was not amused. Newspaper accounts outlined what happened next, and Tinker, Evers, and Fullerton would each fill in the blanks in differing and varying ways over the following thirty years. But there's no doubt that Bedford citizens that day had front-row seats to an internecine free-for-all.

Just before game time, all eyes turned to the middle infield, where Tinker and Evers were squared off in a fist fight. Bob Wicker rushed over from the pitcher's box to break it up, but he got pulled into the fracas. "All three men went into the sod in a clawing, kicking heap," observed an *Indianapolis News* correspondent. Indianapolis fans, worried that their hometown hero Wicker was in trouble, rushed the field. "At one time it appeared as though the players' brawl would involve half the spectators in the grounds."

No one was hurt, order was restored, and the locals returned to their seats. The Cubs went on to play "as if nothing had happened," according to the *News*. The cause of the row was kept secret, despite coverage of the bizarre altercation in newspapers all across the country. Hugh Fullerton finally revealed the triggering episode, but not for another year.

Evers and Tinker each acknowledged that, during warm-ups, Tinker had confronted Evers about the cab and then, in obvious payback, whipped a short peg to Evers from about ten feet away. "It was a real hard ball, like a catcher throwing to second," Evers recalled, waving a gnarled finger on his right hand as lasting evidence. "I yelled to him, you so and so," Evers said, but got only a laugh back from Tinker. "That's the last word we had for—well, I just don't know how long."

The two men cut a deal. "If you and I talk to each other we're only going to be fighting all the time," Tinker told Evers. "So don't talk to me and I won't talk to you. You play your position and I'll play mine and let it go at that." Evers said that arrangement suited him fine, and the two men played side by side in silence almost every game for the next six years. "We never spoke to each other again except in anger," Tinker said.

The two men had more confrontations on the field and in the clubhouse, yet their quarrels seemed only to seal their bond as teammates. "We were fighting all the time," Evers said. "But if anybody on the other club started anything with either of us, we'd both pitch into him." Their feud may even have made them better players, Evers contended, serving as inspiration for seemingly impossible plays. "You simply did not let the other fellow beat you and you either got the ball he threw to you or were knocked down by it."

"People used to wonder how it was we played so well together under the circumstances," Tinker echoed. "They didn't understand the circumstances, that is all." Tinker and Evers had a pact, he said—an unspoken pact, to be sure—to do whatever they could to help the team win. "I could always depend upon Evers to co-operate with me in any play at second and I used to endeavor to do my part toward cooperating with him."

Tinker closed the matter thus: "Baseball is no game for mollycoddles."

"I DON'T KNOW" IS ON THIRD

Baseball history has always been rife with brain-teasing trivia questions, some of them meaningless, others loaded with significance. For more than a hundred years—at least since F. P. Adams penned his famous lines about a "trio of bearcubs"—one of the great stumpers has been: Who was the fourth member of the Tinker-to-Evers-to-Chance infield? The answer, while in one sense trivial, does come with a dose of historic and cultural impact.

In late 1905 Chance saw two big holes in his roster, one in the out-field and the other at third base. In both cases, he wanted heavy hitters and run producers, experienced big leaguers who could provide some wallop in the middle of the lineup. The first move came in December. Eager to show he was a mover and shaker, Murphy was willing to spend handsomely to complete the jigsaw puzzle that Hart and Selee had started to assemble. And Chance had no compunction about giving up a mainstay or two of the current squad to build his team. "We need pitchers, we must have a new third baseman, and a hitting outfielder before we can win the pennant," he told confidants.

Chance looked down his roster for expendables. There was "Doc" Casey, the erstwhile dental school student and senior member of the squad, who had held down the third-base job for the previous three years. Casey had won the respect of his teammates, but Chance knew that Doc was a journeyman at best. Chance also had inherited out-fielder Billy Maloney, whom Selee had acquired a year before from Cincinnati. The speedy Maloney could be sensational performer at times—the "idol of the crowd"—legging out fourteen triples in 1905 and leading the league with fifty-nine stolen bases. But Chance consid-ered him erratic. He told Murphy to dangle both Casey and Maloney as trade bait.

What followed was "one of the most spectacular deals ever recorded in baseball history," according to Hugh Fullerton. Chance had set his sights on Jimmy Sheckard, an outfielder in Brooklyn who had a long track record as a run producer but had fallen afoul of club owners by jumping to the American League during Ban Johnson's "war" of 1902. The subsequent Peace Treaty between the leagues sent him back to Brooklyn, but by then Sheckard was persona non grata with the brass of the Superbas. Rumors of Sheckard's discontent wended through the player network to Chance, who told Murphy to act fast.

Murphy dutifully offered up Casey and Maloney, then tossed in an-other outfielder and a pitcher—plus $2,000—for Sheckard. The deal "stunned Chicago followers of the game," Fullerton said, but it in-stantly made Chance's outfield first-rate. He shifted Frank "Wildfire" Schulte to his natural position in right field and installed Sheckard in left, where he would stay for the next seven seasons while batting in the top half of the order. Along with center fielder Jimmy "Rabbit" Slagle, another Selee import from Boston, this second trio of bear cubs formed a "Tri-Sigma" outfield: Sheckard to Slagle to Schulte.

Wildfire Schulte, from Cochecton, New York, had gravitated to baseball in 1899 despite the qualms of his German-immigrant father that the profession was less than "honest." (Frank turned down his dad's offer of a thousand "plunks" to burn his baseball suit.) The diminutive Slagle, raised in the western Pennsylvania hamlet of Worthville, combined speed with unlikely arm strength, spawning the legend that he could throw a ball over the roof of his house and run to the backyard in time to catch it. Samuel James Tilden Sheckard, of Upper Chanceford, Pennsylvania, was one of the few men of Pennsylvania Dutch heritage to play big league baseball.

Much like their infield counterparts, none of the Tri-Sigma outfielders became a marquee player in his own right. But as a unit they formed a safety net that could chase down almost anything that managed to get past the infield gauntlet. Sheckard was known as "one of the surest, most deadly outfielders on fly balls that ever choked a near-triple to death by fleetness of foot and steadiness of eye and grip."

Doc Casey's departure had left a hole at third base, but there, too, Chance knew who he wanted. Word got around that Cincinnati was not that happy with its current occupant at third base. "Again, inside gossip directed Chance to a man while older managers, not closely in touch with players, listened to other stories," observed Fullerton. Murphy must have been listening to those old hands, too, because he traveled twice to the Queen City to make the trade Chance wanted, though he came back empty-handed. "What third baseman shall we get?" an exasperated Murphy kept asking. The always-blunt Chance kept replying: "Steinfeldt."

Harry M. Steinfeldt would soon take his place in the Cubs' storied infield, where he held down third base for five dynastic years and became the answer to that trivia question. The price was not small: Murphy and Chance had to give up Tornado Jake Weimer, arguably the team's best pitcher over the previous three seasons, to obtain him. Murphy also had to sweeten the pot for the ever-restless Steinfeldt, who made noise about leaving baseball entirely.

But Murphy's investment produced immediate dividends. In 1906, Steinfeldt would led the league in hits (173) and runs batted in (83) and maintained a batting average of .327, second only to Honus Wagner. He also possessed a whiplike arm at third, leading the NL in fielding percentage in three of his five seasons in Chicago. "When it comes to a thrower whose method is a treat to the eye for its grace, speed and unerring airline flight, Harry Steinfeldt . . . is an accomplished actor," said one admirer. "There is a beautiful harmonizing of lift and speed to his flings."

ATHLETE AND ACTOR

Born in St. Louis on September 29, 1877, Harry M. Steinfeldt had moved at the age of four to Fort Worth, Texas, with his German-immigrant parents. His father, Henry, worked for the Anheuser-Busch brewery, which had sent him there to set up a distribution warehouse. Harry, second of five children, was a precocious athlete.

At sixteen, Harry joined in the bicycle craze that was sweeping England and American cities. He must have been pretty good at it: He belonged to the League of American Wheelmen, participating in many of its local and national events. "Craze" is no overstatement in describing the popularity of cycling in the mid-1890s. Almost as soon as the chain-drive "safety bicycle" entered the market, people of all ages and skills learned to ride the increasingly affordable two-wheelers. In every American city, about four times as many people owned bicycles as horses. Bicycle races and riding exhibitions were among the most popular spectator sports in the country, according to urban historian Evan Friss. "Like horse racing, baseball and other sports, bicycle racing attracted a mass audience seeking to experience the thrill of speed and the excitement of competition."

The League of American Wheelmen asserted itself as both advocate for and regulator of this expanding world. Quickly growing to a hundred thousand members, the LAW was at bottom a lobbying organization, formed to goad governments into upgrading the nation's patchwork quilt of graded roadways. The league founded and published *Good Roads Magazine* and encouraged a variety of races and public demonstrations to rally support. Manufacturers and other promoters eagerly staged all kinds of crowd-pleasing exhibitions. These might include country-fair stunts like twenty-four-hour marathons, or contests with cyclists matched against horses and even moving trains. Nothing seemed too outlandish or beyond the pale for the swarms of bicycle enthusiasts who marveled at the speed and maneuverability that cycling afforded its riders. Cycling in the 1890s was "a general intoxication, an eruption of exuberance like a seismic tremor that shook the economic and social foundations of society and rattled the windows of its moral outlook," commented another historian of the sport.

The LAW refused to bless many of these stunts, but Steinfeldt was an eager participant in them. In 1894, LAW officials suspended him for two weeks for competing in an unsanctioned race in Fort Worth. The same officials, however, happily recruited him for a national "cycling brigade" of new riders. His skills earned Steinfeldt a national reputation and even got him his first job (as a bank messenger). But his wanderlust, paired with a typical adolescent rebellious streak, must have called. In the fall of 1894, still only sixteen, he joined a traveling minstrel show. The prime tool of this unusual trade wasn't bat, ball, glove, or bicycle wrench. It was burnt cork.

Blackface minstrelsy—a musical-comedy genre in which white men made themselves up in demeaning caricatures of African American singers, dancers, and comedians—was the most ubiquitous form of entertainment in late nineteenth-century America. Some sixty years after the Christy Minstrels and "Jim Crow" (Thomas Rice) made their first stage appearances in the antebellum South, minstrel revues remained happily ensconced in several theaters in New York City, while a dozen or more touring companies roamed the nation. Suited up in outlandish costumes, their faces smeared black except for white lips and wide bugging eyes, minstrel entertainers "banged and sawed and rattled" through a lively and ritualized set of dance tunes and ditties such as "Jim Along Josey," "Old Dan Tucker," and "Coon, Coon, Coon," interspersed with a rapid-fire banter of jokes told in broad, stereotypical dialect.

Minstrelsy is difficult to appreciate—or even contemplate—today. Yet blackface song and dance was the nation's first indigenous theatrical art form. (Everything else, from opera to classical music to theater, had been imported from Europe.) And it is hard to overstate its impact on all forms of American musical culture: minstrel legacies trace a path through turn-of-the-century ragtime, vaudeville, burlesque and tap dance, musical theater, and improvisational jazz, all the way to rock-and-roll, rap, and hip-hop. "Simply condemning it all as an entertainment that pandered to White racism does not begin to account for its complexities, its confusion, its neuroses," according to John Strausbaugh.

Harry Steinfeldt was one of an untold number of young men who found a perverse kind of refuge in the counterculture world of minstrel entertainment. He hooked up with Al G. Field's Greater Minstrels, a national touring company that tramped its way through Texas every year in the 1890s. The proprietor and star performer, Alfred Griffith Hatfield, was one of the most prominent cork artists and impresarios of his day. "Merely to announce that the famous minstrel and his company were to appear at a given place was practically saying that the minstrel loving population would turn out en masse to greet them," commented a historian in the early twentieth century.

Field intermixed the highly formulaic minstrel routines with never-before-seen musicians and novelty acts; he was one of the first to feature ragtime music pioneers like Harry Van Fossen, for instance. Field also became the first producer to create a separate traveling show of African American actors, giving many black entertainers their first break in show business even if they, too, had to apply burnt-cork makeup and perform absurdist stereotypes of black people. White audiences loved Field's theatrical touches. "Everything they do is original, their jokes are new and upon timely topics, while their singing and dancing and character are as artistic as it is possible for them to be," a Fort Worth critic said in October 1892.

Steinfeldt was probably a cast member or understudy in a motley troupe that grew as large as "½ a hundred," as Field's advertisements boasted. It's not certain what type of showbiz career he thought to pursue—a central role as vocalist, dancer, or comedian; a novelty act like gun-and-sword juggler or "apodal" (footless) contortionist; or a background role as choral singer of "good old fashioned negro melodies." (Fields also had a three-man acrobatic act featuring Jasper the educated mule.)

It turns out, however, that something else caught Harry's restless imagination as he made his way across Texas. At almost every stop he found a way to join an amateur team for a baseball game. Word must have gotten around about his dexterity and skill, because it wasn't long before Steinfeldt was playing shortstop and second base for the Houston Mudcats of the Texas-Southern League. He hopped around Houston, Fort Worth, and Galveston clubs for the next two seasons, playing any number of positions.

Then came a promotion to Detroit in Ban Johnson's Western League, where in one season Steinfeldt played well enough to earn a big league contract with Cincinnati the following year. Steinfeldt played super utility man to the Reds' star-studded infield for a couple of years before cracking the starting lineup at third base. Manager Buck Ewing liked his defensive skills, especially his quick release: "The ball is hardly in his hands before he has it sailing through the air." Steinfeldt's breakout season came in 1903, when he batted .312 and led the NL in doubles, with thirty-two.

But injuries, a revolving door of managers, and his own displays of apathy soon dampened his production. He started to gain weight and lose his edge, and his disenchanted attitude suggested he was bored with baseball.

Frank Chance remembered the untroubled, aggressive player he watched dazzle the crowds in California's winter ball circuit, where Steinfeldt had gone in the off-season a few years back. Chance soon made Steinfeldt more than welcome in Chicago. Shortly after the Cubs announced the trade, Steinfeldt wrote to Murphy and Chance from his home in Marlin Springs, Texas, assuring them he had been working out all winter, would report to spring training at his old playing weight of 170 pounds, and was in "fine fettle."

THE MARCH TO THE PENNANT

Frank Chance's recombination of veterans and newcomers took a few weeks to gel, but it wasn't long before their historic season was off and running. They moved into first place on May 19 with a record of 24–10. "The Giant Killers have struck a run of batting and errorless ball playing that is marvelous," the *Inter-Ocean* crowed.

Then the Giants came to town and brought the Killers back to earth—for the time being. McGraw's boys took three of the four contests to move New York back into first place. However, something occurred during this disappointing series that heralded the Second City's baseball resurgence.

The Sunday game brought a crowd of twenty-five thousand to the West Side Grounds. The Monday game was played before seventeen thousand. And a Wednesday makeup game of Tuesday's rainout delivered twelve thousand more. Chicago had rarely seen such large and passionate crowds. "Every street car . . . was weighed down with humanity," said one account. "Carriages, automobiles and omnibuses kept contributing to the huge army of 'rooters' that had . . . the single purpose—to see the Cubs win another game."

Murphy delayed the first pitch on Sunday for thirty minutes while fans pummeled the gates and police tried to assert control. When that failed, Murphy ordered all the ticket windows and gates closed, shutting out thousands of people, reserved-seat holders among them. The outcasts refused to leave, however, waiting for periodic updates called out by fans seated in the top rows. "Every time a great cheer would arise the outsiders would ask what had happened, and the lucky one would shout, 'Slagle just made a two bagger,' or 'Chance scored.' The one on the outside would groan . . . because he could not see them do it."

The Giants' bitter medicine coupled with the newfound passion of the fans forced all the Chicago players to reevaluate their commitment

The Four Horsemen of the Cubs infield during its great victory run from 1906 through 1910 included former bicyclist and minstrel entertainer Harry Steinfeldt (*left*) at third base. (National Baseball Hall of Fame and Museum, Cooperstown, NY.)

and work ethic. "We were pointed toward the pennant, and we knew it," Evers recalled. "This knowledge, instead of causing us to take our work easy, had the reverse effect. It made us work all the harder."

Chance, Tinker, Evers, and Steinfeldt started coming to the ballpark early every game day, but not for the half hour of casual ball tossing that most teams put in. The foursome would practice elaborate plays over and over again for almost two hours, drilling a single routine for as long as six weeks before trying it in a game. They made a pact that the first to quit a morning workout had to treat the others to lunch or cigars. Chance never initiated a break, so Tinker and Evers colluded to run him ragged at first base with throws in the dirt or over his head. Husk still would not relent, and they got no succor from their new partner. "Strange as it may seem, Steinfeldt, who was the veteran of the quartet, refused to quit until someone else did," Evers said.

Here the Chance combine developed its peerless mastery of the game. This was an era of deep outfields and baseballs battered and worn to the seams, which meant that a game-changing home run was as rare as a triple is today. To score a run—to win a ball game, no less—required constant tactical decision making from the first pitch to the last out. Every player in the Cubs' lineup was expected to be proficient—and ready to execute—a sacrifice, suicide, or "bluff" bunt; a stolen base, a delayed steal, or a double steal; a hit and run, or a run and hit.

At any moment in a game, Chance might signal for some new trick to advance a runner closer to home so that even a weak single might secure a tally. "It is a game of surprises, freaks and accidents," according to Evers. The idea was to eliminate as much of the surprise as possible on your team's end and create as much uncertainty as possible on the other's.

The Cubs disappointing series against New York also convinced Chance and Murphy that they had yet to put a championship lineup on the field, even with Steinfeldt and Sheckard. The remaining weakness, Chance believed, was in the pitcher's box.

Not that they didn't have some outstanding arms already. Mordecai Brown had firmly established himself as a premier hurler—on a par with Mathewson and McGinnity of the Giants. Brown's three-fingered curveball won eighteen games for Chicago in 1905 and led the team to twenty-five victories in 1906, when he held opposing teams to one run every nine innings.

The Cubs' other reliable pitcher was a college-educated, Latin-fluent Hoosier named Ed Reulbach, who had signed with the team in May 1905 and proceeded to rack up eighteen wins, with an earned run average of 1.42. Reulbach was the discovery of George Huff, longtime athletic director of the University of Illinois and one of Selee's and Chance's most reliable scouts over the years. Huff's sleuthing tracked down Reulbach as he moved from Missouri to Notre Dame in Indiana to the "Tall Grass League" of Vermont; he had been attending college classes and playing amateur ball under his real name while pitching semipro games under the aliases of "Lawson" and "Sheldon," to protect his standing for amateur athletics.

To supplement Brown and Reulbach, Chance wanted a third "ace" and had already determined that neither Tornado Jake Weimar nor Bob Wicker was it. He sent Huff on a frantic search for additional talent. Huff came back with Jack Pfiester, a big left-hander from Cincinnati who had also been wandering the bushes from the Midwest to the West Coast. Pfiester was a rare free agent at the time, and so signed with Chicago on the spot. He would go on to win twenty games for the 1906 Cubs and earn the nickname "Jack the Giant Killer."

Chance also tapped into his player network and found out that an old California mate, Orval Overall, of Visalia, was not doing so well with his current bosses in Cincinnati. Chance reasoned that this was a result of overwork and fatigue. "He knew better than Manager [Ned] Hanlon of Cincinnati how to handle the man," Evers said. Chicago said good-bye to the slumping Bob Wicker and got Overall plus $2,000 in the bargain. Overall went on to win twelve games in fourteen starts for the Cubs with an ERA of 1.88.

INSANITY IN THE MAKING

On August 21, after losing three of four games to the Cubs, Muggsy McGraw and the Giants staggered out of Chicago on the late-night train for Pittsburgh. Broken and embittered, they had fallen nine games behind Chicago with only forty-six games remaining. The reigning world champions had been taunted, ridiculed, and belittled on four successive days by crowds estimated at twenty-eight thousand, twenty-seven thousand, sixteen thousand, then ten thousand. In game 3, southpaw Pfiester had outpitched Iron Man McGinnity to post a 3–0 shutout under a sweltering sun, which seemed to sap what was left of the Giants' spirits. "Jack the Giant Killer worked through the humidity and heat of the West Side baseball park before 16,000 perspiring fans without dampening his uniform collar," according to one account, "and that is what made the New York Giants fume and stew." Eddie Heeman and the Board of Trade Rooters had come out for game 4 to watch Miner Brown put down the Giants for the second time in a week. "So long Muggsy, we hate to see you go!" they sang.

The Cubs were at 81–31, a .735 winning percentage that, incredibly, would only improve as the season wound to a close. The Cubs went on to win twelve straight games after the Giants left town; then, after a solitary loss in St. Louis, they reeled off another twelve. They lost only four more games in the final two months of the season to finish 116–36. Their .763 winning percentage has never been matched, and their 116-win total has never been topped, even after teams began playing a longer schedule in 1962. The Cubs of 1906 were a bona fide juggernaut, with no apparent weakness.

The Cubs were also a sensation in Chicago that year. The team drew a record 654,000 fans to West Side Grounds, for an average of 8,300 per game, up from 6,300 the year before and almost twice as many as in 1902, the year Selee and Hart took over the team. The second-best NL attendance in 1906 was in New York, where the Giants drew 402,000, or 5,400 a game, while the rest of the NL clubs averaged 290,000, or about 3,100 a game, a third as many as turned out daily for the Cubs. C. W. Murphy was a happy man; he privately boasted that he was able to repay his entire $105,000 loan from Charles Taft within the first full year of business operations.

Only one other team in the major leagues came close to matching the Cubs' popularity in 1906. That was Charlie Comiskey's White Sox. Another 585,000 fans, or 7,400 a game, came out to root for the White Sox against their American League opponents. The combined Chicago franchises drew 1.24 million fans to their ballparks that season, topping the combined attendance of all three New York clubs (Giants, Yankees, and Brooklyn Superbas).

"Nearly Everybody in Chicago Is Crazy about Baseball," a *Tribune* headline declared on September 9, under a five-column photograph of a crowd of people packed into the grandstand of the West Side Grounds. "There is so much interest in baseball here and now that at a game played by either of the two big teams more money is taken in at the gate than any race meeting, theatrical performance, or circus ever played to."

The *Trib* also took note of the changing demographics of a typical baseball fanatic. "Out of the crowd at any big baseball game could be pressed a delegation that could try the most intricate lawsuit, perform the most delicate operation, build the highest skyscraper, sell the largest bill of goods, and swing the biggest deal on the market."

THE HITLESS WONDERS

No one, even Sox partisans, expected the Chicago AL team to win the pennant and qualify for the third staging of a World's Championship series. On August 1, their record had been only 50–43, in fourth place behind Philadelphia, New York, and Cleveland.

Fielder Jones, Comiskey's player-manager, had been an elite performer since 1896, patrolling center field first for Brooklyn in the NL and then Chicago in the AL. Jones became manager in 1904 and subsequently earned a reputation for his innovations, "one who understood the rule book and was unafraid of taking chances," according to one profile. Jones needed to employ every tool he had that year. The team had injury and personnel problems all year—only one starter played the entire season. Still, the Sox had a first-rate pitching corps, led by the "huge, pink-faced" right-hander Ed Walsh, a former coal miner whose specialty was a mystifying spitball, still legal in those days. "Big Ed" had a break-out year in 1906 with seventeen wins and a 1.88 ERA, leading the league with ten shutouts. Jones could also call on stalwarts Frank Owen, Guy "Doc" White, and lefthander Nick Altrock. Together the Sox hurlers gave up only 2.13 runs per nine innings in 1906, second best in the league.

The feeble White Sox offense, however, was as remarkable as the team's strength in pitching and defense. The *Tribune*'s acerbic sports columnist Charles Dryden has long been credited with calling their punchless lineup the "Hitless Wonders," although that phrase had been used before by him and others. Yet Hitless Wonders so accurately described the 1906 Sox that it soon was attached exclusively to Jones's ball club for posterity. The Sox had a team batting average of only .230, last in the AL. Only three starters hit over .250 for the season, and their best hitters, including future Hall of Fame shortstop George Davis, never exceeded .280.

But the Hitless Wonders had an uncanny ability to get runners across the plate. They were third in the league in runs scored, third in stolen bases, and first in walks. They also led the league in hit batsmen, putting another fifty runners on base. Cleveland manager Jimmy McAleer called them "the luckiest bunch of ballplayers" he had ever seen. "If the team wants a base on balls to win, it gets it; if an error is needed someone is sure to boot the ball. I never saw or heard of a club that can do as little in the hitting line and get away with it as those Chicago boys."

Something finally clicked for the White Sox in August. They proceeded to win nineteen straight, including eight games in a home-and-away exchange with the first-place Highlanders, with a climactic 10–0 victory on August 18. During the streak the Hitless Wonders scored 5.26 runs a game while their parsimonious pitching staff gave up only half a run per game, aided by nine shutouts.

The Sox finished the season with a respectable 93–58 record, three games in front of New York. They were playing in St. Louis on October 2 when they learned they had clinched the pennant, and they returned to "delirium" for their final home stand. "Nobody can talk, think or dream of anything but great games [as] both teams win," exclaimed the *Chicago Daily Journal*.

The two Chicago victors would now face each other in baseball's first cross-city World's Championship. C. W. Murphy could see the turnstiles churning. "I don't know of any team I would rather play than Comiskey's," he said.

THE WORLD SERIOUS

The biggest sporting event the city of Chicago had ever seen was just days away, and it seemed as if all two million denizens were carried away by the moment. City Council passed a resolution declaring a holiday for the Tuesday opening game. "This is the first time in the history of the national game, so far as is known, that the council of any city in the country ever extended its official thanks to a baseball club or to a sporting or amusement enterprise of any character," the *Inter-Ocean* reported.

The *Tribune* ran a full-page human-interest feature purporting to have found "the only man in Chicago" who didn't know about the World Series. Immigrant butcher Ulrich Schulte, a father of three girls, may have remained oblivious to the great occasion, but everyone else was on tenterhooks. "All through the weary night frail women tossed nervously upon their downy couches, while strong men . . . lay with eyes wide open staring vacantly at the ceilings of their hall bedrooms," an *Inter-Ocean* editorialist rhapsodized on the eve of the first game. "The great city was sleepless."

The Cubs and Sox were not unfamiliar with each other even though National and American teams did not play each other during the regular season. As sanctioned by the National Agreement, the two teams had played for local bragging rights in the year-end City Series, an annual exhibition they continued through 1942. The Cubs had won the 1905 match, four games to one, before capacity crowds teeming with such enthusiasm that Murphy acted as if the City Series trophy were more valuable to him than finishing first in the National League.

The Cubs entered the 1906 World's Championship as prohibitive and evident favorites, based on the way the team had outclassed every other club in the senior circuit and crushed the reigning champions. "The Cubs are top-heavy favorites," reported the *Washington Post.* Hardly anyone other than hard-core South Siders dared to dispute that judgment, and many were even predicting the Cubs would sweep four games straight in the best-of-seven format.

Only one Chicago sportswriter dared to think otherwise.

Hugh S. Fullerton of the *Chicago Tribune* had covered both teams that season and was known among his colleagues as the leader of a new breed of objective, fact-based baseball "dopesters." (Years later Fullerton's instinctive skepticism moved him to call foul on the 1919 World Series, instigating the notorious Black Sox investigation.) As the 1906 World's Championship approached, Fullerton stuck his neck out: He said the Hitless Wonders might surprise everyone.

At least, he tried to say as much. Shortly before the first game, Fullerton typed out a column with the unflinching forecast that the White Sox were going to win four of the first six games. He compared the two teams point by point: their talents at each position, their psychological makeups, even the impact that overflow crowds might have on fielders' range of motion—all of which led him to conclude that the White Sox actually had an advantage. This was an outrageous analysis, contrary to all conventional wisdom. City editor Jim Keeley refused to publish the column. He was afraid readers would think the *Trib* staff was insane.

It was left for the two teams to play each other and resolve any remaining argument. While newspapers made fun of the enmity that Cubs and Sox fans had for each other, a sense of shared excitement seemed to be filling up city streets, offices, saloons, ward rooms, and living rooms. "Baseball is talked about more than it ever was before," noted the *Tribune*. "More people are interested in it. More people are acquainted with the minutiae of the game, the biographies of the players and the fortunes of war, as they are exemplified in the activities of the two baseball teams upon the uniforms of which appear "C-H-I-C-A-G-O."

The first game of the series fell on October 9, which happened to be the thirty-fifth anniversary of the Great Chicago Fire of 1871. All Chicago was there, in spirit if not in the flesh. "More people than the grounds can hold yearn to see the game," wrote Dryden.

Here's how the cross-town series played out:

GAME 1: TUESDAY, OCTOBER 9, WEST SIDE GROUNDS
FINAL SCORE: White Sox 2, Cubs 1
PITCHERS: Mordecai Brown v. Nick Altrock
SERIES STATUS: Sox 1, Cubs 0

GAME ACCOUNT: A total of 12,693 rabid fans braved snow flurries and bitter cold for a pitchers' duel, each side held to four hits. In the top of the fifth, substitute third baseman George Rohe, playing only because George Davis had been injured in the final week of the regular season, lashed a triple into deep left field. He scored on the next play. Each team scored a run in the sixth, but otherwise southpaw Altrock shut down the great Cub machine, its lone run coming on a wild pitch.

SIDEBAR: "The air in the ball park was ideal for putting up ice. Snow fell in ladylike quantities, yet it was the real goods," waxed Dryden. "Wise fanatics came rigged out like Peary parties. Men in bear skin coats and carrying extra wraps squatted in the boxes and on the open field seats."

GAME 2: WEDNESDAY, OCTOBER 10, SOUTH SIDE PARK

FINAL SCORE: Cubs 7, White Sox 1

PITCHERS: Ed Reulbach v. Doc White

SERIES STATUS: Sox 1, Cubs 1

GAME ACCOUNT: The Cubs jumped out with four runs in the first three innings behind the hitting of Steinfeldt and Tinker. Reulbach took care of the rest, pitching a one-hitter. A crowd of 12,595 watched in near-freezing temperatures.

SIDEBAR: Hotel managers in the Loop estimated that more than two thousand visitors had come to witness the games. "It is the biggest bunch of baseball fans I ever saw," said one clerk.

GAME 3: THURSDAY, OCTOBER 11, WEST SIDE GROUNDS

SCORE: White Sox 3, Cubs 0

PITCHERS: Jack Pfiester v. Ed Walsh

SERIES STATUS: Sox 2, Cubs 1

GAME ACCOUNT: Spitballer Walsh allowed a single and a double in the first inning, and later a base on balls, but otherwise no other Cub managed to reach base, as Big Ed racked up twelve strikeouts. Once again, understudy Rohe was the star of the day, delivering a two-out, bases-loaded triple off Pfiester in the sixth. Attendance: 13,667.

SIDEBAR: The *Chicago Tribune* hosted four thousand people at the city Auditorium and another 2,500 fans at the First Regiment Armory, where announcers relayed every play of the game almost instantaneously, using megaphones and a direct connection to a Western Union telegraph operator at the ballpark. "The moment the telegraph instruments would tick[,] tumult would change to silence, then would come to tumult again."

GAME 4: FRIDAY, OCTOBER 12, SOUTH SIDE PARK

SCORE: Cubs 1, White Sox 0

PITCHERS: Brown v. Altrock

SERIES STATUS: Sox 2, Cubs 2

GAME ACCOUNT: The weather warmed up enough to bring out 18,384 fans for the best-played contest in the series. Brown pitched a two-hitter, while Altrock spaced out seven hits. The lone run came in the seventh inning on a single by Chance, sacrifice bunts by Steinfeldt and Tinker to move him around to third, and a clean shot to left on the first pitch to Evers. Cubs rooters sent up a "deafening roar."

SIDEBAR: Cap Anson, the former White Stockings patriarch recently elected city clerk, attended the game and played the role of impartial pol to perfection. "Although it was not like this in the olden days, I can't say I've seen many better games than today's," Anson said. "It's anybody's series now."

GAME 5: SATURDAY, OCTOBER 13, WEST SIDE GROUNDS

SCORE: White Sox 8, Cubs 6

PITCHERS: Reulbach v. Walsh

SERIES STATUS: Sox 3, Cubs 2

GAME ACCOUNT: An almost picture-perfect day delivered a capacity crowd of 23,257, with perhaps as many more turned away. Neither starting pitcher lasted the outing, as both lineups busted loose with several run-scoring rallies. George Rohe went three for four, including a double. A final Cubs rally fizzled in the ninth when Pat Moran, pinch-hitting for Evers with Chance on second, failed to deliver.

SIDEBAR: An agent for song-and-dance impresario George M. Cohan, whose play *Popularity* was appearing on Broadway, presented managers Chance and Jones with a pair of watch fobs, each bearing a gold pendant studded with diamonds, etched with their respective names and the inscription "From George M. Cohan, a lover of baseball."

GAME 6: SUNDAY, OCTOBER 14, SOUTH SIDE PARK

SCORE: White Sox 8, Cubs 3

PITCHERS: Brown v. White

SERIES STATUS: Sox 4, Cubs 2

GAME ACCOUNT: A bright and warm Sunday elicited 19,249 fans as the White Sox delivered the coup de grâce in rather short order. Miner Brown, working on one day's rest, gave up eight hits and a walk in the first two innings as the Sox scored seven runs.

SIDEBAR: An estimated five thousand people who went to the ballpark but failed to gain admittance got a unique description of the game. An African American fan mounted a telegraph pole and managed to "splice himself to the crosstrees," where he barked out game developments through a megaphone. "He announced every move in the game with . . . accuracy and fluency," the *Inter Ocean* reported. Grateful fans took up a collection and gave the play-by-play caller $25 when he dismounted.

AFTERMATH

The moment the Sox recorded the last out in the ninth, retiring Wild-fire Schulte at first, thousands of South Side Park fans erupted. "The crowd surged over the field cheering the individual players, the players collectively[,] and thumping said players on the backs with such enthusiasm that every one of them had to fight a way to the waiting carriages," *Sporting Life* reported. A crowd of small boys waiting outside broke into the park at game's end, racing onto the field "merely to stand on the historic ground and share in the excitement." Men and boys paraded with tin horns and cowbells and carried man-sized canvas "socks" filled with straw.

Cubs fans in the stadium gathered around team president Murphy and pleaded for a speech. "The best team won," Murphy responded gamely. "They won because they played the better ball." At the end of his remarks Murphy called for "three cheers for Comiskey and his great team." Murphy also sought out Comiskey and offered personal congratulations. "If we had to lose I would rather see your team the victors than any other club in the country," the Cubs magnate said. Comiskey didn't miss a beat: "Yes, and I would rather beat any club in the country than yours." A hearty handshake followed.

Even stoic and sorely disappointed Frank Chance was gracious. "It was a hard series to lose and, naturally, I don't feel very happy," he told

reporters. "White, Walsh and Altrock are three of the toughest propo-
sitions I ever went up against, and there lies the cause of our defeat." He
closed his comments by noting the irony of the Hitless Wonders' effort:
"They outbatted us and won."

Baseball officialdom was as happy as ever. Attendance over the six
games totaled fifteen bodies short of a hundred thousand, with receipts
of $106,550 almost evenly distributed between the two ball clubs. The
players' share was $33,402, and Comiskey threw in another $15,000 for
his boys from his take. Each Sox player took home $1,875 and each Cubs
player $440 for his efforts that week.

And society at large took note of this once-disdained form of popular entertainment. Postseason series had previously generated the suspicion that the players merely tilted the outcomes toward each other on
alternating days to string out the sequence and fill their pockets with
extra cash. League presidents Ban Johnson and Harry C. Pulliam tried
to preempt that tendency, first by having the National Commission
run the series and then by limiting the players' share of gate receipts to
the first four games. The powers-that-be hoped fan excitement would
only increase as the best-of-seven series unfolded.

Paradoxically, the Hitless Wonders' unlikely victory over the "invincible" Cubs may have elevated the World Series to its apotheosis as
baseball's crown. From then on, with the exception of the 1919 Black
Sox plague, the World Series has rarely been questioned for its authen-
ticity and faithfulness.

"It is the glorious uncertainty of baseball," exclaimed an *Inter Ocean*
editorial, "and the practical impossibility of corrupting a baseball team
that have brought the sport to a level of popularity where in the United
States today probably two-thirds of the people hang in anxiety on the
outcome of the present world's championship."

The editorial writer waved off any remaining skeptics and concluded, no doubt to citywide agreement: "The Chicago clubs are just
now giving as perfect examples of ball playing as this country has
ever seen."

PART THREE

Dynastic Cycles

Chicago stands as probably the fourth city
of the world in population. . . . But she is the
first city of the world in many things—in
enterprise, in growth, in energy, and in her
indomitable optimism and self-confidence.
Nowhere else is there such human voltage.

NEWTON DENT,
Munsey's Magazine,
April 1907

CONQUEST INTO CULTURE

1907

You have advertised Chicago not only as the home where reside the men of brawn, muscle, and sinew, of art, dexterity, and science, sufficient to achieve over all competitors and write upon their shields "conqueror" as against the world, but you have done more—you have won your trophy without a suspicion of unfair play, without an intimation of unjust conduct, and with the whole of the country conceding that it was won by courage, by accomplishment, and in bravery with honor. **JAMES HAMILTON LEWIS**, at a victory banquet for the 1907 World Champion Chicago Cubs

Just after sunset on Thursday, October 17, 1907, 350 Chicagoans, dressed in their best, gathered at the Auditorium Annex building on South Michigan Avenue, just across from Grant Park. Stepping along to an orchestra's spritely accompaniment, the party entered the gold-and crystal-laden banquet hall, for a feast and an evening's entertainment of songs, cheers, tall tales, and victory speeches.

The printed programs at the elegant table settings let the guests know they would dine in high style: *consommé* Rachel, puff-pastry *bouchée à la reine*, sea bass Dorothy with potatoes Laurette, and a beef tenderloin *forestière* topped with larded mushrooms and wine sauce. An appetizer of Blue Point oysters would precede the main courses, with fancy ice cream, cakes, and cheese bringing up the rear. Liquid refreshment would flow from beginning to who-knew-what-end, kicking off with Manhattans and progressing through carafes of Pommery & Greno Champagne and an 1893 Sauternes. For those with less affected tastes, there came bottomless cups of "Cubs Punch."

Five days after the completion of the 1907 World's Championship series, the high society of the nation's second-largest city hosted a victory banquet for their newly crowned Cubs.

The Auditorium Annex, or Congress Hotel, as its owners preferred to call it, was part of a complex constructed in 1893 to house visitors to the great World's Columbian Exposition. The original twelve-story north tower of the Annex was designed to complement Louis Sullivan's pathbreaking Auditorium Building across Congress Street, one of Chicago's early architectural masterpieces. The Annex boasted a state-of-the-art concert hall, luxury hotel rooms, office suites, and a large observation tower that jutted another ten stories above the city's rising skyline. A tunnel under Congress Street connected the Annex to the Auditorium with a glass-and-marble passageway, which had become known as Peacock Alley for the famous actresses and opera stars who paraded daily through it. As Joseph M. Siri describes in *The Chicago Auditorium Building*, the architectural wonder went on to play a central role in the city's social history.

A fourteen-story south tower, an annex to the Annex, had just opened in 1907, and it featured the ornate banquet hall, or Gold Room, where "the walls and ceiling are literally plastered with gold leaf," according to a reporter. "We do not know of any other large room anywhere that makes such a show of gold." It was the crowning showpiece to a dining and entertainment complex that would become the largest gathering place of its kind in America. At the time, and until it fell into disrepair between the world wars, the Congress Hotel was a destination among captains of industry, politics, and culture, including presidents Grover Cleveland, William McKinley, and Theodore Roosevelt. Their frequent visits gave it the name "Home of Presidents."

The Gold Room seemed an appropriate venue for the city's newest champions. "No civic event," the *Tribune* reported, "has been given greater or more representative recognition by Chicago than that of Chicago's National league triumph on the diamond in the season just finished." The limited seating and high price of entry ($10 per person, or about $300 today) made it a rather exclusive affair, with representatives of industry, retail, the Board of Trade, and state and local government leading the guest list. But it was not without a few everyday fans.

At the head table sat manager Frank Chance, club owner C. W. Murphy, National League president Harry C. Pulliam, and former Chicago newspaper reporter George Ade, by that time one of the best-known playwrights and humorists in the nation. All eighteen players from the Cubs' pennant-winning roster were on hand, led by Johnny Evers, Joe Tinker, Mordecai Brown, and Harry Steinfeldt. A flamboyant and well-traveled orator named James Hamilton Lewis, a Chicago city official with a long political résumé, handled toastmaster duties.

"Gentleman, the City of Chicago honors itself in honoring you," Lewis intoned in a deliberate baritone, the vowels long and plaintive, the Rs rolling melodiously. "It greets you tonight in the most sacred festival man ever invented as a sign of friendship to man, that where man breaks bread with his fellows."

And that was just to clear his throat.

J. Hamilton Lewis — "J-Ham" to his many acquaintances in politics and judicial halls — gave some of the most eloquent speeches in America. "One of the world's most gifted spellbinders," the *Tribune*'s I. E. Sanborn had promised. Lewis had only recently settled in Chicago after a long career as a lawyer and politician in Washington State. A man of slight but erect bearing, he might appear in public in a dark suit with a cream-colored waistcoat and a bright-green tie with matching handkerchief and socks. Even then, his most arresting feature was a lush Vandyke, neatly combed, parted, and waxed. J-Ham presumably dyed both whiskers and matching toupee as he aged; his contemporaries referred to their "pinkish" hue.

In Chicago, Lewis had just served as the city's corporate counsel in the brief, two-year term of reformist Democratic mayor Edward F. Dunne. Lewis had previously done a tour as U.S. senator from Washington, and he would later return to the nation's capital as a senator from Illinois, where he would rise to the post of Democratic whip.

Lewis certainly knew how to take center stage. Even though some of the more illustrious men on the speakers' list, including Illinois governor Charles S. Deneen and federal judge Kenesaw Mountain Landis, had begged off, it was no matter to Lewis or to the crowd. Lewis read aloud their letters of regret and felicitation with a flourish that the less-gifted authors could never have delivered. Lewis knew how to capture the spirit as well as the import of the Cubs' accomplishment.

"There never has been a time in the history of the recorded ages," Lewis declaimed in his arched, Mid-Atlantic-trained accent, "when the heroic athlete was not received with honor and greeted with praise." He was just warming up:

> The gratification you afford the community is not alone in tendering amusement and offering attraction, but in giving the illustration of that which builds character, strengthens physical manhood, and shapens [sic] to perfection the proportions of God's noblest creation—the man. . . .
>
> You have displayed to the world of athletes how men can play baseball and come forth without stain upon character or reflection upon the profession. For this Chicago is doubly proud of you and greets you as her honorable and deserving sons. At this table tonight we not only proclaim you as victors in a contest of sport, but as men who have obtained the crown of personal approval of those who love honor above victory, but who worship more those who obtain victory with honor.

The Chicago Cubs, Hamilton made sure, were the toast of the town.

A SINGLE-MINDED OBJECTIVE

Six months earlier, the city of Chicago had greeted the 1907 baseball season with far more fanfare than usual. In the wake of their historic showdown in October 1906, the world-champion White Sox and the record-setting Cubs had earned local regard for their prowess on the field—and newfound prestige as models of clean baseball. Both ball clubs had even won the respect of the rest of the baseball world, grudging as it might be in some quarters. "Every big league city is insanely jealous of Chicago's two wonderful teams and is out for revenge," crowed the *Inter Ocean*.

The pennants flying over South Side Park and West Side Grounds conferred on the Sox and Cubs a measure of glory beyond the sporting world. As they traversed the country, playing in front of large, eager crowds, they became the city's ambassadors to America.

By early spring, expectations were running high. "If Chicago was baseball mad last year the present season is likely to see a frenzy to cause comparison with 1906 to appear ridiculous," predicted the *Inter Ocean*. The prospect of another pair of pennant showdowns with the two Gotham clubs only heightened the city's fervor.

Chicago in that decade was continuing to grow bigger and faster than its leaders could manage with any real sagacity. Yet through an almost haphazard combination of business ingenuity, rising social conscious-ness, and nascent if incremental political reforms, the sprawling city on the lake was becoming the epitome, if not the ideal, of modern American life.

In terms of commerce, no other city pulled as much weight. It was the center of the nation's transportation infrastructure, moving grains, livestock, and timber. It was the manufacturing home of the McCormick and Deering harvesters, the revolutionary machines that created industrialized agriculture. And it was a packing house for the nation, annually processing more than three million cattle, four and a half million sheep, and eight million hogs into dinner fare for every city east of the Mississippi.

"Every State in the Union hurries at the call of Chicago," wrote New-ton Dent, a popular magazine writer. "'Bring me your lumber,' she demands. 'I want two billion of it a year. Bring me every weekday fifty thousand of your farm animals and a million bushels of your grain. Bring me your ore and oil and cloth and paper and tobacco, and be quick, for I am Chicago—the City of Speed!'" To Dent, the people of Chicago were the standard-bearers for a new century, as characterized by their success in financial arenas as on the playing field. "Whether the game is business or baseball, they carry off the pennants," he said.

Frank Chance, meanwhile, restrained himself. He was more deter-mined than ever to reach the ultimate prize that had eluded the 1906 team. From the moment he gathered his charges in West Baden, Indiana, for spring training, he spurred them to a singular mission—winning it all. "I do not see any team in the National league that has a chance to beat us out for the pennant," he told reporters in March: "After winning the pennant I do not think we will be beaten for the world's championship."

It would be a long, 154-game campaign before he could make good on that prediction. The team won its first three games against St. Louis and Pittsburgh before losing to the Pirates, 1–0, despite Miner Brown's two-hit pitching. That game's lone run came in the third inning, when Jimmy Slagle in center field let a ground ball slip between his fingers. The runner took second, and two neatly placed bunts later he crossed the plate. "It was a tough lemon to hand Brown, and a squeezed lemon at that," reported Sanborn in the *Tribune*. The writer then added with a wink: "That makes it impossible for them to win more than 153 championship battles this season."

Yet by the end of April, the Cubs had lost only one other game, winning thirteen, putting them in first place. Cubs pitchers gave up three or fewer runs in all but one of those games, a telling indicator of their style of play. Over the summer, opponents would manage to score four or more runs in only thirty-four contests. The pitching staff, led by Brown, Ed Reulbach, Jack Pfiester, Orval Overall, and Carl Lundgren, would allow only 390 runs for the season, best in the league. Their stingy combined 1.73 ERA, led by southpaw Pfiester at 1.15, is mind-boggling even for the deadball era.

They were bolstered by a stonewall defense that also finished first with a .967 fielding percentage, led by Johnny Evers at .964 and Harry Steinfeldt at .967. So even while the Cubs team's batting average of .250 and 571 total runs scored were nothing to tout, its matchless pitching and defense enabled low-scoring Chance lineup to outpace their opposition over the course of the season by a 181-run differential, which was low even by the standards of the era.

John McGraw's Giants, meanwhile, were just as determined to reclaim the throne. They kept pace with the Cubs through April and even moved a game ahead of them in May. But in their first head-to-head matchup, in late May, the Cubs served notice that McGraw's re-gime was passing away. The Cubs took two of three games in the Polo Grounds, leaving both teams with 25–6 records. The Cubs then began to pull away in early June, leading by two and a half games, and fans felt unusually confident when the Giants pulled into town for a series be-ginning June 5. Three games later, the Giants limped away to St. Louis a badly beaten team; the Cubs had taken three straight, putting them up in the standings by five and a half games. They never looked back.

The new expectation of success for Chicago baseball teams placed a burden of responsibility on the players, not only for their performance on the field but also for their personal comportment. Like Comiskey's White Sox and other American League clubs that played under the stern watch of Ban Johnson, the Cubs under Frank Selee and Frank Chance had earned a reputation for playing "clean" baseball. And now that they had proved they could prevail over the likes of McGraw and his foulmouthed practitioners of dirty ball, the Cubs had a higher stan-dard of behavior to uphold than most other clubs.

In the second of the Cubs' May 1907 contests at the Polo Grounds, after Miner Brown had bested Christy Mathewson 3–2, more than a thousand of the twenty thousand fans had followed umpires Hank O'Day and Bob Emslie off the field, hurling epithets and solid objects at them for their calls against the Giants. Outside the park, police fired gunshots into the air to disperse the mob. New York players joined in on the rescue efforts, surrounding the umps and escorting them to a nearby elevated train station, where they hid unharmed "until several trainloads of bloodsuckers had started off on a wild goose chase," as a bemused Charles Dryden described the scene for the *Tribune*: "Hoo-ray for the national pastime, which is a pot of boiling vitriol in this man's town."

McGraw's Giants notwithstanding, most NL teams jumped aboard the clean-ball bandwagon. The magnates had decided to give Harry C. Pulliam the same broad powers to enforce the rules as Ban Johnson had been wielding in the junior circuit. Pulliam and his band of newly emboldened umpires saw to it by means of ejections, fines, and suspensions for the most egregious offenders. They received moral support from members of the sporting press, who, if not actually in league with the baseball magnates, were eager to help promote the emerging celebrities among the players.

Less compliant in this campaign were the spectators in the grandstands and bleachers—the cranks, fans, or "bugs," as some writers called them—who began not only filling up the seats and sidelines but also tying their self-esteem to the fortunes of their teams. This led to some notably rowdy behavior—which the magnates were not necessarily inclined to control, even if they could. The only way to enforce order in the stands would have been with more police presence or their own security details, both of which cost more money than anyone cared to spend. Indeed, New York's police commissioner, Brigadier General Theodore A. Bingham, refused to assign any of his officers to private "amusement" venues. So as stadiums swelled and routinely overflowed with tens of thousands of fans each afternoon, the potential for aggression and outright hostilities grew as well.

THE BOTTLE INCIDENT

Having won Chicago's admiration for clean play, the Cubs were surprised by the venom that awaited them on the road the next year. Every crowd wanted a piece of them. The enmity was palpable whenever they set foot in New York, where fans of both the Giants and the Brooklyn Nationals, also known as the Trolley Dodgers, reserved special animosity for their Second City adversaries. McGraw egged his partisans on, insisting that the Giants were a better team when healthy (though they had won only two home games against the Cubs in 1906). "You know there's lots of difference in the way a club plays when it's ten games ahead and when it's a neck and neck fight," McGraw told one newspaper.

For their part, Brooklyn fans were working themselves into a lather when the Cubs showed up at Washington Park in mid-July 1907. Repeated taunts from the bugs along first base, both profane and vicious, soon had the desired effect, though not on the usual suspects. Hot-blooded Johnny Evers wouldn't take the bait, for instance, nor did Joe Tinker. The man they tipped over the edge turned out to be the solid, imperturbable rock of the infield, Frank Chance.

New York and Chicago reporters gave conflicting accounts of who and what started the "bottle incident" of July 8. The brouhaha unfolded with two outs in the ninth inning, with the Cubs leading Brooklyn 5–0 in the rubber match of a three-game series. Some fans in the "cheap" twenty-five-cent seats along the right-field line were razzing Chance. He must have returned their ribald comments in kind, if not worse in tone of voice.

All of a sudden, a small shower of pop bottles landed near the heels of Chance and nearby umpire Bill Carpenter. Chance could take no more. He picked up one of the bottles and turned to face his tormenters, at which point more bottles came flying. Chance chucked his bottle back into the crowd, most of whom were then standing on their seats. All-out war followed. "For an instant it rained streaks of glass," observed the *Tribune*'s Dryden, "and in the midst of the fusillade stood the peerless leader like Mr. Ajax—defying said bottles. More than a few of them just missed his head."

Then Chance made a second, and potentially lethal, mistake. He turned toward the "expensive" fifty-cent seats behind the players' bench and fired another bottle (or two) into the thick of the crowd. One apparently found a target, a boy named Tony, who later said he was hit on the head. Both Chance and the crowd had completely lost their senses. Chance would have been mobbed and mauled but for the wire netting that separated the field from the stands, along with the quick response of some club-wielding police. Brooklyn owner Charlie Ebbets intervened as well, bravely rushing into the melee, where he "soothed the bloodseekers by promising to have Chance arrested," Dryden wrote.

Meanwhile, Tinker ran up to Chance from behind and wrapped him in a bear hug. The rest of the Cubs ran toward the stands and faced down the crowd, refusing to be intimidated. "Bottles flew at their heads like bullets in a battle," wrote an astonished New York reporter. "But they never flinched, and finally the mob in the stands, ashamed to attack men who were not fighting back, stopped."

A police detective hustled Chance into the clubhouse, and other officers finally cleared the field. The Cubs then recorded the final out of the game. Chance and his minders stayed out of sight for a couple of hours while the seething mob drifted away. "Police Captain Maude told Chance he would have pinched him had he seen him heave either of the bottles," Dryden wrote.

Chance was contrite. "That's all right," he told the cops. "I did wrong to lose my temper and act the way I did." But even then, Husk could not suppress his deep-seated frustration. "It is hard to be cursed and made a target and not lose patience with a senseless crowd, sore because we beat the home team."

Chance trudged down to National League headquarters in lower Manhattan to face the music from Harry Pulliam. The two men had a long, candid talk. Yet the damage had been done to Chance's image. "That Chance was provoked to throw the bottle into the bleachers is not denied," opined *New York Evening Telegram* sports editor John B. Foster, "but that he added anything to his reputation by doing so is very seriously questioned." Foster credited Chance's apology and sincere regret, but even Chance would probably agree with Foster's bottom line: "Any ball player who attempts to get back at the spectators makes a sublime ass of himself."

The boy in the stands apparently came out unhurt. Pulliam suspended Chance for a week, but only after conducting a personal investigation, including a visit to the scene of the riot and taking testimony from the umpires. A week in limbo was far too soft a penalty to many Chance haters, but Pulliam bowed to Chance's otherwise spotless on-field behavior over the previous ten years and gave a nod to Chance for turning himself in.

Meanwhile, even New York writers remained aghast at the sordid behavior of their hometown crowds. "The whole bottle throwing episode was a disgrace to Brooklyn," judged Robert Edgren, sports editor of the *New York Evening World*. "We have been used to talking disparagingly of Western 'savages,' and when a New York ball team visiting the hustings is stoned or mobbed on leaving the grounds we howl long and forcefully over the unsportsmanlike behavior of the people in the rural districts. This time it is on us."

The proxy war between America's two biggest cities was fully engaged. When the Cubs visited New York again later that summer, Chance found a strange letter waiting for him at the Polo Grounds. A drawing of a bony hand with clawlike fingers appeared at the bottom of it, signed "Black Hands," a reference to the La Mano Nera extortion rackets of southern Italy. In broken English, it read in part: "Your club must not get again Pennant this year 1907 from the New York. . . . Your club are too coward, but 'Poor Giants.'" Then followed a direct threat: "If you not let the Giants from the first place this year, Gang of Black Hands will see you after, will help you for your life. We will use bomb on your players team on train wreck and we will follow your team traveling." Said the writer in conclusion, "We are cranky on the Giants."

That afternoon, the Cubs won a tense, twelve-inning game, 3–2, with Brown once again outdueling Mathewson. The teams eventually split the four-game series, though by this time the Cubs had a fourteen and a half game lead in the standings. Chance's Cubs left New York with the Giants—and presumably the Black Hands—eating their dust.

FROM THE OBSERVATION DECK

Charles Dryden—the razor-edged wit behind tall tales like "Percy the Trained Flying Fish"—could see absurdity in almost any situation. But going to the ballpark every day as beat reporter for the *Chicago Daily Tribune* never failed to feed his taste for irony. Dryden rarely offered his readers a who-what-where account of the contests. To him, baseball was a "diamond stage" and players simply actors in the roles of heroes, knaves, and goats—depending on the day, the weather, and the circumstances.

"Real athletes in real uniforms scared the Cubs back into their proper stride," began one of his accounts in June 1907. He was covering a Monday-afternoon home game. "The champions entertained Boston at home for the first time this season and beat them 2 to 1 in a game better than the Sunday show was bad. The going fairly sparkled." By the third paragraph, Dryden's metaphors were in full flower. "Our peerless leader [Frank Chance] unkinked his spine and shone like a new chop suey sign at first base. Had Chance been laid up with locomotor ataxia the pastime of the last few days would have cured him just the same. It was up to the P.L. to get well quick."

Dryden was the first and probably the best humorist in the nascent craft of sports journalism, which was not so much a profession as a boneyard for ink-stained hacks. Increasingly, however, the sports pages were becoming a way station for young urban strivers seeking literary fame. Dryden's style of reporting made him famous as the Cubs and White Sox rose to prominence—ballplayers read his work as closely as fans.

His game accounts were a map of his oddball mind. In this instance, Dryden was foreshadowing that Chance, who had been out the previous day with a back injury, had come back to drive in the first run and factor significantly in the winning run. Brooklyn had pummeled the Cubs, 11–1, the day before, but Chance was determined to get back on the field in the first of four games against the Boston Doves, né Beaneaters, to steer his ball club toward winning ways.

Chance had come to bat in the seventh inning, the score knotted 1–1, with two outs and two on base. For most of the game, the Doves' fresh-faced pitcher, Irvin "Young Cy" Young, was nervously holding his own against the great Mordecai Brown. Dryden watched with amusement as Boston catcher Tom Needham called time and walked to the mound to confer with his rattled pitcher. Dryden offered this curious account of their "conversation":

Said Tom to Cy: "These champs of the N.L. and breakers of the world's record are up against it hard. We are too swell for them. To date they have eleven swats, mostly solid smashes, and one run. If we do not use force they will lose."

"Just as you say," replied Mr. I. Young, better known as Cy. Thereupon he walked Chance and Randall and forced in the winning run. Clever idea.

The foregoing may not be a verbatim report of what Tom said to Cy, but the main doings are a facsimile of what Young did for the struggling Cubs.

A quick recap of the day's results followed, but another diverting tableau had caught Dryden's eye. He devoted the next long section of his dispatch to a description of Boston's new plaid uniforms, their posh hotel accommodations, and their pregame parade to West Side Grounds, where they had arrived "in a new yellow bus with No. 7 on the bow." Cubs fans were captivated by the tony Eastern team's grand entrance. "No more stylish outfit has visited our fair city," Dryden went on, slyly. "Time was . . . when those heavy boys roomed under high sidewalks and took window board in front of the best restaurants. When they did take a hotel it was the kind at which either teams would not let their watches stop. Look at them now."

Dryden loved to hand out nicknames—Chance was the "Peerless Leader," while Charles Comiskey became "The Old Roman," presumably for his protruding schnoz. The Sox's lumbering but prideful pitcher, Ed Walsh, was "Big Moose," whom Dryden would also describe as "the only man in the world who can strut standing still."

Some of his epigrams were indeed worthy of an Oscar Wilde: "Washington, first in war, first in peace, and last in the American League," was his most famous and lasting quip. Dryden was the Mark Twain of baseball, his contemporaries agreed, and as Richard Orodenker notes in his history of sports writing in America, he turned baseball reporting into its own art form. "The casual tone, the air of self-confidence, the compactness of the sentences, and their classical rhythms are all hallmarks of the light essayist."

Sports reporting was working its way up the ladder of journalistic re-spectability at the same time that "clean" baseball was helping resusci-tate the image of the game. One phenomenon fed the other, it would seem. Fans came to see the teams and the players first, but with read-ership numbers that counted in the hundreds of thousands, led by the penny *Examiner*'s circulation of 170,000 on weekdays and 650,000 on Sunday, and the two-cent *Tribune*'s 162,000 and 320,000, sportswriters could capture and hold an audience that far outstripped the few thousand fans at any one home game.

Sports reporting also benefited from technological and cultural progress. New printing presses made it possible to add photographs and editorial cartoons to game coverage. More people, including young children, could read and write. And, as a result, the practitioners of the sensational yellow press looked to spectator sports as a ready, if unpredictable, source of daily events. By 1906, publishers realized that baseball stories in particular—packaged with scores, statistics, photos, and illustrations—sold newspapers.

There had been a core audience for sports coverage ever since the *New York Clipper* began as a weekly entertainment sheet in 1853 and gave Englishman Henry Chadwick (the "father" of baseball) a platform for his studious coverage of baseball's evolving rules and behaviors. Francis C. Richter's *Sporting Life*, a weekly tabloid published in Philadelphia, and brothers Al and Charlie Spink's the *Sporting News*, a competitor out of St. Louis, came along in the 1880s, nurturing a generation of beat reporters in both major and minor league cities. Influential writers such as Tim Murnane in Boston, Harry Weldon in Cincinnati, Joe Vila in New York, and Leonard Washburn and Charles Goodyear Seymour in Chicago emerged in this era.

In Chicago, where as many as nine daily newspapers competed for readers in the 1880s and 1890s, a group of literary-minded writers had broken away from their elders in the staid Chicago Press Club to form their own social club. Meeting in the rear room of Henry Koster's saloon, at the corner of LaSalle Street and Calhoun Place (also known as Newsboys' Alley), Charlie Seymour and some buddies concocted the Whitechapel Club, named after Jack the Ripper's neighborhood in London. Among Seymour's compatriots were Finley Peter Dunne, whose "Mr. Dooley" sketches were filled with trenchant observations on society and culture. Another was George Ade, the future humorist and playwright in the mold of Mark Twain. Whitechapel members were "wild and erratic geniuses," said one contemporary. It "was young with hope, and it was bizarre."

The Whitechapel Club lasted only five years, but it shaped the image of the Chicago newspaperman well into the twentieth century, according to journalism historian Alfred Lawrence Lorenz. The club's legacy was a new generation of willful writers and eager readers from across the economic and demographic spectrum. And by the turn of the century, no one had the circulation reach or the editorial freedom of Charles Dryden.

A modest and reclusive man, Dryden was an unlikely superstar. His daily dispatches always carried his byline—a rarity before his day—and the *Tribune* even bought large billboards at the ballparks touting his daily column. Dryden protégés included Ring Lardner, whom Cubs players called "Charley's Hat" because they only saw him at Dryden's side in those years. Lardner would go on to national fame as a literary satirist and short-story writer, though he would always insist that he was a baseball writer first and last. When New York critics once complimented Lardner for his humor-filled columns, Lardner replied: "Me, a humorist? Have you guys read any of Charley Dryden's stuff lately? He makes me look like a novice."

Aside from Lardner (and another literary acolyte named Damon Runyon), few of Dryden's contemporaries could match his writing prowess or his biting wit, always delivered on deadline. But many of them, particularly those covering the Cubs and White Sox, developed their own followings, taking advantage of the reams of column inches afforded them. "The papers of Chicago in those days were unlike any printed anywhere else," explained Hugh S. Fullerton. "They were written largely in the language that the wild growing young city understood. . . . They were boisterous, at times rough; they lacked dignity, perhaps, but they were readable, entertaining and amusing."

Fullerton and other scribes took Dryden's cue and found their own ways to mix point of view, breaking news, and a dose of skepticism into their scribblings. They wrote for the everyday reader, using slang and team or player nicknames (often inventing them) in a descriptive style that brought the game and its players to three-dimensional life. Sportswriters of this era also served as willing promoters for club owners, mythologizing local stars, promoting games and special events, and generally reinforcing the growing cult of baseball celebrity. Charles W. Murphy, a former sports editor in Cincinnati, expected no less from

Sportswriter Hugh S. Fullerton was known as a baseball "dopester" who relished the scientific elements of the game. (New York Public Library.)

the reporters who covered his ball club's games, traveled on their trains, and ate and slept in the same hotels. Those who followed clubs at home and on the road acted like they were part of their teams; on some occasions, fights broke out in the press box between warring factions.

But the sportswriters were also developing a fan base of their own, and their names quickly became prized commodities in the cutthroat newspaper market. Many of them changed mastheads from year to year as a Hearst or a Pulitzer or other competitor offered a hot writer a bigger salary to jump ship.

Hugh Stuart Fullerton III was a case in point. His brand of baseball reporting combined the narrative journalism with statistical analysis. A native of Hillsboro, Ohio, Fullerton began covering baseball as a teenager. He worked for the *Tribune* from 1897 to 1907, then jumped to William Randolph Hearst's chain before moving to New York in 1920. He was also one of the first sports beat reporters to branch out into magazine journalism, writing feature stories for the *American Magazine*, *Liberty Magazine*, and the *Saturday Evening Post*.

Unlike Dryden, Fullerton was more methodical than humorous, and he never considered himself a wordsmith. But he also wasn't afraid to venture into the clubhouse to talk to players, something the diffident Dryden rarely bothered to do. Players gave Fullerton exclusive interviews as well as scoops. He was known in his day as a "dopester," or a reporter of detail and behind-the-scenes gossip. In 1906 and 1907, as the Cubs became the best team in baseball, Fullerton wrote a weekly feature column for the Sunday *Chicago Tribune*. He would usually focus on an otherwise unseen aspect of the game, such as "Tricks That Win Ballgames." "To have the correct answer one must know Fullerton," said Grantland Rice, another understudy of both men.

Fullerton, Dryden, and their contemporaries were storytellers above all. They used their daily platforms to bring drama, comedy, intrigue, and suspense to an Industrial Age populace hungry for diversion as well as shared passion. Their stories took various guises and formats—everything from profiles, scoops, and gossip to old-timer reminiscences and boyhood nostalgia—which collectively helped to elevate baseball from a cult of aficionados (and gamblers) to a popular craze of unprecedented scale and devotion across generations.

They did not invent the profession of sportswriting or perfect it, by any stretch. But these scribes built a bridge from one century to the next, setting the stage for a generation of writers such as Lardner, Runyon, Frederick C. Lieb, Westbrook Pegler, Heyward Broun, and the legendary Grantland Rice to cover baseball and other sports in the Ruthian golden age of the 1920s and 1930s. But the trailblazers set the tone and the range of coverage. "There have been brilliant writers since those days," Fullerton recalled in 1928, "but somehow the pioneer writers got more of the atmosphere of the game, more of the scent of the dugout, into their stories than the moderns do."

THE WORLD'S CHAMPIONSHIP

The Chicago Cubs met the Detroit Americans in the second week of October for the best of seven World's Championship series, which began with two games at West Side Grounds. The Tigers had led their league with a .266 batting average, 696 runs scored, 75 triples, and 1,745 total bases. The team's headliners were their center fielder, Nebraska barber "Wahoo Sam" Crawford, and rookie sensation Ty Cobb. Their pitching staff, led by twenty-five-game winners Ed Killian and "Wild Bill" Donovan, had finished third in the AL with a 2.33 ERA.

Except for the outcome, it may have been the least memorable World Series ever:

GAME 1: TUESDAY, OCTOBER 8, WEST SIDE GROUNDS
FINAL SCORE: Cubs 3, Tigers 3 (game called after 12 innings due to darkness)
PITCHERS: Orval Overall, relieved by Ed Reulbach, v. Donovan
SERIES STATUS: 0–0

GAME ACCOUNT: This taut game was the best played one of the series. The Cubs had trailed 3–1 heading into the ninth but rallied for two runs, including a score by Steinfeldt, when pinch hitter Del Howard's swing-and-miss on a third strike got by the Tigers' catcher.
SIDEBAR: A crowd of 24,377 turned out on a crisp, partly cloudy day. Sam Crawford drove in two runs and scored another, but Cobb went 0-for-5. The Cubs wore their road grays in an effort to break their 1906 series jinx at home.

GAME 1 REPLAY: WEDNESDAY, OCTOBER 9, WEST SIDE GROUNDS
FINAL SCORE: Cubs 3, Tigers 1

PITCHERS: Jack Pfiester v. George Mullin
SERIES STATUS: Cubs 1, Tigers 0

GAME ACCOUNT: The Cubs broke a 1–1 tie in the fourth inning with two runs when Jimmy Sheckard doubled home Joe Tinker and Jimmy Slagle.
SIDEBAR: Attendance was only 21,901 despite much warmer weather. Game hero Slagle almost became a goat when he became the only player in World Series history to fall victim to a hidden-ball trick, tagged out at third by Bill Coughlin.

GAME 2: THURSDAY, OCTOBER 10, WEST SIDE GROUNDS
FINAL SCORE: Cubs 5, Tigers 1
PITCHERS: Reulbach v. Ed Siever
SERIES STATUS: Cubs 2, Tigers 0

GAME ACCOUNT: Reulbach limited the Tigers to six hits, while Johnny Evers's two doubles and a single led the Cubs. Cobb blamed the loss on pitcher Siever's "Lady Godiva ball"—there was never anything on it. Yet Cobb and Crawford managed only a single apiece off Ruelbach.
SIDEBAR: A chilly damp wind and temperatures in the forties limited attendance to 13,114. One Chicago writer dubiously blamed the small showing on the opening tie game, claiming that fans had long planned on the date being an away game and so couldn't get off work.

GAME 3: FRIDAY, OCTOBER 11, BENNETT PARK, DETROIT
FINAL SCORE: Cubs 6, Tigers 1
PITCHERS: Overall vs. Donovan
SERIES STATUS: Cubs 3, Tigers 0

GAME ACCOUNT: Overall pitched a five-hitter and drove in two runs in the fifth inning to stake the Cubs to a 2–1 lead.
SIDEBAR: Five special trains left Chicago's Michigan Central and Polk Street stations the night before, ferrying two thousand Cubs fans to the game. One of the passengers was Major Gobel of Blue Island, Illinois, just south of Chicago. He brought forty carrier pigeons to the ballpark and

turned some of them loose at the end of each inning to carry news 260 miles to Blue Island.

GAME 4: SATURDAY, OCTOBER 12, BENNETT PARK
FINAL SCORE: Cubs 2, Tigers 0
PITCHERS: Brown v. Mullin
SERIES STATUS: Cubs 4, Tigers 0

GAME ACCOUNT: Brown pitched a seven-hit shutout, and Harry Steinfeldt knocked in Slagle in the first with the only run needed.
SIDEBAR: Sportswriters before the game wondered whether Cubs owner Murphy would instruct his players to take a fall in this game because he had already sold twenty-five thousand tickets to game 5 at West Side Grounds the next day. When Miner Brown caught wind of the rumor, he told reporters: "To blazes with that crowd in Chicago tomorrow. I'll finish it today."

ELECTRIC MAGIC

Chicago's most rabid baseball fans had begun showing up downtown a full two hours before game 4's opening pitch, rapidly filling up the streets and sidewalks. An estimated eight thousand men, women, and children nestled shoulder to shoulder, paying little heed to the forty-seven-degree temperature or the twenty-two-mile-an-hour winds off Lake Michigan. They had come out for one of the biggest public spectacles in civic memory, and the Cubs rooters quickly grew hoarse from yelling for the hometown boys. To this horde, it hardly mattered that none of their local heroes, not Tinker or Evers or Steinfeldt or "Three-Finger" Brown, were present and visible.

At 2:30 p.m., eight thousand faces craned upward and stared intently at a large, rectangular billboard mounted above the second-floor windows on the Dearborn Street side of the *Chicago Tribune* building. The object of their attention was a bizarre-looking contraption to anyone who didn't understand baseball. It was dominated by a baseball "diamond" painted on a large wooden backdrop. Electric light bulbs flashed on or off at each base and fielding position. The team lineups were listed on opposite sides of the "playing field" with lights to show which man was at bat and who was on base. One row of lights on the bottom showed the pitch count and how many outs, while another row kept track of the innings and score. This facsimile of the baseball diamond and its batters, baserunners, and defenders gave almost every spectator in the street a clear, luminous view of every pitch, play, and run, virtually as soon as they occurred in distant Detroit.

This was, in a way, an electrified version of a promotional stunt the *Tribune* had tried the year before. On that occasion, the company had rented two concert halls accommodating five thousand or more fans, and it had "re-created" the six Cubs–White Sox games on stage using placards, blackboards, and chalk. An announcer shouted out the play-by-play through a giant megaphone. The *Tribune* also had contracted with Western Union for a direct connection from the ballpark to the venues. Two telegraph operators stationed behind the real home plate tapped out messages recording each ball, strike, out, hit, base achieved, and so on. Other operators then relayed each development to the auditorium audiences—all just moments after it happened. It was like "watching" a play-by-play account by radio, except that this was fifteen years before such audio broadcasts were possible.

The main drawback to the 1906 megaphone version was the size of the crowds. Fans in the back rows had a hard time following the rapid-fire announcements, resulting in rolling queries of "how's that?" crashing into a backwash of shouted replies from the front seats—all while the man on stage was booming out the next pitch or play. Still, the *Tribune* liked what it had started, although in 1907 it wanted to improve the presentation in both size and scale. Electricity-powered bulletin boards promised a visual spectacle and would allow for thousands of fans to "watch" the game from a distance.

Chicago wasn't the only city to take advantage of this newfangled technology. The *Washington (DC) Evening Star* would also set up such a board outside of its offices at Eleventh Street and Pennsylvania Avenue. Spectators filled up that American League city's downtown blocks, most of them rooting for Detroit. The federal government had closed for the afternoon, sending hundreds of clerks scurrying toward the *Star* building. Though the game didn't go the Tigers' way, the crowd seemed pleased with the presentation. "Everybody saw what was going on in Chicago," the *Star* reported the next day with self-satisfaction. "Those in the rear had just as fair chance as the ones in front, and right there was emphasized the superiority of The Star's electric board over the old megaphone system."

Back in Chicago, the "real fans," as a *Trib* reporter called them, "to whom the weather conditions were as nothing and the game everything," filled the downtown streets and sidewalks. The assembled mass blocked all traffic, stopping streetcars in their tracks. The fans ultimately commandeered the entire intersection of Dearborn and West Madison Streets, with latecomers piled up in the side streets. The seventeen-story, steel-framed skyscraper that was home to the *Tribune* provided ample backdrop and sunshield for the electric display lights. In the tall office buildings across the street, eager spectators poked their heads out of the windows—a multitiered audience "from the ground floor to the uppermost stories."

Once the game was underway, the massive crowd cheered in unison at each instant of action: they let out whoops when the flashing lightbulbs showed four balls and a walk to leadoff hitter Rabbit Slagle; more cheers when the lights showed him stealing second base, and yet again when they showed him crossing home plate and scoring the first run on a base hit to left by Harry Steinfeldt. The Cubs quick lead seemed to galvanize the city: "Passersby and pedestrians in the adjacent streets and avenues heard the tumult, wondered, and then joined in the demonstration."

The electric bulletin boards did something else for baseball. No small number of the partisans who filled the streets were women, who were keen to display their enthusiasm in dress as well as voice. They waved small Cubs pennants and wore "varicolored sleevelets" tied around their arms, each marked with "CUBS" in large letters. The ladies' fervor took their male escorts aback. As one *Trib* reporter condescendingly noted, "They rooted for the Cubs with an enthusiasm that displayed a truly marvelous feminine lung development."

THE BASEBALL TICKER

Newspapers, which had long-standing contractual relationships with telegraph companies like Western Union, led the way in deploying bulletin boards powered by electricity and fed by telegraph. The telegraph had been the breakthrough technology of the late nineteenth century; among many other qualities, it gave news organizations a way to share stories and information with their readers amid a hotly competitive daily news cycle. Afternoon baseball results from telegraph "tickers" became a valuable commodity, and many a newspaper would highlight even partial, late-inning scores in its afternoon street editions.

Skeptical baseball owners, hooked on the extra revenue they could scratch out from selling printed scorecards at their ballparks for a nickel or a dime, initially failed to appreciate the drawing power of constantly updated scoreboards. The magnates feared the potential cannibalization they foreshadowed. "There was a growl over the bulletin boards," conceded Pittsburgh Pirates owner Barney Dreyfuss in 1906. "The old regime held that bulletins cut down the attendance at games when the team was at home."

Western Union, meanwhile, saw nothing but dollar signs. The telegraph company had long counted on a particular class of information consumer for a major part of its revenue—a class best described by the term "investor," if it encompasses illegitimate as well as legitimate commerce. In 1887, Western Union president Norvin Green told U.S. postal officials that three classes of customer depended on its ticker services: speculators in commodity options and futures contracts, "bucket shops" where patrons wagered on the price movements of stocks and commodities, and "pool rooms" that took bets on horse races and other sporting events. Indeed, according to historian David Hochfelder, Green all but admitted that "a majority of Western Union's ticker business came from gambling."

By the turn of the century, Western Union saw the demand for sports information as a growth market. The invention of the quadruplex in 1880 had made possible the simultaneous transmission of four messages at a time over one wire; a shorthand method called the Phillips Code, which abbreviated the most commonly used phrases to simple one- and two-digit numerals, made rapid transmission of news reports a relative breeze; and more recent advances made it easy to set up ticker machines and keyboards at remote locations. Western Union nurtured close ties with saloons that hosted betting "pools" on both horses and ball games. The company leased proprietors of pool rooms a wire and ticker at $1 a day. As a result, between 1893 and 1903, the company's annual income from horse racing and other sporting events grew to $8 million out of a total ticker income of $17 million. Sports alone generated $2 million a year above expenses.

Baseball and the telegraph benefited each other, prompting Western Union officials to offer the baseball magnates a sweetheart deal: free telegraph service for their personal business communications, in exchange for exclusive rights to their major and minor league ball games. Western Union could then sell its game feeds to newspapers, business offices, union halls, theater and opera houses, and any other venue (including saloons) where fans might shell out their dimes and nickels to follow or even "watch" a ball game as it took place just across town or in some faraway city.

As a result, baseball was soon everywhere. Even the lordly *New York Times* had to bow to the grip that baseball had come to hold over the American public's imagination. "The one ever-dominating topic of conversation in this broad country from May to October is baseball," it remarked in an editorial. "Financial upheaval, political controversy, a noteworthy visit of royalty, a social scandal, or a great disaster may once in a while drive other subjects out of the public mind, but the crowd around the baseball bulletin boards never dwindles."

THE OLD BALL GAME

In November 1907, with Chicago still rejoicing in the Cubs' first World's Championship, the Tomaz F. Deuther Music Publisher released the sheet music for a new song. Its cover leaf, bearing the inscription "Dedicated to Frank Chance" across the top, included a photo inset of the

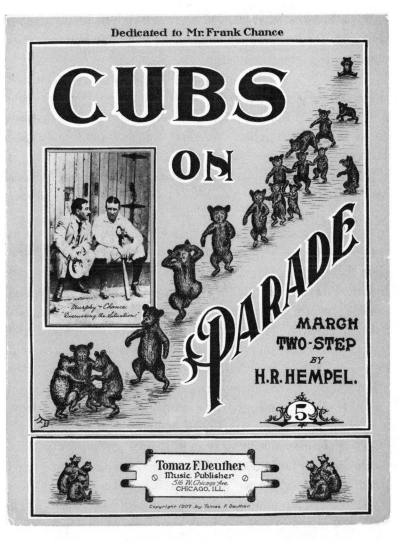

At the close of the 1907 season, a Chicago music publisher came out with the "March Two-Step" tune featuring the World Champion Cubs. Pictured are owner C. W. Murphy and manager Frank Chance. (Courtesy of the Lester S. Levy Collection of Sheet Music, Johns Hopkins University Library.)

Peerless Leader seated casually next to C. W. Murphy. That image was surrounded by a cartoon drawing of a line of dancing bears marching down the page on their hind legs.

"Cubs on Parade" is the only known composition of H. R. Hempel, who wrote the piece in the march two-step style made popular by John Philip Sousa's "Washington Post March" of 1891. It wasn't the first song about baseball in America—there had been as many as sixty songs about the sport, perhaps beginning with "Base Ball Polka," written in 1858 by an amateur ballplayer from Buffalo. But Hempel's dance tune, coupled with the Cubs' dynastic rise, may have helped set a musical craze in motion.

Sheet-music publishers like Deuther dominated the music industry in the days of primitive phonographs. Popular songs and dances, especially those arranged for piano and amateur singers, were all the rage in parlors across America. Song culture was part of everyday life, from lullabies, hymns, and march two-steps to popular ditties like "My Gal Sal" and "Shine on Harvest Moon," making the piano a central piece of furniture in most middle-class homes. In the 1890s, U.S. piano manufacturers produced more than two hundred thousand new keyboards a year, most of them large uprights, and music teachers were giving private lessons to as many as half a million children at a time. Parents and children alike were eager for new songs to play and sing.

Print publishers, operating in tandem with the still-vigorous blackface minstrelsy and the emerging vaudeville industries, recruited performers and songwriters to gin up new songs and dances. William Randolph Hearst reprinted sheet music in his newspapers, as did *Ladies' Home Journal* and other popular magazines. In New York a string of publishing houses specializing in sheet music congregated downtown in a neighborhood called Tin Pan Alley, where they cranked out hundreds of five- and ten-cent copies of new tunes every year.

One of the leading music publishers in Chicago was Will Rossiter's firm on West Lake Street; his greatest hit was "Meet Me Tonight in Dreamland," released in 1909. But Rossiter also composed and published a tune in July 1908 called "Between You and Me," billed as "a Home Run Song Hit by Johnny Evers and Joe Tinker." It's a romantic number that begins "Two lovers stroll together, two lovers hand in hand." Perhaps assured they wouldn't have to actually collaborate on the words and music, the silent rivals agreed to pose for the cover and add their facsimile autographs—and take the credit for the song—even though neither was known to possess a lick of musical skill.

As these music publishers churned out more and more songs and dance numbers in the 1890s and early 1900s, composers like George M. Cohan and Irving Berlin scoured American culture for inspiration. Along with the timeless staple of young love, they also wrote about longing and nostalgia. They came up with odes to leisure activities like carriage rides, picnics in the park, bicycling, and bowling ("Spars and Strikes"), but also invoked some of the new touchstones of modern life, as in "In My Merry Oldsmobile" and "There's a Wireless Station Down in My Heart."

Rarely, however, had songwriters thought of baseball as a subject. Only two baseball songs came out in 1902, "The Baseball Fiend" and "Three Strikes Two-Step"; only one in 1903, "Boston Americans March (Two-Step)," celebrating that team's World Series victory; and just one more in 1904, "Husky Hans," acclaiming the Pirates' great shortstop Honus Wagner. The 1905 season saw a slight increase as five new song sheets hit the market, including "Baseball Cake Walk" and "The Umpire Is a Most Unhappy Man." But 1906 brought none, even with baseball insanity overtaking Chicago. By the time the Deuther house issued "Cubs on Parade" in November 1907, it was only the fourth baseball song of that year.

Something must have changed the industry's perception of baseball during 1907 and 1908. A young entertainer named Jack Norworth, no baseball fan, could see the opportunity plain as day. Norworth was a songwriter and blackface minstrel artist on Tin Pan Alley, where he collaborated with piano player Albert Von Tilzer. They wrote several hit songs together, including "Honey Boy" and "Good Evening Caroline," and each had his own hits, Von Tilzer with "My Old New Hampshire Home," and Norworth with "Shine on Harvest Moon." Von Tilzer and his brother opened York Music Company in 1903, and they went on a hunt for new songs to publish.

Norworth had a brainstorm. "Quite simple," he would recall. "I thought it was time for a baseball song, and an idea struck me which I thought was pretty good." What Norworth came up with in the spring of 1908, as told in *Baseball's Greatest Hit*, the definitive history of the song, was a simple lyric composed in a typical two-part, verse-and-chorus structure. Only the eight-line chorus is well known now:

> Take me out to the ballgame,
> Take me out with the crowd.
> Buy me some peanuts and Cracker Jack,
> I don't care if I never get back.
> Let me root, root, root for the home team,
> If they don't win it's a shame.
> For it's one, two, three strikes you're out!
> At the old ball game.

Norworth showed the lyric to Von Tilzer, who came up with a tune for it in about the same amount of time that Norworth had taken to scratch out the words. Tin Pan Alley veterans didn't waste much time on finer points, relying on instincts and tried-and-true devices to get a song into circulation. In this case, Tilzer crafted a simple waltz that moves briskly along and stays within a single octave, making it easy for almost anyone to sing along. And it reaches a rewarding climax in the seventh line, where the singers get to shout "ONE, TWO, THREE strikes you're out!" "Think about it," marveled a modern-day music theorist. "You're singing along like a nightingale and all of a sudden you're not singing a song anymore—you're shouting out strikes!"

"Take Me Out to the Ballgame" became an instant hit. By October 1908, it was in the top ten for the year, and its first recording, a ten-inch shellac disc rendition on the Victor label by the Haydn Quartet, spent seven weeks at No. 1 during the months the Cubs and New York Giants were fighting for the National League pennant. Other music publishers tried to cash with immediate copycats, such as "Take Your Girl to the Ball Game." None reached the heights of the pathbreaker, but at least thirty baseball tunes would follow in the next year and a half, including "He's a Fan, Fan, Fan," "The Baseball Man for Me," and "Let's Get the Umpire's Goat."

Ironically, the song got little play in big league ballparks. It found its real favor in early movie houses, which needed material for the long intervals when projectionists were changing reels. Hence the short-lived phenomenon of "illustrated song plays"—illuminated photo slides of a new song, sung by a house vocalist and accompanied by the house pianist, who urged the audience to sing along. Movie houses across America reverberated with this new tune about baseball.

"Take Me Out to the Ballgame" has since been featured in more than 1,200 films, television shows, and commercials, and of course has become the anthem of baseball's seventh-inning stretch, sung more than 2,500 times a year in major league ballparks and inestimable times and places in the minor leagues.

VICTORY REDUX

Perhaps "Cubs on Parade," written in the immediate wake of the World's Championship, received an early premier at the October victory banquet. The news reports don't say. But the celebratory banquet and toasts, "further enlivened by vocal and orchestral music," captured the spirit of the times nonetheless. The speeches and dancing continued into the early morning hours. Cubs rooters worked themselves into spasms of delight, and "left the hall hoarse from cheering the great ball players and their greater leader."

And so, barely nine years after organized baseball had devolved into a funk of foul play and fouler spirit—a stain on society—and only six years since Frank Selee had come in to reverse the team's sagging fortunes, the Chicago National League Baseball Ball Club of Frank Chance, Johnny Evers, Joe Tinker, and others was declared world champions in both deed and merit. What 116 wins in the previous season could not quite validate, four straight victories in the 1907 postseason finale had accomplished: the Chicago Cubs were perched atop of the nation's imagination and approbation.

No one wanted the occasion to pass unnoticed. The six-page banquet programs left one page blank for autographs. The players' signatures, each as distinctive as their backgrounds and personalities, still jump off the page with cheer and bonhomie. Artie Hoffman slyly added his "Circus Solly" nickname to his mark. Johnny Evers wrote in "Shoes" next to his, a proud callout to his new shoe store in downtown Chicago.

Frank Chance's speech that night was not recorded, but he probably told the assemblage something similar to what he told Francis Richter at *Sporting Life* just before the series began. "We won the pennant because we have the greatest team in the National League," Chance said. "That is the first and principal reason. But there are two others. First, the Chicago National team is composed of manly fellows who do not have to be watched. Their manager is at liberty to devote his time to baseball. Second, there is harmony on the team. You can't win a pennant with knockers in your organization. One of our men enjoys seeing another make a good play as much as if he had made it himself."

J. Hamilton Lewis seemed to recognize the Cubs' unique traits as he wound up his remarks at the Victory Banquet. Near the end, he turned to the men seated in front of him—to Johnny Evers, twenty-six years old; to Joe Tinker, twenty-seven; to Harry Steinfeldt and Mordecai Brown, thirty; and to Chance, the old man at thirty-one—and addressed them directly.

"You start out young, strong, supple, and hopeful," Lewis told them. "You afford for millions the hour of merriment, a day of satisfaction and a season of delight." Yet as the crowds disperse and the season comes to an end, "you are no longer in the light of attraction, nor do the multitude cheer you to accomplishment. In such hour as this too often you are forgotten. It is against this injustice I speak."

The majestic orator then offered a personal reassurance. "Let it be understood," J-Ham concluded, "that this dinner is not only to certify the high esteem in which you are held as players, but the great regard in which you are to be held hereafter as men."

TEAM OF DESTINY

1908

New York and Chicago—queen cities of the East and West—tussling for the laurels that an ability to toss and bat a little leather ball around a couple of acres of land bring. [This] was the secret of the feverish anxiety which kept fans from Maine to Monterey and from St. Augustine to Sitka gluing their eyes to the tickers all summer. REX LARDNER, "Cubs' Road to Third Pennant Is Hardest of the Three Paths," *Chicago Inter Ocean*, October 9, 1908

Baseball has always been a mathematical sport. The game is defined by questions of shape, relative position of figures, and properties of space—geometry; it's driven by the convergence of infinite sequences to a well-defined limit—calculus; and the athletic skills required to play it are exhibited, and constrained, by kinetic motion through space and time—physics. Playing or even watching a baseball game requires a working knowledge of its conceptual underpinnings.

Henry Chadwick, the first reporter to cover baseball games, understood this instinctively. He invented the "box score" to sum up, in abstract terms like hits, runs, outs, assists, and errors, the incremental actions in each game. He recorded the results of every play so he could track these actions through time in the form of cumulative batting averages, fielding averages, and other statistics that measure individual and team performance. Chadwick was the consummate baseball fan:

he wanted to follow the action astutely *while it was in play*, not just after the fact. To do so, he reckoned, both fans and players needed a way to grasp the basic concepts of the sport, intellectually and instantly.

In July 1866, Chadwick authored the game's first comprehensive manual: *The Base Ball Player's Book of Reference*, which had been commissioned by the emergent National Association of Base Ball Players as it sought to govern organized baseball competition across the nation. This 140-page booklet, small enough to fit into a player's back pocket, covered practical necessities like the duties of umpires, how to score a game, and how to practice, among other fundamentals. In the first twenty-five pages, Chadwick sought to rationalize the differing versions of baseball played up to that time. He put forth a unified set of rules and sought to explain the theories behind them.

Chadwick's booklet codified the accepted rules of play, from the size of the ball and bat, to the number of bases (four) and the number of paces between them (ninety feet each), to which direction one runs the bases (counterclockwise). Another was the difference between a fair ball and a foul ball—a distinction that is unknown in one of baseball's cousins, cricket. Understanding fair and foul required rather abstract thinking. Fair territory is demarcated by an infinite extension of the two lines connecting the point of home plate with the points of first base and third base.

Chadwick's *Book of Reference* also included some second- and third-order concepts that were difficult for players and fans to internalize, in part because they were fairly arbitrary: each team alternated turns in an "inning," three outs to each turn, with nine innings to a game. Another, somewhat puzzling rule declared the "striker" (batter) out if a batted ball was caught on the fly or on one bounce; this rule was soon changed to caught flies only.

Chadwick expressly codified the difference between a force out and a tag out after a ground ball. Earlier versions of baseball had allowed fielders to retire a baserunner by "soaking," or "plugging," him before he could reach base. From here on, Chadwick declared, a runner would be out only if a fielder touches him with ball in hand or—and here's his conceptual twist—"if . . . the ball is held by an adversary on first base, before the striker touches that base." The force out was an important concept that Chadwick felt compelled to explain further:

> It should be distinctly understood by all that the ball must be held by the base player with some part of his person on the first base, "before" the striker touches it, or he is not out. . . .

Here the rules and the concepts of baseball start to get dicey—and, more important, they take a shape that will one day affect the fate of the Chicago Cubs. The concept of a force out, as applied by Johnny Evers, was to bear directly on the outcome of an epic, jaw-dropping game played forty-two years later, on September 23, 1908, at the Polo Grounds in upper Manhattan, pitting the Chicago Cubs against the New York Giants.

The end of the 1908 game—indeed, the result of the entire 1908 season, many believe—turned on the disputed interpretation of a force out. The ultimate ruling, made by a National League court of final appeal in favor of an abstract argument first put forth with singular conviction by one John J. Evers Jr., climaxed a baseball story for the ages. And like all stories for the ages, this saga hinges on a long-forgotten origin story: Father Chadwick and his 1866 rule book.

In section 22 of his tome—"Vacating Bases.—Putting Players Out."—Chadwick draws on another abstraction that players and fans take for granted today. "Players must make their bases in the order of striking," Chadwick declared, "and when a fair ball is struck, and not caught flying, the first base must be vacated, as also the second and third bases, if they are occupied at the same time." This requirement—to vacate a base and advance to the next one when the bases behind are occupied—seems elemental. But it was not always so.

Chadwick needed to explain baserunning rules because they also differed from those of cricket, where neither the striker nor the runner in front of him has an obligation to run for the next wicket on a batted ball unless the lead runner thinks he can make it safely. Chadwick delivered a logical and all-important clarification for the situation of a runner forced to advance to the next base: "Players may be put out on any base, under these circumstances, in the same manner as when running to the first base." That is: a simple force out, not a tag out, pertains if the runner must vacate his bag on a base hit and move to the next base, no matter which one.

Here is where the regulation and its precedents come full circle. First, take note of Section 28—"Running Home after the Striker Is Out"—in which Chadwick states: "If two hands are already out, no player running home at the time the ball is struck can make a *run to count in the score of the game* if the striker is put out by a fair catch by being touched between home and the first base, or by the ball being held by an adversary at the first base before the striker reaches it." The implication is clear, though it requires the same leap of logic that Chadwick articulated in section 22. If a runner cannot score from third when the defense completes the third out of an inning by a force-out at first, then the same concept should apply if the forced third out occurs at second or third base. The run does not count even if a runner crosses the plate ahead of the play.

Father Henry Chadwick died on April 20, 1908, at the age of eighty-three, just days into a momentous baseball season. He did not live to see how the campaign turned out, who won or lost, or why. But his words and precepts, laid down forty-two years earlier in his pocket guidebook, would ultimately decide the season—and provide a century's worth of glory—for the 1908 Chicago Cubs.

NEW DIGS ON THE WEST SIDE

Two days after Father Chadwick's passing, Charles Webb Murphy staged a grand reopening of the renovated West Side Grounds. He spared little expense in his desire to commemorate the Cubs' ascension to baseball's summit. The afternoon festivities, graced by balmy weather, promised plenty of pomp and circumstance, speeches, flag raising, and multiple offerings of long-stem roses to the new heroes—all packed into an hour-long run-up to the home opener.

Murphy had many surprises in store for the legions of Cubs fans.

Before there was a Wrigley Field on Chicago's North Side, the Cubs played all their home games at the West Side Grounds, located on a block bounded by Taylor, Wood, Polk, and Lincoln (now Wolcott) streets. The standing-room-only crowd at this August 30, 1908, game against archrival New York Giants was typical. (Bain Collection, Library of Congress.)

An impressive two-story brick edifice greeted them at the entrance on South Lincoln Street. On the roof of the ticket office perched two heroic statues: one depicting Frank Chance, the Peerless Leader, in his familiar batting stance; the other a generic Cubs pitcher in the act of hurling a ball to the plate. Murphy had commissioned a local sculptor, Osborne T. Olsen, to produce the eight-hundred-pound cement megaliths. (The pitcher had to be guy-wired to the building to keep the right-hander from toppling off its mooring.) Spread out along the entrance pavilion stood fourteen more oversized statues by Olsen—each portraying a bear cub climbing up a giant cement baseball bat.

More evidence of Murphy's lavish ambitions appeared inside the stadium. He had doubled the size of the grandstand to accommodate six thousand seats, a new wooden canopy offering protection overhead. He had Olsen line the upper boxes with iron rail piping, ornamented with four hundred gilded cast-iron baseballs. Olsen also found a way to fashion more than a thousand regulation Spalding baseball bats into a balustrade guarding the stairways. The game itself wasn't going to be the only drawing card. "That new playground on the west side is a poem of beauty and comfort," Charles Dryden marveled.

More than fifteen thousand fans turned out for the spectacle, which included a brass band with three loud snare drums "that made folks sit up and ask for more," according to Dryden. Fans who couldn't acquire a ticket milled about outside the gates; a few agile types climbed trees and telephone poles to sneak a look into the ballpark. Even braver souls went next door, where opportunistic property owners had erected wooden bleachers on the roofs of buildings overlooking the ball field. One newspaper photograph shows more than two hundred people huddled shoulder-to-shoulder, at least ten rows deep, on forty-five-degree risers teetering high atop a five-story brick structure.

Murphy had made a lot of money on the Cubs over the previous two years, enough to pay back his original loan from Charles Taft and pocket a tidy sum for himself. Now that he was flush, fully in charge, and getting a public relations lift, he went into full P. T. Barnum mode. The renovation of West Side Grounds was just the start.

A few weeks before Opening Day, Murphy had unveiled a new Ladies' Day policy, giving free admission on Tuesdays to any female accompanied by a man. He was not the first to stage a Ladies' Day—the White Sox sponsored one on Fridays—but he put no limit on the number of women who could come along on the ticket-paying arm of a "gentleman escort." Hundreds of women in brightly colored outfits would soon burst out among the sea of dark suits, brown derbies, and straw "boaters" that had typified crowds at Cubs games.

The presence of fashionably dressed women at the ballpark soon created its own kind of problem for the men and women who actually wanted to see a baseball game.

That spring in New York, the German operetta *The Merry Widow* had taken Broadway by storm. Lily Elsie, a premier singer, had already ignited a craze in Europe by wearing an oversized plumed bonnet in the English production. The American producers decided to give away a replica of her hat to every woman who came to opening night at the New Amsterdam Theatre. A "battle of the hats" erupted after female theatergoers discovered there weren't enough hats for everyone. Within weeks, demand for the Merry Widow hats spread across the country.

At the height of their popularity, the resplendent confections could reach up to eighteen inches in diameter and hold all kinds of trimmings around the brim, including flowers, feathers, fruit, even whole stuffed birds. When women began showing up at the ballpark in these outsized creations, they posed something of an obstacle for those unlucky enough to have seats behind them. "A girl with a white dress and immense purple hat got behind the catcher," the *Chicago Daily Journal* reported after one Cubs game, "and over 900 fans lost all sight of the game." Another woman sitting up front in her bedecked bonnet "trimmed with several acres of foliage" unwittingly created an inviting target for the gents behind her, who tossed wads of newspaper and hot peanuts atop her Merry Widow. Two men gallantly stood up as protection. They "withstood the bombardment," mocked a reporter, "and incidentally cut off the view of several more people."

The battle of the hats continued through most of the summer, until the "MWs," as the male writers then called them, started diminishing in size and as some women caught on to the hullabaloo they had created. "A number of thoughtful women removed their expensive millinery creations during the game, gaining the gratitude of many spectators," came an approving report in May. "At a ball game you can tell whether a woman is a real lady or just a plain female by noting whether she has her hat on or not."

THE CUBS OF 1908

The Cubs found out quickly that the 1908 season was going to be tougher going than the previous year's cakewalk. The Pirates and Giants were each out for revenge and redemption, and both teams eyed Frank Chance's squad as their enemy. By the end of May, the Cubs were 23–13, enough to put them in first place, but seven of those thirteen losses had come at the hands of the Pirates and Giants, including a 13–3 drubbing by Pittsburgh in the second game of a double header on May 31.

Chance had the same, now-veteran group that had won two NL pennants and a World's Championship: Evers, Tinker, and Steinfeldt in the infield; Johnny Kling behind the plate; and the Tri-Sigma unit of Sheckard, Slagle, and Schulte patrolling the outfield. Miner Brown, Ed

Reulbach, Jack Pfiester, and Orval Overall provided a fearsome pitching armada. Together they had won 223 games over that two-year span and seemed poised to win another 100 or more.

Then something quite strange happened that shook the Cubs' close-knit clubhouse to its foundations. While nursing their wounds after the twin loss to Pittsburgh, Jimmy Sheckard got into an argument with a utility infielder whom Chance had picked up near the end of the previous season. His name was Henry Zimmerman, though everyone called him Heinie. His parents were German immigrants who had settled in the Bronx. As a teenager, Zimmerman had earned a reputation on New York City's semipro circuit. But he had always been an eccentric man, with a short fuse and a sometimes-violent temper.

As Sheckard and Zimmerman traded words, whatever they were arguing about suddenly turned vicious. A fist fight followed, something usually ignored by their teammates as a not-so-unusual consequence of a tough loss on a hot day. Sheckard then threw something at Zimmerman, who retaliated by grabbing something similar, which happened to be a bottle of ammonia. The glass shattered as it hit Sheckard in the forehead and the liquid splashed into his eyes.

Sheckard's wild shrieks got everyone's attention, Chance first of all. Sheckard was his outfield captain, one of the team's best hitters. Zimmerman was a promising rookie, but his odd ways, perpetual sneer, and meager production hadn't won him many friends. Husk jumped onto Zimmerman and pummeled him with a boxer's fury. Zimmerman didn't back down, however, holding his own until several others joined in the beating. They nearly killed him.

Both Sheckard and Zimmerman were rushed to a hospital; each stayed out of the lineup for several days without explanation to the press. Sheckard would eventually recover his eyesight, but he remained out of action for several weeks. Zimmerman recovered, too, and after a suspension eventually returned to the roster as a reliable part-time player. In the meantime, the shorthanded Cubs lost the next two games to the Pirates, raising Pittsburgh to second place. By the end of June, the Pirates had climbed to the top of the standings by half a game, with the Cubs in second and the Giants in third.

A great pennant race was stirring. It would continue to the final weeks, days, and even hours of the regular season (and then some). The teams fought a three-way war of attrition, a battle royal for the ages, with a bizarre, helter-skelter finishing lap that modern-day baseball mavens, even with more than one hundred years of hindsight, are still trying to explain.

THE INQUISITIVE FAN

Johnny Evers had earned the nickname "Human Crab" in large part because of his constant arguing with umpires, especially over their knowledge—or lack thereof, in his mind—of baseball rules. Perhaps his biggest beef as a notorious "kicker" of the men in blue was that he was usually right. "All there is to Evers is a bundle of nerves, a lot of woven-wire muscles, and the quickest brain in baseball," Hugh Fullerton said.

Evers was the most unlikely of baseball brainiacs. He was infamous for his hot head and short fuse on the field, a nonstop motormouth of insults and umpire diatribes. "His tongue knew neither fear nor control when he was crossed," said umpire Bill Klem, who called balls, strikes, and outs for thirty-six years, "and he thought everybody within eye or ear range was crossing him."

Evers would not dispute Klem's assessment ("My favorite umpire is a dead one," he said), but he also operated against type when off the field and out of uniform. He was an obsessive student of the game, its history, and its complexities. When Evers teamed up with Fullerton to write a baseball instructional manual in 1910, they included eight geometric diagrams one or the other had devised to show how fielders should position themselves for different batters in different hitting situations. They were baseball's first "sabermetricians," calculating percentages of getting a batter out on the basis of hitting "grooves," defensive angles, and other factors. "The geometry of the game becomes more complex the deeper it is studied," they wrote. "As Mr. Euclid, who invented diamonds, would say: If X covers 24 feet with his arms and legs and 18 with his brain, Y, the base-runner, is out, provided Z, the umpire, does not call him safe. Q.E.D."

Evers's bedside companions on the road were the *Troy Times*, *Sporting News*, and baseball rule books. "In the evening before I go to my room I buy the final baseball extras of all the evening newspapers and read them before I go to sleep," he once said. He would also stockpile large amounts of candy, then lull himself to sleep eating chocolate bars and studying the inside game. He wasn't the only one in his pursuit of a competitive edge, he insisted: "Every ball player in the business spends hours of time and thought to see how he can beat the rules, to discover some way to gain an extra base, or some slight advantage over their opponents," he said. But if Evers wasn't alone as a student of the finer points of the game, he was surely the most obsessive.

The Cubs were at home the weekend of July 18–19, so Evers no doubt saw the "Inquisitive Fans" column that appeared in its usual place in the *Chicago Tribune*'s Sunday sports section. This forum allowed readers to ask about arcane situations that might come up in the course of a ball game. The anonymous editor's terse answer to one fan's query, buried in agate type near the end of the column, would have struck a nerve in a baseball crab:

> In the last half of the ninth, with the score tied, two men out and a runner on third, the batter hits to left and the runner scores. The batter, seeing the runner score, stops between home and first. The ball is thrown to first baseman, who touches his base before the runner reaches it. Can runner score on this?
>
> JOSEPH RUPP

> No. Run cannot score when the third out is made before reaching first base.

The *Tribune*'s unequivocal answer derived from rule 59 in the "Scoring of Runs" section of that year's rule book. The text rings with a clear echo of the edict put forth more than forty years before in Chadwick's section 28: "One run shall be scored every time a base-runner, after having legally touched the first three bases, shall legally touch the home base before three men are put out. Provided, however, that if he reach[es] home on or during a play in which the third man be forced out or be put out, before reaching first base, a run shall not count."

Johnny Evers knew ballplayers observed this rule mostly in the breach, particularly when the situation involved a force-out at second. It was common practice to permit a baserunner to halt his progress if the batter had knocked in a game-ending run from a runner on third. A forced runner leaving first or second would habitually turn away and run back to the team's bench, or to its clubhouse in the outfield.

Thanks to "Inquisitive Fans," the baseball world had been properly alerted. It gave Evers the ammunition he needed to put its principle up for trial.

NEW YORK V. CHICAGO

New Yorkers and Chicagoans shared no love for each other at this time. Chicago had long passed Philadelphia as the second-largest city in the country, behind New York, and it had become the business and manu-facturing hub of the entire country—its central railway depot; its lead-ing grain broker, lumberyard, and meat packer; and home to its larg-est retailers. Chicago seemed poised to overtake New York and even London, not just in population and wealth but as the center of modern civilization. "Young as she is," averred a New York literary magazine's profile of the city, "Chicago has become the pace-maker of the world."

The diverse peoples who filled Chicago's streets, plants, skyscrapers, and homes were beginning to internalize, even unify, around this notion of the city's emerging primacy. They took encouragement in 1906 from the success of Chicago's two big league baseball teams, which both beat their New York counterparts. The Cubs' victory in the 1907 World Cham-pionship series solidified the city's regal image of itself. By the middle of 1908, as Chance and Co. competed furiously for a third consecutive NL pennant, the rivalry between the New York Giants and the Cubs took on more psychic freight than mere baseball bragging rights. This was becoming a contest of civic pride and identity. "If you didn't honestly and furiously hate the Giants, you weren't a real Cub," said Joe Tinker.

Newspapers in each city thrived on the rivalry, as contests between the Cubs and Giants sold papers. In light of the high degree of human drama and daily suspense, publishers and editors gave their sports pages more space to cover baseball contests, and editors in turn assigned more reporters to cover baseball games. Chauvinistic writers in both burgs found a resonating metaphor in baseball and played it to the hilt. Their regional conceits focused on what the differences between the Cubs and the Giants said about each city. New York was educated and influential, Chicago the workingman's town. "The Giants had their good looking, college-educated pitching ace: Christy Mathewson," notes baseball historian Cindy Thompson. "Chicago's ace embodied the common man: the former coal miner with the deformed hand, Mordecai 'Three Finger' Brown."

For Chicago partisans, the vile Muggsy McGraw was the perfect villain against the morally righteous working stiffs on stoic Frank Chance's club. Cubs fans had spent the better part of four years hating, ridiculing, and demonizing McGraw, with Eddie Heeman's Board of Trade Rooters setting the tone and level of intensity. And Muggsy did everything he could to uphold his venal image. When the Giants made their first 1908 appearance in Chicago in late May, McGraw put on yet another show as his club lost a close, bitterly fought contest, 8–7, in ten innings. Muggsy wasn't around at the very end, thrown out of the game by umpire Bob Emslie "after the boss kicker had filled the air and the ears of a portion of the spectators with choice selections from his famous repertory of vilification," according to I. E. Sanborn.

McGraw never backed down, of course. The Giants won the next three games, serving notice that the Cubs would have no clear path to the pennant. "The Cubs have never been in a real fight," McGraw told a sympathetic writer for *Sporting Life* the following week, taunting Chance, his favorite target. "So long as things are breaking well there are some players who do brilliant work, but when luck turns and they are forced to fight every day they give way under the strain." Then macho Muggsy laid down his gauntlet: "Whether the Cubs are fighters has yet to be proven. If they are not fighters, there is not a chance for them to win a close race."

The Cubs lost another three out of four games when they traveled to New York in June. The teams split their next four-game matchup in Chicago in mid-July. On Tuesday, August 11, which started out as a fair, sunny day, an estimated thirty-five thousand fans lured by the promise of a doubleheader filled up the Polo Grounds beyond its capacity more than an hour before game time. "It was without doubt the greatest midweek crowd that had ever seen a baseball contest in the United States," an *Inter-Ocean* reporter gaped. Another ten thousand to fifteen thousand screaming partisans crammed onto Coogan's Bluff, the 175-foot escarpment overlooking the hollow of land along the Harlem River, at 155th Street and 8th Avenue.

Then the clouds appeared and unloaded a crowd-drenching downpour in the middle of the first contest. The Cubs won the rain-shortened game, 4–0, behind the rock-solid pitching of "Giant Killer" Pfiester. Once again, McGraw took an early shower, ejected in the fourth inning. "He was like a madman," according to the *Inter Ocean*. "Mac tried every means of vituperation to get the goats of the visitors after they had forged to the front." The *Tribune*'s I. E. Sanborn recounted one of the more civil exchanges between the two managers: "Muggsy shouted at the Peerless Leader: 'You've got a bunch of Germans with their heads down.' To which Chance retorted: 'Aw, why don't you go out and pay some of the debts you owe.'"

The victory left Chicago with a 57–42 record, good enough only for third place, a game and a half behind New York and trailing Pittsburgh by a full four games. During the next two weeks, the Cubs would claw their way back into contention with nine straight wins. But the Giants and Pirates were winning, too.

THE GILL AFFAIR

It had been a few weeks since the "Inquisitive Fans" column had planted the seed of the rule-book insurrection that Johnny Evers would soon incite. The Crab found his opening in September when the Cubs were visiting the Pirates at Exposition Park. The Pirates, Cubs, and Giants were still locked in a three-way race for the pennant with only four weeks to go in the season.

Umpiring that afternoon was Henry M. "Hank" O'Day, one of the most experienced and respected arbiters of his era. A native of Chicago, O'Day was a baseball man through and through, one of the few umpires in history to play and manage in the big leagues as well as adjudicate. He was loner by nature, never married, and showed little interest in anything but baseball—a "misanthropic Irishman," one fellow umpire called him. O'Day did not like being challenged by ballplayers or managers. Arguing with him, said mild-mannered Christy Mathewson, was like "using a lit match to see how much gasoline was in a fuel tank." Even so, it was generally allowed that O'Day had the courage to make a tough call no matter how unpopular, and no matter who was doing the arguing. As was customary, O'Day was the only umpire working the game, a point of contention for Cubs owner C. W. Murphy, who had been unable to persuade his fellow barons to pony up the expense of two umps for every game.

This day had seen a corker of a pitching matchup. Miner Brown had a shutout going through nine innings, but the Pirates' Fred Willis had also put up goose eggs, so the score was tied at zero going into the bottom of the tenth. The sun was fading when Fred Clarke reached base on an error. The next batter dutifully laid down a sacrifice bunt in front of Brown to move Clarke into scoring position at second. The great Honus Wagner came to the plate next, his Popeye arms flexed and cowpuncher's legs bowed. Wagner was as fearsome as any hitter alive. The "Flying Dutchman" promptly slapped a curveball toward right field, a sharp grounder that Evers could only knock down with his glove hand. Clarke might have scored but the coach at third "lost his nerve," according to a local scribe, and threw up a stop sign. Evers hurried throw to the plate let Wagner advance to second.

The next batter was rookie first baseman Warren "Doc" Gill. He should have been easy pickings for Brown's stub-fingered curveball, but on the second pitch Brown spun a slow hook right into Gill's leg, sending the kid to first. The bases were full, with only one out. Brown snuck a curveball past the next batter for a called strike three. Two outs, with John Owen "Chief" Wilson, another rookie, coming to bat. "What did this recent graduate from the minors do but soak the first ball Brown pitched him on the nose," reported Sanborn in the *Tribune*.

Wilson's smash whistled past Evers and the ball dropped safely into short center.

Clarke trotted home easily, as could have the speedy Wagner if his run were needed. But it wasn't, so Wagner headed straight to the bench as many of the eight thousand fans poured down onto the field to congratulate their hero, Chief Wilson, as he touched first. "Everybody thought, of course, the game was over and started for the clubhouse," Sanborn observed. O'Day watched Clarke cross the plate and, satisfied that the game-winning run had scored, headed for a drink of water from a faucet and hose behind home plate. He did not turn around, did not see—did not seem to care—that the runner who had been at first, Doc Gill, had also presumed victory and slowed halfway between first and second before turning away toward the sidelines.

The only person who did care was Johnny Evers. "Evers, seeing Gill's break for the bench, yelled for Slagle to throw in the ball," according to Sanborn, who watched the entire scene. "Jimmy did and Evers touched second base with it, then wheeled to claim a force out on Gill, only to see Umpire O'Day making fast tracks for an exit with his back turned completely to what had been pulled off."

Evers ran over to O'Day to make his case—heatedly—that Gill was out and therefore the inning should be over and Clarke's run nullified. O'Day would hear none of it. "He wouldn't even wait for argument or to ascertain the real facts, which he probably did not grasp at this time," according to Sanborn. Evers would remember O'Day's words to him long afterward: "Cut it out, Johnny. The game is over." Evers shot back: "It isn't over until that man touches second base! Why don't you wait until the game is over, you big fat head."

They didn't part friends. Evers believed O'Day was mad at him for his constant kicking that summer, but he kept his beef going all the way to the hotel and into the night. Murphy got wind of it and decided to use the occasion to revive his long-argued point to the league that one umpire couldn't cover the entire field of play.

The next morning Murphy filed a formal protest with the NL's president Pulliam, including testimony from several witnesses to back up Evers's account. "Chicago claims Gill should have touched second base before he ran to the clubhouse, and will prove by affidavits . . . that he failed to do so," stated his telegram to the league's headquarters.

Pulliam, chief champion of the umpire's absolute authority on the field, was not about to countermand his man on the scene. After calling O'Day for his account, Pulliam issued a statement: "The umpire in this case, by allowing the winning run, ruled that there was no force at second, because if there had been the run could not have been scored. The protest is denied." End of story.

Except for one thing: by rejecting the Cubs' protest, Pulliam endorsed the old Chadwick concept that a run cannot be counted on a forced third out. As Pulliam stated plainly to Murphy: If there had been a force-out, "the run could not have been scored." With these fateful words, Pulliam essentially forced his own hand on an almost identical—and much more consequential—play in New York just days later. Even O'Day half admitted in a hotel lobby argument with Evers and Tinker that he may have missed the call, and while he bore Evers no love, he signaled that he might rule differently if the circumstance should arise again.

The next time Pulliam, O'Day, and Evers would show up to the same ballpark, the Cubs would get their chance to put Chadwick's arcane concept to its ultimate test.

A PEERLESS PEP TALK

By mid-September in this seesaw race, Chicago and Pittsburgh had each fallen three games behind New York when the Cubs traveled to Philadelphia for a series against the fourth-place Phillies. After they dropped the first game, 2–1 in ten innings, they learned that the Giants had just beaten St. Louis, leaving Chicago now four and a half games back with only seventeen to play. The players were dejected and feeling hopeless on the ride back to their hotel, according to Evers. "We were pretty thoroughly licked that evening," he said. "We didn't have a thing to say, for it seemed that our last hope had vanished and that we could not possibly get into the World Series."

Tinker broke the silence, addressing Chance: "Well, Cap, we are done and we might as well celebrate our losing tonight." Chance looked up, paused a moment, then locked eyes on his teammates. "No, we won't," said the battle-tested trail boss. "Boys, we have been pretty good winners. Now let's show the people that we can be good losers. Let's show them that we never give up; that we are never beaten. Let's show them we play as hard when we lose as when we win, and that we fight for the pure love of fighting, whether it means victory or defeat." Evers, who often chafed under Chance's overbearing direction, remained forever in the Peerless Leader's corner after that speech. "Chance is without an equal in putting fight into a team," he said.

Whether Chance uttered those exact words or Evers later embellished them, the effect was breathtaking. The already-exhausted Cubs went on to play three doubleheaders in the next three days, four games in Philadelphia on September 19–20 and two more in New York on September 21. Except for a 0–0, ten-inning tie game suspended by darkness in the first twin bill, they won all of them.

The nightcap of the Giants' doubleheader crystalized for Chicago fans the merits of having Frank Chance in charge. His hand grew steadier the more McGraw went haywire. "The whole Chicago team is clever, machine-like, and game," commented the *New York Evening World*, impressed with Chance's situational play calling—sacrifice bunts, stolen bases, and the like—while disdaining McGraw's failures at his own small-ball tactics. McGraw, meanwhile, kept resorting to other gimmicks, like warming up one starting pitcher but replacing him with another just before the first pitch. (The substitute got pummeled anyway.) "The 'Napoleon of baseball' was outgeneraled all the way yesterday," observed the McGraw-hating *Chicago Daily News*, "and to his bad judgment may be charged the loss of the second game."

Charles Dryden best captured the new sense of optimism that seeped into the Cubs clubhouse and once again infected its fan base. "Tonight the walls of despair floating over Harlem cracked the ancient rocks of Coogan's Bluff, but what do the Cubs care for that?" he smirked. "To the victors belong the glad noise."

A MAN NAMED MERKLE

The Cubs had inched to within a half game of the Giants by winning the doubleheader. A victory on Wednesday afternoon would leapfrog the Cubs into first place with only a week and a half to go. Everyone assumed the next two games would decide the pennant. (To Murphy's delight, Pulliam even assigned two umpires to the series: Hank O'Day and Bob Emslie.) The sense of anticipation was palpable in both cities. The *Chicago Tribune* placed a three-column advertisement in the sports section announcing that its electric scoreboard would reproduce "every play of the game" as it happened in New York.

Chance had used up Miner Brown's arm in Tuesday's double bill, so he threw Jack Pfiester out to face Mathewson. Though no longer a consistent winner, Pfiester was 4–2 against McGraw's club so far that season. But Mathewson was on his way to one of his best seasons: thirty-seven wins against only eleven losses, with a league-leading 1.43 ERA. Eleven of his wins were shutouts.

Four innings breezed by without a run and only a couple of base-runners. Then Joe Tinker came up in the fifth and did what he often managed to do with Mathewson's drop curves. He drove the ball "like a cannon shot" over the second baseman and deep into right center, past right fielder "Turkey Mike" Donlin. The ball bounded to the back of the yard and Tinker sped around the bases for an inside-the-park home run. Turkey Mike redeemed himself two innings later when he singled home Buck Herzog, who had reached third on a Steinfeldt throwing error and a sacrifice bunt. That tied the score, 1–1, where it stayed through two and a half more innings.

The Giants mounted a charge in the bottom of the ninth. Pfiester induced a ground out for one away, but then gave up a single to Art Devlin. Moose McCormick followed with a "grass cutter" to Evers, who flipped to Tinker for a force at second, but they had no time to get McCormick at first. There may have been a reason for that. "Tinker did not like the way Devlin came into the bag," noted one reporter on the scene. "The two had some words and bristled up to each other pugnaciously." The New York partisans were getting agitated, as if they weren't already, and gave the Cubs players another earful of jeers.

To the plate next came a little-used and less-known rookie named Fred Merkle. Within minutes his name would go into the history books with a label that still lives in infamy.

Just nineteen years old, Merkle was a late season call-up from the minors and had played in only thirty or so big league games. Born in Watertown, Wisconsin, to German-immigrant parents, Merkle had played high school baseball in Toledo, Ohio, and he had a reputation as a bright, aggressive ballplayer—a "gentleman and scholar" and a "voracious reader." He was also an aggressive baserunner during his long tenure with McGraw and the Giants, which lasted through 1915.

Standing tall at six feet, one inch, yet to fill into his 190-pound playing weight, Merkle surprised everyone, especially Pfiester, by plugging a hard drive into right field. It landed deep enough to get McCormick around to third. Everyone in the Polo Grounds could sense that the Giants were getting ready to make the kill. Two outs, runners on first and third, the crowd going wild, Cubs in a jam.

"Then came the bone-headed finish," wrote Dryden for the *Tribune*, "which left the bugs puzzled and wondering." What actually happened has been challenged, debated, gnawed at, chewed over, regurgitated, and then rehashed for more than a century, from the moment the bizarre sequence unfolded to the present day. Reporters and other eyewitnesses took sides from the start, depending on their hometown allegiances. The actors on the field all replayed it for newspaper accounts in the following days and for the historical record for decades afterward. Historians have sifted through the testimony and inspected the sketchy evidence. Yet even today, no one seems able to say with certainty what happened at the Polo Grounds on the afternoon of September 23 in the bottom of the ninth inning. And yet, if one evokes the holy writ of Father Chadwick, then heeds the parable of Pittsburgh's Warren Gill of nineteen days prior, and credits the lawyerly homework of Johnny Evers, it's self-evident that this moment of baseball lore and its startling outcome were inevitable, if not preordained.

The next batter to face Pfiester was Al Bridwell, the Giants' shortstop. Left-hander Pfiester worked from a stretch, less worried about Merkle facing him at first than he was about keeping McCormick, the potential game-winning run, from wandering too far off third base behind him. On Pfiester's first offering to the plate, Bridwell swung hard and made contact. The ball sailed over Pfiester's head, just out of reach. It almost hit the midfield umpire, knocking him off balance. Bridwell had "pasted a neat but not gaudy single to center," as Dryden drily phrased it.

From third, McCormick had bolted for home at the crack of Bridwell's bat, seemingly scoring the winning run, to loud and mad delirium from the New York fans. The horde rose up as one and rushed the field to hoist McCormick and Bridwell on their shoulders. The Giants on the sidelines—Mathewson, Herzog, Tenney, Donlin, Devlin, and others—didn't hesitate, all bolting from their bench toward their clubhouse in right field, desperate to elude the clutches of the victory-crazed mob. There may have been fewer than ten thousand fans present that day, "but the crowd looked bigger when the tumult broke loose on the field," Dryden reported.

Meanwhile, the earnest, fresh-faced Fred Merkle, following in the footsteps of Doc Gill and countless rule-book-oblivious ballplayers before him, watched from just off of first base and doubtlessly leaped with a child's glee as he saw McCormick cross home plate. Merkle could also see the rabid fans climbing over the railings and pouring onto the field. He could see his teammates racing for cover in right field. His instincts must have told him to follow their lead, so he took advantage of his head start. Still only halfway between first and second, Merkle veered right and hightailed it for safety.

John J. Evers Jr., who like any good litigator knew better than to ask a question he didn't already know the answer to, leaped to attention. His fully prepped partners, Frank Chance, Joe Tinker, and Harry Steinfeldt, also jumped into action, as did Arthur "Circus Solly" Hoffman, the backup center fielder known for his acrobatic catches and swift feet, though perhaps not for so accurate a throwing arm.

Evers watched Merkle recede into the outfield, then rushed over to second base, arms waving frantically. "Solly! Solly!" he shouted. The alert Hoffman raced in to pick up the ball, firing it as hard as he could toward Evers's waiting glove. His throw didn't come close its target.

Watching the scene from the coach's box at first base was the Giants' other star pitcher, Joe "Iron Man" McGinnity, a ten-year veteran and future Hall of Famer. He had quickly wised up to Evers's nefarious plot, so he, too, jumped into action. Circus Solly's chuck sailed high over Evers's head, into the infield, hitting Tinker in the back and falling to the ground somewhere between second and third. Evers kept screaming for the ball at second base. McGinnity rushed onto the madcap infield, where Pfiester, Chance, Tinker, and Steinfeldt were all lunging for the ball among the legs and feet of the fans. Somehow the Iron Man got hold of it.

Whether out of instinct or instant premeditation, or both, McGinnity tried to heave the ball into the grandstand. But Tinker, or maybe it was Pfiester, happened to be tightly wrapped around McGinnity's arms, so his toss couldn't travel far. The ball fell somewhere near the sideline bullpen amid the sea of reveling New Yorkers and, as fate would have it, a Cubs relief pitcher. Someone there—a fan, most likely, though no one knows who—reached down and grabbed the ball, or *a* ball. No one is quite sure since there was also a bag of used balls lying around in the bullpen for warm-up use. Whatever it was this man had in his clutches, he wasn't about to let go of it.

Steinfeldt and Floyd "Rube" Kroh, the rookie southpaw in the Cubs bullpen, raced up to the nameless fan and screamed at him to give up his prized possession. He refused. So Kroh "solved the problem," said Evers, by slamming his fist down on top of the man's head, smashing his stiff brown derby over his eyes. "As the gent folded up, the ball fell free and Kroh got it," Evers recalled. Kroh picked the ball up, or picked *something* up, or perhaps it was Steinfeldt, or even Tinker, one of whom ran toward second and flipped the ball, or—again, *a* ball—to Evers.

The man of the hour, standing on second with a swarm of New York bugs buzzing around him, held *this* ball high over his head to show umpire Bob Emslie, the second ump working that day, that he had forced out Merkle. But Emslie, who was already getting an earful from Frank

Chance about the whole proceedings, claimed ignorance of the actual play at second because of his stumble and his subsequent efforts to keep his eyes on Bridwell's hit into the outfield.

Evers turned his gaze toward home plate. Running toward him was Hank O'Day—yes, that Hank O'Day, perhaps the most astute baseball adjudicator of his day, a native of Chicago but no particular lover of the Cubs, arch nemesis of Crab Evers for sure, and most recently a veteran of the Warren Gill affair in Pittsburgh. This time O'Day had seen everything, and Evers knew that O'Day knew what he knew.

That's when all hell broke loose.

Frank Chance swooped down on O'Day and insisted that McCormick's run did not count, that the score remained tied after three outs, and that the playing field must be cleared so the game could proceed into extra innings. O'Day seemed to agree. But by then hundreds, if not thousands, of fans "had swarmed upon the diamond like an army of starving potato bugs," according to Dryden. Enough fans, easily egged on by McGinnity's protests and Muggsy's standby crew of private security goons, had gotten wind that something had suddenly turned sour, and they fixed their ire on the umpires.

The mob surrounded O'Day before he had time to gather his wits. "Those within reach began pounding him on all available exposed parts not covered by the protector, while the unfortunate attackers on the outskirts began sending messages by way of cushions, newspapers, and other missiles," according to a *New York Herald* reporter. A "flying squadron" of city police rushed in and barely managed to get the umps to safety under the grandstand. "He had to run for it," Evers said of O'Day. "So did the rest of us."

O'Day testified later that he had already reckoned that even if he and Emslie could have managed to restore order, the fading sunlight would have disappeared by then. So he had decided (no doubt as he and Emslie were running for their lives) to suspend the game anyway.

By rule, then, a tie game suspended due to darkness or other non-weather-related causes must be replayed in its entirety, not from where it left off. (Suspended games were a recurring feature of Wrigley Field until the Cubs finally installed lights there in 1988.) Chance and C. W.

Murphy were not about to let the Giants off the hook so easily. They argued vociferously that the home team had an obligation to clear the field, and by failing to do so, the Giants should have to forfeit the game to the Cubs, an automatic 9–0 score. But by this time O'Day and Emslie had been spirited away.

The first newspaper accounts of the game carried different scores, depending on whether it was a Chicago or New York publication. "Bridwell's Hit Wins for Giants; Riot Follows at Polo Grounds," insisted the *New York Evening World* in its late edition, declaring that the Giants had won, 2–1. The *New York Herald* and the *New York Times* were more circumspect the next morning, hedging on the outcome. But the *Chicago Tribune*'s banner headline over Dryden's dispatch had it the other way: "Battle of Cubs and Giants Ends in Row. Umpire Calling It No Contest." The *Pittsburgh Post*, fully aware of the precedent that Evers, O'Day, and league President Pulliam had established on its home turf two weeks earlier, stayed neutral: "Chicago and Giants Mix Up in the Ninth; Protest Game." Almost every newspaper in the country carried some version of the story. Way out in Phoenix, the Arizona *Republic* gave the game page-one play under the headline "The Verge of a Riot."

Oddly enough, many people in New York had remained oblivious to the Warren Gill affair in Pittsburgh. The *New York Globe* was the only New York paper to mention the Cubs' protest at the time, but with no explanation. Word of the Gill affair had gradually slinked along the baseball grapevine to some New York insiders, including Christy Mathewson; but not to young Merkle, obviously, or even to McGraw, the great baseball trick artist—who, if he'd known, surely would have browbeaten his young charges to stay on guard against Evers.

McGraw's flacks in the press were spitting bile. The Cubs were protesting the game on a "cowardly technicality," fumed Sam Crane in the *New York Evening Journal*. The *New York Herald* lectured the next day: "An enormous baseball custom has had it from time immemorial that as soon as the winning run has crossed the plate everyone adjourns as hastily and yet nicely as possible to the clubhouse and exits."

Chicagoans, as one might expect, took a dim view of New York's grievance. The *Tribune*'s I. E. Sanborn, who covered the Pittsburgh game but was not in New York for the Merkle episode, gave no quarter: "Outside of Manhattan island, where baseball is considered a national pastime and not a form of paying tribute to New York, it is a recognized fact that the Giants lost that victory over the Cubs by a blunder."

An hour or so after the game, umpire O'Day confirmed to Chance and McGraw that McCormick's run did not count, and that their game had ended in a 1–1 tie. The two teams were already scheduled to play again the next afternoon, and so could have replayed the game then as part of another doubleheader. But Murphy and Chance let Pulliam know they would insist on a forfeit and appeal O'Day's decision on those grounds. That made it impossible to schedule a makeup game the next day.

COURTS OF APPEAL

The wheels of justice moved slowly, and inexorably, over the course of the next few hours and days. Pulliam had been at the Polo Grounds and witnessed "the scene of great confusion," as he called it, even if he did not discern the precise movements of the players and umpires. Pulliam, now thirty-nine years old, handsome, and still an eligible bachelor, was described as "an idealist, a dreamer, and a lover of solitude and nature." He was an eccentric dresser, one reporter said, as "all the colors of the rainbow were utilized by him in the color scheme of his fancy waistcoats." Other couched descriptors said he had "never been associated with any woman." Pulliam's relationship with the NL magnates was tenuous, at best. He was, however, decisive, firm in his convictions, and true to his word.

On the evening of the Merkle game, Pulliam called O'Day and Emslie to his residence at the New York Athletic Club. The umpires gave him their accounts, and O'Day scratched out a handwritten memo giving his version of events: "The ball was fielded in to 2nd base for a Chicago man to make the play, when McGinnity ran from the coacher's box out in the field to 2nd base and interfered with the play being made.

Emslie, who said he did not watch Merkle, asked me if Merkle touched second base. I said he did not. Then Emslie called Merkle out, and I would not allow McCormick's run to score." Pulliam didn't reveal his thinking at the time, but he did say that any formal appeal to the umpire's original decision would draw the process out another five days to give both teams time to respond.

Ironically, the next day the Giants beat the Cubs, 5–4, in the rivals' last regularly scheduled matchup of the season, putting New York in sole possession of first place. The day after that, however, McGraw's club dropped both games of a doubleheader with lowly Cincinnati, while the Cubs defeated Brooklyn. The Pirates were still running neck and neck with the Cubs and Giants for the top spot going into the final hours of the season.

Pulliam continued to seek testimony from players, including the upright Christy Mathewson, who initially asserted that he had personally escorted Merkle back to second base before the ball reached Evers. Pulliam rightly discounted such "memories." Pulliam had little room to maneuver, since in the Gill affair he had already established the legality of Evers's force play and had already established the umpire's on-field authority. Moreover, he knew that O'Day's ruling was founded upon the Gill precedent. As long as O'Day's ruling conformed with baseball's rules, Pulliam would not countermand him.

Over the rest of his career, O'Day rarely discussed the Merkle play. But he did confirm something in his first public comments, six years after the event, that sheds light on his ruling. Never a fan of Evers, O'Day insisted to the *Chicago Tribune* that the Little Trojan shouldn't get credit for what had transpired. The decision to nullify McCormick's run, O'Day maintained, was not based on Evers touching second. Rather, said O'Day, he and Emslie made the ruling because Joe McGinnity had illegally entered the field and interfered with the play. Consequently, the dispute over whether the ball that Evers finally received was the original is moot, since the run was nullified upon McGinnity's infraction. Finally, "If McGinnity's interference had not given us that clear point to rule on[,] the credit for the play on Merkle would have gone to Hoffman," O'Day said, since Hoffman "threw the ball in when most fielders, following custom, would have kept it and fled to the clubhouse, in the belief that the game was over."

In other words, McGinnity was the real culprit, for trying an old-school trick that might have been tolerated in the 1890s, when Mc-Graw's goons ruled the baseball roost. The only question in O'Day's telling was whether Merkle had touched second base before the Iron Man touched the loose ball in the infield. What O'Day failed to mention, of course, was the legal precept that Evers had first prosecuted: that the game itself is not over when the runner crosses home, but only after the forced runner (Gill, Merkle) touches the next base. Merkle's failure to do that kept the play "live" during McGinnity's blatantly illegal run onto the field.

Pulliam had no choice but to back O'Day's remedy as well as his judgment. On Friday, October 2, he handed down his ruling, expressly citing rule 59 and the Pittsburgh precedent as the underpinning of his reasoning. Pulliam affirmed the tie game and ordered it replayed at the end of the regular season *if* the two clubs were still tied for first place.

There remained one last court of appeal: the National League's Board of Directors. League bylaws stipulated that this body could overrule a league president's decision, but only by unanimous vote. Garry Herrmann, owner of the Reds; George Dovey, owner of the Boston Doves, and Charlie Ebbets of Brooklyn served as a supreme court. The three men agreed to meet in Cincinnati on Monday, the day after the Cubs and Pirates would close their seasons with a game in Chicago.

In the meantime, the teams and their fans could only wait. "A hush fell upon 80,000,000 people," lamented an overwrought reporter for the *New York Evening Mail*. "The wheels of industry had ceased their whirr . . . husbands halted on their homeward ways, wives let the dinner grow cold . . . in a stilled and silent wait for the decision on that tie game." The debate raged on, but New York partisans gradually lost the battle for public opinion. A few McGraw apologists like Crane of the *New York Evening Journal* kept carping about the "technicality" of the Merkle play, but the more other New Yorkers learned about the rules, the more they questioned the basis of the Giants' grievance. The editorial board of the *New York Times* opined that O'Day's decision "seems to an unprejudiced outsider fair and impartial," adding that Merkle clearly should have known better. "Such an error of judgment could scarcely be overlooked in an amateur sport. It would be foolish to expect professional players to overlook it."

THE SEASON WINDS DOWN

On Sunday, as Chicago hosted the Pirates at West Side Grounds, 30,247 "maddened" fans showed up to cheer on their Cubs. Hugh Fullerton, now a roving correspondent for Hearst's *New York American*, was on hand. "Before the greatest crowd that ever saw a baseball game, the teams engaged in one of the most desperate and determined games in the history of baseball," he wrote.

New York could stay alive only if Chicago were to beat the Pirates and the Giants won all three of their remaining games against the Doves. A Pirate win over Chicago would end the season for both the Cubs and the Giants. So, New Yorkers did what they had to do—they rooted for the Cubs. Some 3,500 Giants fans made their way that day to the Polo Grounds, where the Cubs-Pirates game was reproduced on two electric scoreboards placed near home plate. "By following the twinkling of small bulbs the fan could figure out play by play," reported a somewhat astounded *New York Evening World*.

In the event, the Cubs won, 5–2, behind Brown's pitching and offense, helped by the defensive handiwork of Evers, Tinker, and especially Chance. With the scored tied at 2–2 in the sixth, Tinker drove a two-out pitch into the standing-room-only crowd in left field, a ground-rule double on a ball that might have been a triple, Fullerton said. Pirates manager Fred Clarke ordered a free pass to Johnny Kling to get to the next batter, pitcher Brown. The proud Hoosier took offense at this disregard for his batting skills—"Brown is one of those men who get mad when others affect to despise them," said Fullerton—and promptly lined a "screaming" single to right. That scored Tinker and gave Chicago the lead for good.

A couple of neat defense stops by Tinker and Evers in the late innings kept the Pirates from mounting a comeback. Then Chance delivered the decisive stop in the eighth "with one of the most astounding plays ever made," according to Fullerton, never easily impressed. Third-baseman Tommy Leach, batting just ahead of the fearsome Wagner, belted a hard line drive over first base, a surefire double, except for Chance's running, diving leap to his left, snaring the ball while spinning backward toward the outfield. The game ended an inning later when Tinker calmly grabbed a hard bounder to short and flipped to Evers at second for the forced third out. "Chicago outplayed, outhit and outran the Pirates," Fullerton wrote. "They won the game on class and nerve, and demonstrated that they have the best ball team in the league."

The outcome in Chicago put no fear in New Yorkers, however. On news of the final out, fans at the Polo Grounds shook hands all around. "The Giants will get them yet," they beamed.

The Giants put down the Doves following afternoon, 8–1, and won again the day after, 4–1, leaving their record at 97–55, just one win behind the Cubs, at 98–55. Later that night, Herrmann, Dovey, and Ebbets agreed to affirm Pulliam's ruling: Merkle out, run nullified, game tied. If New York ended the season on Wednesday with another win—and the same record as the Cubs—the Giants and Cubs would replay the Merkle game on Thursday, October 8, in the Polo Grounds, to decide the pennant.

The directors were not kind to Merkle: "There is no question but that the game should have been won by New York had it not been for the reckless, careless, inexcusable blunder of one player, Merkle," their joint statement read. Sportswriters, fans, and historians have vacillated over the various accounts of the play ever since, but history's verdict has been severe: it is today and will forever be known as "Merkle's boner."

A year later, Dovey would reveal confidentially to a *New York Tribune* writer, W. J. Macbeth, that he, Ebbets, and Herrmann had been "up a tree" until they came to a sworn statement by Christy Mathewson that contradicted his earlier account. "Mathewson swore that Merkle did not touch second base," Macbeth said Dovey said. Macbeth didn't publish Dovey's account until years later, after Dovey's death.

McGraw and Brush thought they had gotten the raw end of the deal, but they agreed to show up for the single playoff game if needed. The Giants then blitzed Boston, 7–2, on Wednesday, October 7, to force a final showdown with Chicago the next afternoon at the Polo Grounds. The stage was set for one of the biggest, meanest, and most violent baseball grudge matches of all time.

THE PLAYOFF GAME

On Wednesday afternoon, Frank Chance and the Chicago Cubs boarded the Twentieth Century Limited out of downtown Chicago, destination New York City. They would sleep on the train during the eighteen hour trip, "the fastest train ever taken by a baseball club," the *Tribune* assured its readers. They would arrive at 9:30 the next morning, in time to "catch their baseball legs" and prepare for the winner-take-all playoff game at 3 p.m.

As the train sped toward Manhattan, the Cubs displayed an air of quiet confidence. The "champs" had boarded the train "as if they were going on the sweetest sort of a pleasure jaunt," according to the *Inter Ocean*. Chance sought to reassure the reporters with them that fans had nothing to fear. "Whoever heard of the Cubs losing a game they had to have?" Husk asked.

Many Cubs fans couldn't believe this reprise of the Merkle game was needed at all. "If the Cubs don't win the pennant—tragedy! Despair, insanity, suicide, coroner's inquest," cried a prophecy attributed to the city coroner Peter M. Hoffman. "Why, to tell you the truth, I shouldn't be surprised if we had a suicide or two right here in this office," he winked. Giants fans were also working themselves into a tizzy in anticipation of yet another do-or-die moment. "That the game will be a struggle to the death is certain," announced the jittery *New York Her-*

ald. "The town is in the grip of the greatest excitement, fringed with nervous prostration. It is rumored that several sanitariums are constructing additions to take care of baseball 'bugs.'"

Fans were lining up at the gates of the Polo Grounds long before the Cubs' train pulled into New York on Thursday morning. A special overnight watch of security men had been guarding the bleachers and "spent most of the night digging small boys from under seats," reported the *New York Times.* The first ticket seekers got there by daylight, shivering in the morning frost, and within hours, hundreds of people were "clinging to the outside of the tall yellow gates that guard the entrance like bats to rafters." By 10 a.m. they numbered a thousand, an hour later at least seven thousand, by one reporter's estimate. Each quarter hour delivered hundreds, if not thousands, more from the trolleys and elevated trains that served the ballpark.

The early arrivals were droplets in a bucket compared with the deluge to come. When the doors opened at noon, a sea of fans came streaming through. By 12:45 p.m., more than two hours before game time, "the last inch" of standing and sitting room had been filled, reported the *New York Times,* which estimated the crowd at thirty-five thousand to forty-thousand people. That was far more than capacity, so it wasn't long before thousands of people who had crammed into aisles and passageways burst over the barriers guarding the field.

Many scrambled for a better vantage point behind the ropes in the oblong stadium's cavernous center field. Hundreds more climbed up to the high-pitched roof of the grandstand and claimed precarious viewing spots far above the diamond. Orders came to close the outside gates, locking everyone inside, as yet another crush of people—thousands of paid ticket holders among them—were still trying to gain entry.

And still they came. By midafternoon, as many as 250,000 people had mustered inside and outside the ballpark, according to various newspaper and police estimates. "Toward the sky the crowd seemed to pile, and over the highest fringe of fans reared the 155th Street Viaduct and Coogan's Bluff, higher yet and dense with men, women and children," according to the *Times.* The view from the press box, added the *New York Evening Telegram*'s correspondent, showed "the skyline everywhere was human heads," their faces peering down from roofs, fences, train tracks, and light poles, and even in the far distance, on smokestacks, chimneys, advertising signs, and apartment buildings. A fireman named Henry T. McBride wanted to see the game so badly he climbed an elevated train pillar, but lost his grip and fell to an instant death, "his vacant place quickly filled."

The Cubs players arrived well before game time and, fearing for their safety, furtively made their way to the visitors' clubhouse to dress and get some batting practice. The taunts began as soon as Chance and his charges emerged on the field in uniform. "Robber," "bandit," "quitter," the crowd howled. Chance acted as if nothing was out of the ordinary. "Roars, hoots, hisses, jeers are showered upon him as he advances, but he smiles pleasantly as if the freedom of the city had been conferred upon him," nodded the *Chicago Tribune*.

Onto the field marched McGraw and his troops, producing an even greater roar. The crowd urged each Giant to doff his cap before they would let up their collective yells. "It puts you in your blood all right. All right," said one fan to another. They hurled more epithets the Cubs' way: "O, you robbers! You brigands!"

With both teams on the field, ready to play, the gamesmanship began.

By custom, Frank Chance had waited until the Giants finished their twenty-minute batting practice before calling his players onto the field. But the umpires, without his knowledge, had decided to start the game fifteen minutes early, at 2:45. Only five minutes into the Cubs' practice session, Iron Man McGinnity, bat in hand, approached Chance and re-claimed his right to the plate for fielding practice. Chance refused to be bullied, standing erect and brushing up to McGinnity, who said something harsh in return and then spit at him. Iron Man raised his bat as if to strike Chance's head. "The fighting blood is up," the *Tribune* reporter feared. Several players from both teams saw what was happening and rushed to home plate, while spectators hushed in anticipation of a pre-game brawl. "Instantly the Polo Grounds are aflame."

What happened next remains in dispute. New York witnesses said McGraw walked up to the budding fracas and quickly calmed things down, ordering McGinnity to back off. But Chance and other Cubs suspected something more nefarious at work, and they were convinced that the Cubs had barely avoided a lethal trap. McGinnity was a decoy, they insisted, sent up to provoke Chance because McGraw wasn't going to start his No. 2 pitcher that day anyway, and so could afford to lose Iron Man to an ejection if they could get Chance thrown out (or injured) in the bargain.

But Chance had been tipped off. The Giants had a "dozen prizefighters" waiting in the wings to jump in and "cripple several of our men before the game," he told the *San Francisco Chronicle* two months later. "The starting of the fight would have been the signal for them to jump in."

Mordecai Brown and Joe Tinker both had gotten wind of the ruse, which a Giants player owned up to years later. "Muggsy McGraw was laying a plot to beat us," Brown recalled. Earlier, in the clubhouse, Chance had told his team: "Cross 'em up. No matter when the bell rings to end practice, come right off the field. Don't give any excuse to quarrel." Once McGinnity raised his bat on Chance at home plate, Brown said, "Husk stepped back, grinned and wouldn't fall for their little game." Yet again, Frank Chance had won the day, according to his troops, and earned their eternal admiration. They gave him full credit for showing calm leadership in one of the most pressure-filled situations of their careers.

Finally, it was time to settle this feud with a baseball game.

PLAY BALL

The game itself was anticlimactic, though it also proved to be cathartic for the forty thousand partisans inside the stadium and the more than two hundred thousand watching, listening, or just kvetching outside. "When the word came, 'Play,' a silence fell over all," recounted the *Inter Ocean*, whose correspondent described the general mood as "a tenseness which could be felt." Thousands of cowbells and horns went silent. The game was on. "It held the crowd by a spell."

The Cubs played quietly through the first inning, offering two lazy fly-ball outs by Sheckard and Schulte, sandwiched around Evers's ground out to second—a quick one-two-three inning. The Cubs would not be so efficient in the Giants' half; the first ball Pfiester delivered to Ed Tenney plunked him on the arm for a free pass to first base. Tenney soon came around to score the game's first run on a liner over first base that Chance tried to contest as foul. No dice, said umpire Bill Klem. Giants led 1–0, still only two outs.

A subsequent base on balls by Pfiester was all Chance needed to learn about the Giant Killer's arm that day. He called time out and, without hesitation, took the sore-armed lefty out of the game. Chance signaled for his workhorse, Mordecai Brown, who ignored a shower of boos and hisses as he walked confidently from bullpen to pitcher's box, two runners on base to contend with, and dangerous hitter Art Devlin at the plate.

"Unconscious of everything, careless in his bearing," Sanborn described Brown's dramatic entrance, "the man who had faced and touched off many a death dealing blast in the depths of Indiana's coal mines walked to his position, hurled a few balls to Kling to assure himself of his accurate aim. Then he was ready!" Despite having pitched more than three hundred innings already that year, winning twenty-five of his thirty-one starts and doing double duty by saving another five games as the league's top relief pitcher, Brown's three-fingered curveball hadn't lost any of its mystery. The big right-hander promptly struck out Devlin.

After the relative calm, the second inning riled both benches and stirred up the crowd again. Chance walked to the plate under a storm of hisses—"not boos, like you hear in modern baseball," Brown recalled, "but the old, vicious hiss that comes from real hatred." Chance couldn't have cared less, Brown said, and "choked the hisses back down New York's throat" by sending a line drive into right field for a single. But Chance then did something quite stupid: He wandered too far off first base and let Mathewson get the jump on him. As Chance dived back to the bag, umpire Klem threw up his arm, "Out!" That jolted the crowd, which mocked Chance without mercy. Matty proceeded to strike out the next two batters. The Cubs put up another zero on the scoreboard.

But the steady Brown quieted the restive multitude in the bottom of the second, inducing two harmless fly balls and a ground out. The Cubs badly needed a rally in the top of the third inning, and fortunately the first batter would be Joe Tinker. No doubt Mathewson had to take a deep breath. Once upon a time, Tinker was "putty in my hands," Mathewson would say in the opening sentences of his autobiography, published just a few years later. For two years Matty considered Tinker the least dangerous hitter in the Cubs lineup; and indeed, Joe had managed only two hits off him in 1904 and none in 1905.

But Tinker changed his approach in 1906. He took up a longer, heavier bat, readjusted his stance, and learned to wait out the wicked "fadeaway" that Mathewson used to make a right-hander look foolish as he lunged for the ball. Tinker's readjustment had immediate effect. "Then he had me," Mathewson marveled. A middling hitter against the rest of the league, Tinker proved one of the most fearsome hitters that Big Six would ever face from then on, hitting just under .400 against Mathewson from 1906 through 1908, even higher in later years.

No better illustration of Tinker's dominance over Matty came than at this momentous occasion. On Mathewson's first pitch, Tinker lashed a roping liner that carried deep into center field. It sailed over the head of Cy Seymour, who had to chase it down quickly just to limit Tinker to a stand-up triple. Johnny Kling didn't waste time letting Mathewson get his bearings, knocking Tinker home with a hit to left field.

The Cubs small-ball machine then got moving. Miner Brown moved Kling to second with a sacrifice bunt. Mathewson got Sheckard to fly out, but Johnny Evers refused to go fishing for any of his waste pitches and drew a four-ball, semi-intentional walk. "Wildfire" Schulte came to bat next, two on with one out, and he pushed a ball into left field that bounced into the stands for a ground rule double. That scored another run and put Evers on third. The Cubs had the lead, 2–1.

As he came to bat, Frank Chance got more full-throated razzing from his New York tormentors, but as usual they only inspired him: "The wrongs he and his team had suffered rankling in his breast and a thirst for revenge," waxed Sanborn. Husk greeted a Mathewson curveball "squarely in the middle of its break" and drove it into right field.

Evers trotted home, with Schulte right behind him, and the crowd collapsed in a despairing sigh, the Cubs leading, 4–1.

And that was pretty much all there was to see. Miner Brown trudged back to the mound in the bottom of the third, putting out a brief fire here and there, helped by some nice defensive work by Tinker. Otherwise Brown mowed through the Giants' lineup until the seventh, when he allowed one more run on a sacrifice fly. That got the crowd back into the game for a moment, but their cheers belied a lack of confidence. "The yelling which swelled out was no longer the joyous p[a]ean of the first inning," observed Sanborn. "It was rasping and raucous with anger of hope deferred and of anxious moments of fear and dread."

No other Giant reached first base. Brown needed only four pitches to secure the final three outs in the bottom of the ninth. Only one big challenge remained for the victorious Cubs: get out of there with their lives.

The Cubs had "stolen" the pennant, screamed the mob, with the game over and the season lost. The bad feelings ran so high, acknowledged a New York paper, that "the Chicago men were bombarded as they left the field, kicked and reviled." Hundreds of rabid fans took to the field, growling and out for blood. Tinker, Sheckard, and others took hard knocks to the head, while someone slashed Pfiester on the shoulder with a knife. Another hooligan chased down Chance from behind and delivered a wicked chop across his neck. The blow broke some cartilage and temporarily snuffed out his voice.

When the team finally made it to relative safety in their dressing room, the doors barricaded, armed guards had to stand outside to hold the mob back. The Cubs eventually were secreted back to their hotel in a patrol wagon with two cops on the inside and four more riding the running boards. They hustled out of town that night for Detroit, site of the upcoming World Series, by slipping out the back door and running down an alley, escorted by a swarm of policemen.

The Chicago Cubs had won the National League pennant for the third year in a row. The New York Giants and their frustrated fans returned to their homes that night with nothing to show for the season but hard feelings and a national reputation for sore losing.

AFTERMATH

Frank Chance and his Cubs didn't have much time to reflect upon their triumph as they rushed west on an overnight train. But this year's World's Championship also proved rather anticlimactic, as the Cubs took four out of five games, winning all three played in Exposition Park and splitting the two games at home. Ty Cobb performed better this time than the year before, stroking seven hits with four runs batted in and three runs scored. But he managed to steal only two bases over the five games and was thrown out once. Frank Chance, meanwhile, had eight hits and four runs scored, and he stole five bases without a miss.

More interestingly, watchful eyes in Chicago and New York began to ponder the implications of the violent showdown at the Polo Grounds for baseball and for society at large. "Chicago is proud of the baseball team," the *Chicago Tribune* editorialized, "and of the men who have shown such perseverance and courage in the face of such disheartening obstacles, and who now have their reward in the satisfaction of a triumph over masterful adversaries on foreign territory."

Even more significant, perhaps, was the generous response in New York—though not from Muggsy McGraw, who continued to gripe that the rug had been pulled out from under him. "I don't feel badly," he said disingenuously. "My team merely lost something it had honestly won three weeks ago." His Giants would not win another pennant, or even finish ahead of the Cubs, for three more years. But McGraw's wasn't a consensus opinion among more reasonable New Yorkers. "The Cubs played better ball," said the *New York Herald*. "It was the general opinion of those who watched the game without favor that Chicago was not well treated, either in the matter of decisions or by the crowd." A columnist for the *New York Evening Journal* was disgusted with the treatment New Yorkers gave the Cubs. "The scene yesterday was really the most disgraceful ever pulled off around here," he said. "Gee whiz! If we can't lose a pennant without dirty work let's quit altogether."

Hearst's *New York American* may have summed up a nationwide sentiment on its editorial page the day after the Giants' bitter loss. "A people who can become as excited about anything as the majority of

New Yorkers can about the baseball pennant is far from being lost to hope," its editor opined. "We know now that we *can* become excited, energetically, masterfully excited, and as soon as we understand how properly to apply that tremendous dynamite force to the really important things of life, we will get what we ought to have, individually and collectively, and no thieving corporations, no swinish bosses, no bludgeon-bearing election thieves can stand a minute before us."

President William Howard Taft Jr. brought along his retinue to take in a ball game at West Side Grounds in September 1909. When he stood up in the middle of the seventh inning to stretch his legs, the entire crowd rose with him. (Library of Congress.)

DESTINY DISSOLVES

1909–1912

And now it is said, far and wide, that this famous Chicago Club is again a wreck and will have to be builded anew. Time alone—that inexorable judge of teams and men—will round out the story of this great machine which, while it lasted, was invincible. WILLIAM PATTEN AND J. WALKER MCSPAD-DEN, in *The Book of Baseball*, 1911

They called him "Big Chief," or sometimes "Big Lub." He was an enormous man for his day, topping six feet and three hundred pounds. The bulbous face and receding hairline only added to an overall impression of rotundity. But then he would flash a quick, happy grin, his blue eyes squinting over plump and rosy cheeks. The broad smile curled along the borders of his handlebar mustache and seemed to extend "to the back of his ears," according to one smitten observer. A hearty laugh and some easy banter loosened up everyone around him, even the starched-collared dignitaries in his entourage: the "silk-hatted" governor and secretary of defense, the "gold-laced" general with his uniformed aides-de-camp, assorted members of Congress, foreign ambassadors, judges, and city officials. Everyone got into the spirit of the occasion by dint of their Big Chief's prodigious charm—if not by his insistence that they spend an afternoon together at the ballpark.

William Howard Taft, twenty-seventh president of the United States, had arrived in Chicago on the morning of September 16, 1909, on the front leg of a thirteen-thousand-mile tour across a growing, forty-six-state union. It had been less than six months since Taft, a Republican, had taken the oath of office. Arriving that morning from Washington by special train, the president's packed agenda mixed public relations with political coalition building. His twelve hours in the Windy City included receptions, banquets, and meetings with financiers and other business elites, topped off by a motorcade along Garfield Boulevard, lined with two hundred thousand singing schoolchildren.

A key point of contact for this high-level expedition was Charles Webb Murphy, whose former backer and minority partner happened to be the president's older brother, Charles. All three men had grown up as baseball fans rooting for the Cincinnati Reds. And so, at the president's insistence, his schedulers blocked out a full hour and a half in the afternoon so Big Lub and his minions could drive out to West Side Grounds and take in a Cubs game.

An animated crowd, estimated at twenty-nine thousand people, had turned out on the bright and sunny Thursday afternoon, as much to gawk at the nation's chief executive as to watch their two-time world-champion Cubs take on the reviled New York Giants. Murphy had rescheduled the game to accommodate Taft's compressed timetable, but that had not deterred a swelling crowd, or its passion for patriotic pomp. Flags and bunting decked the stadium while a sixty-two-piece band blared "Hail to the Chief" upon the president's entry. When the ensemble struck up "The Star-Spangled Banner," a wildly popular march tune but still years away from being declared the national anthem, the music mesmerized the gathering crowd. "The first notes were all there was heard to the anthem because the sea of human beings had risen to its feet, heads were bared, voices were raised in a great volume of sound which paid earnest tribute to the man who showed his democratic spirit by taking the greatest interest in a democratic game," according to a breathless report in *Harper's Weekly*.

Murphy had erected a special box for the president and his party, but Taft asked to "sit with the 'fans.'" When Big Chief and his retinue took their place behind the first base bench, photographers, both professional and amateur, turned their lenses on "the fleshy, cheery man in the grandstand." The president chuckled when a man in an Uncle Sam costume marched past him. A little girl in a star-spangled dress got close enough to earn a handshake. Two boys brought lemonade, which Taft drank deeply. Then he munched on popcorn while the cameras continued to click away. "Now you fellows hurry up and get through," he chided the photographers. "I want to see the game."

Once play was under way, Taft took care not to show favor for either the Cubs or the Giants. But reporters took note that he kept his eyes glued to the field, discussing business only between innings. "President Taft is not a baseball fan because it is the popular pastime," wrote an approving I. E. Sanborn in the *Tribune*, "but because he is one, and because he not only likes the game but knows it."

The Giants were up 2–1 in the seventh inning—the "lucky seventh," as Cubs fans had been calling it for years as Frank Chance's resourceful squad found ever new ways to win ball games late in the day. As the teams changed sides and the Cubs ran to their bench for the bottom half, President Taft suddenly stood up. He felt like stretching his legs, the big man explained. But the patriotic crowd felt compelled to follow their leader. "Immediately the thousands of spectators stood up and waited until the president had reseated himself," Sanborn reported. Taft may only have been mimicking a midgame custom he learned as a boy. But when the president repeated his "seventh-inning stretch" the following year, during a Washington Senators game, a new baseball tradition took root.

Unfortunately for the Cubs, the Big Chief had no effect on the careening course of the 1909 season. The Giants held on to win that game, 2–1, stifling any hopes that the Cubs might be able to climb back to the top of the standings in the remaining three weeks of the season. The Pittsburgh Pirates had all but run away with the pennant that year behind Honus Wagner's league-leading .339 batting average and hundred runs batted in. The Bucs would finish the regular season with an insurmountable 110–42 record. It didn't matter that the Cubs would take thirteen of the next nineteen games on their schedule, including two of three against Pittsburgh, to finish with a noteworthy 104–49. That was five more victories than in their great 1908 championship season, but it was only enough to place second in 1909.

As the presidential visit demonstrated, however, professional baseball had become a national passion, and its players, from Tinker and Evers and Chance to the aging Honus Wagner, a young Ty Cobb, and the ever-popular Christy Mathewson, had become heroes to people of every age, income, and region in the nation. "Even the President of the United States is a 'fan' and has placed his seal of approval on the national sport," noted *Harper's Weekly*, adding that the Taft imprimatur had not only lifted the game's reputation in high society, but that his winsome fellowship with all strata of baseball fans had opened the way to a new era of communal fellowship.

"Business and professional men forget for the time their standing in the community and, shoulder to shoulder with the street urchin, 'root' frantically for the hit needed to win the game," the *Harper's* correspondent declared.

EARLY DEPARTURES

On July 5, 1909, Frank Selee, who had assembled and directed the early Cubs dynastic line, died of tuberculosis in the Oakes Home, a Denver treatment center run by the Elks Club. He was forty-nine. Selee had been following the Cubs from afar since leaving the ball club four years earlier. He and May had settled in the high-desert climes of Colorado and New Mexico in hopes of repairing his lungs. When his condition deteriorated, he moved into the tubercular facility. "He died just as he had lived," said George Morrison Reid, a Colorado businessman and sports team backer who was at his bedside. "Up to the last minute he was perfectly conscious and the last five minutes of his life he spent in dictating telegrams to all of his old friends in the big leagues. . . . He knew the end was near but he met it just as he had always met everything else—smiling and confident."

A contingent of Elks brothers accompanied May as she transported the body back to Melrose, Massachusetts, for a family funeral at the First Methodist Episcopal Church. Following a scripture reading and a rendition of "Rock of Ages" by the all-male Arion Quartet, the Reverend Dr. Willard T. Perrin's solemn eulogy extolled the game of baseball along with its model practitioner: "No one can thoroughly understand

American life without realizing the great hold the national game of base ball has on the people," Perrin began: "Small boys begin to play it; then when they are young men in the high school and college they continue to play it with greater interest. The public likes it, as shown by the large number who attend the games. The ministers, doctors and all sorts of professional men witness the games, and even the women are seen at them in large numbers. The American people are to be congratulated on having such a wholesome sport."

Less than two weeks after Selee's funeral, baseball lost another pivotal force in its societal transformation. Harry C. Pulliam, the strong-willed and innovative president of the National League, who in 1902 had forced its owners and players to clean up their act and make the game presentable to a wider audience, died by his own hand on July 29. Just forty, he shot himself in the right temple in his living quarters at the New York Athletic Club.

Although he had been in poor health for several months—earlier that year he had suffered a nervous breakdown, leading to an extended leave of absence—many people speculated that Pulliam was still distraught over the heavy criticism that came his way after the Merkle affair. No doubt there was more to it than that, including insinuations that the dandified bachelor was a closet homosexual and at odds with some of the owners, John Brush and C. W. Murphy top among them, who thought he was partial to players and umpires and not loyal enough to his magnate bosses. Some have even conjectured that he was being threatened with blackmail. Former Cubs owner James A. Hart, an old friend, was saddened but not surprised, hinting that something deeper in the troubled man's psyche was at work. "Pulliam told me two years ago that he would end it himself some time," Hart told the *Tribune*. "His friends have feared such an act. I'm sorry, for I had a great liking for him."

THINKING BALLPLAYERS

As they approached the 1910 campaign, marking their eighth consecutive season together, Tinker, Evers, and Chance were widely regarded as the best infield combine in the business. But the three men, now aged twenty-nine, twenty-eight, and thirty-three, respectively, were also gaining reputations as exemplars of a new brand of baseball integrity.

Perhaps it took a woman writer to note the extent of the game's transformation in just ten years. Baseball in the 1890s, observed Margaret Brown for *Pearson's Magazine*, had no appeal in genteel society, where it was looked upon as little more than "a rough-and-tumble game played by a nine of rowdies for the benefit of a crowd of hoodlums." By the end of the first decade of the twentieth century, however, ball parks had a much different character. "The 'mob and hoodlums' that hurled epithets and missiles at the umpire, that waited with stones outside the ball grounds to make it pleasant for the opposing nine, have passed away," she declared. "The 'rowdies' who filled the air with profanity, who made the game a slugging match in which brute strength and arrogance were the only assets—they, too, have departed."

In their stead, a new breed of professional ballplayer had taken over, one who "plays the game on lines that are purely scientific—he is thinking all the time," and one who prizes fair play over crass opportunism. "He may be a college man, he may have other interests to look after, nevertheless, he is no longer ashamed to step out on the diamond and show the public how the great national game ought to be played." Heading her list of eight exemplary players was Frank Chance, "the sort of man who would have made a success in any business." She liked the way Chance played the game and managed his players with a mixture of toughness and compassion. "Chance is straight-forward, quick-tempered, and absolutely candid in saying what he thinks. He despises the player who cringes or tried to shirk his duty, but the man who is in trouble can go to Frank Chance and find a sympathetic, warm-hearted friend."

Brown's other new-age role models included college graduate Mathewson, humble Dutchman Wagner, and, right up there among the elite, "Little Johnny Evers, Chicago's whirlwind at second base." She singled him out as "one of the slickest, quickest youngsters in the game," struck by the energy he brought to the ballpark every day. "Evers is the sort of fellow that doesn't grow old, always a boy," she effused, "always clever, enterprising, nervy—that's it. Little Johnny's nerves are responsible for his eternal youth."

The whole tone of the game as played by Chance, Evers, and her other "transformers of baseball" had raised the morale of players and fans alike, Brown concluded. "A player is no longer tabooed in society. Some of them have high social standing," she said. "The professional game's supreme popularity is due to the present type of the players, the men who lifted the embargo of respectability."

The emergence of a consensus that "scientific" baseball had finally replaced crude rowdyism would surely have touched a nerve in John McGraw. The Napoleonic field general had always considered himself the premier mastermind of the inside game, insisting all along that his cheating and umpire baiting were merely side effects of an unrelenting will to win. But the Giants were no longer winning—indeed, they had not finished higher than the Cubs in the standings for four straight years, with another runner-up finish to follow in 1910. Even McGraw must have realized that he needed to rehabilitate his public image, so at odds with the magical aura of world champions Tinker, Evers, and Chance.

Coming to McGraw's aid was a new general-readership monthly, *Baseball Magazine*, which had launched at the conclusion of the 1908 season in response to the growing fascination with the game and its players. The publication featured player profiles and human-interest stories about aspects of the game that might not be readily apparent to casual fans. McGraw, remarkably, made himself available for an exclusive interview. What followed was a rather transparent attempt to give the man called Muggsy a personality makeover.

"He is a gentleman in every sense of the word, just as most of the players on his team are," began the fawning profile writer. The article describes a generous, good-natured humanitarian who eagerly gives up his sleeping birth to a child, a woman, or an old man and spends the night sitting up in the train's smoking room; who gives "hundreds of dollars every year" to charities that help down-and-out newspapermen, actors, and pugilists; and who "takes defeat as a matter of course." McGraw should never be described as a "sore loser," this writer maintained. "On the team there are several such losers, but McGraw is not one of them."

CELEBRITY STATUS

A wider fan base for baseball seemed hungry for insider views of it. All three Cub heroes found themselves in demand for newspaper and magazine features, and even as authors in bylined articles. Their growing fame led them down some unusual avenues of popular culture.

Joe Tinker and Johnny Evers, the erstwhile "songwriters," also posed in uniform for a garter manufacturer: "Holds your sock smooth as your skin," the ad boasted. Evers collaborated with Hugh Fullerton on the baseball how-to book, *Touching Second*, in 1910, adding his marquee name and first-hand knowledge to Fullerton's explication of the inside game. Fullerton also was the likely ghostwriter that same year for Frank Chance, who published a young adult novel, *The Bride and the Pennant*, at a time when mass-market authors like Zane Grey were taking up baseball themes to attract readers young and old.

Tinker took his rising celebrity status in yet another direction. He launched a widely publicized theatrical career that provided him with lucrative winter employment for years. He made an inauspicious debut, in November 1908, at Chicago's People's Theatre as a bit player in a light comedy, *Brown of Harvard*, a play about the travails of a varsity crew squad. Sportswriters and fans laughed it off at first, but the *Tribune*'s theater critic conceded that Tinker had the makings of a genuine thespian: "Joe could straighten out some of Bill Shakespeare's curves."

Tinker took his new calling seriously, working hard to memorize his lines and taking care to enunciate them clearly. Word of his not-so-bad performances soon caught the attention of vaudeville agent Jake Strand. He signed Tinker to an eight-week winter run as "headliner" in a big-time act.

In those days, vaudeville playbills ranged from trained seals to J. M. Barrie's *The Twelve Pound Look*, starring Ethel Barrymore. Strand wanted something in between for his handsome young shortstop, so he shopped around for a one-act baseball sketch. Strand doubted his novice could command the stage by himself; he would have to appear on stage in uniform, and he would need a female costar. Strand engaged Sadie Sherman, an attractive young actress and well-known ragtime singer, to share the playbill with Tinker. But that still left the socially delicate problem of how to introduce his character into a lady's parlor in his baseball togs. Strand called in Charles S. Adelman, a Chicago theater critic and veteran sketch artist, in search of a plot conceit that would prove at once prim, proper, and crowd pleasing.

Adelman came up with a script he called "The Great Catch": Sherman's character lives near the ballpark and is anxiously watching a Cubs-Giants game through her window. She is describing the action to a friend on the phone. Suddenly a Giant batter rips into a fastball from Mordecai Brown, and the Cubs appear doomed. "It's all over!" Sherman screams. "We lose! What a blow! That ball is never going to come down." Of course, it does come down, smashing through the window. The game seems lost, but "footsteps are heard rushing up the stairs accompanied by a frenzied roll of the drums," Adelson said, "and in skids our hero, spearing the ball with one hand and shouting, 'he's out!' Triumphant screams from off stage. Sadie throws her arms around his neck and kisses him." Songs, cheers, and happy ending follow.

Strand loved the concept and took Tinker and company to a small-town vaudeville house for a short tryout. A small audience, mostly children, watched with glee as Tinker rushed into Sherman's parlor, only to lose sight of the ball in the floodlights. "The world's greatest shortstop missed it by a foot and it dribbled into the pit," Adelman recounted with dismay. The curtain dropped and Tinker fumed: "I couldn't even see it!" Strand saw a public relations disaster awaiting them in Chicago. But they persevered, rehearsing the scene for hours as Tinker practiced catching the ball from all angles. "Needless to say, he never muffed it again," Adelman said.

"The Great Catch" opened at the Haymarket Theater in Chicago and then toured the Midwest vaudeville circuit to wide acclaim. Tinker was "a refreshing change from most athletic champions who took to the stage—good looking, bore himself like a gentleman, and neither clumsy nor obstreperous," according to a Chicago critic. Tinker followed up that success with a second play, *A Home Run*, costarring another well-known Chicago actress, Elsie Crescy. He went on to perform in a variety of vaudeville sketch and monologue vehicles over the next six baseball off-seasons, earning much as $1,000 a week.

ONE LAST PENNANT RACE

One hundred and four wins may not have been good enough to catch Pittsburgh in 1909, but that same number of victories proved more than enough for the Cubs to seize the National League pennant in 1910 for the fourth time in five years.

During this season the major league powers decided to introduce a baseball with a cork center. The new ball traveled farther and faster than the old version. One of the first players to take advantage of the souped-up pellet was Frank "Wildfire" Schulte, the longtime Cubs right fielder. For most of the deadball era, batters had typically used bats with thick, bottleneck handles, which they would grip high on the handle as they tried to make contact. For this livelier ball, Schulte fashioned his bat with a thin handle and gripped it down on the knob to generate more bat speed. The result that season was a league-leading 10 home runs to go along with 68 runs batted in and a .301 batting average. Schulte would go on to lead the league in 1911 with 21 home runs, 21 triples, and 107 RBIs, making him the first major leaguer to hit more than 20 home runs since Buck Freeman in 1899, and the first to complete the season with more than 20 home runs, 20 triples, and 20 doubles—a rare feat to this day.

By the end of September, the Cubs were cruising to the pennant, leading by ten and a half games with only thirteen to play. Exhausted after two weeks on the road, the team had a leisurely two-day train ride from Boston to Cincinnati, for a four-game series against the fifth-place Reds. The first game on Saturday, October 1, got off to a promising start. But then, in the fifth inning, their luck went sour. If there was to be one moment that heralded the end of the great Cubs dynasty, this may have been it.

The Cubs had scored two runs in the fifth to take a comfortable 5–1 lead when Johnny Evers came to bat and drew a pass to first. A sacrifice bunt and a single moved him around the bases and homeward. Ring Lardner of the *Tribune* described what happened next. "Evers could have scored standing up but did not know that," Lardner observed. As he approached the plate, Evers hesitated in midstride as he began to slide. "As his right foot came in contact with the plate everyone in the stand could hear the bone crack, and also could hear John's cry of pain," Lardner said. The Cubs rushed Evers to the clubhouse, where a surgeon diagnosed a broken ankle. Evers would be out of action for at least six weeks, far past the end of the season and the World Series. "The accident took most of the pepper out of the Chicago players," observed Lardner.

The Cubs did win the NL pennant in a rout, setting them up to face the American League champions, Connie Mack's Philadelphia Athletics, in the World Series. The A's had run away from their junior circuit competitors on the strength of the hitting of second baseman Eddie Collins and the pitching of Jack Coombs, a pair who would soon bedevil the Cubs. Coombs, who had won thirty-one games that year, pitched three complete-game wins in six days. The Athletics coasted to their first World's Championship.

LONG GOOD-BYE

The 1911 season was the beginning of a precipitous end to the great Cubs machine.

The first clue that this campaign would be different came in March, when Frank Chance sold Harry Steinfeldt's contract to St. Paul of the American Association. Chance believed he had better, younger replacements at third base, and he turned out to be right. Steinfeldt's best days were behind him. Catcher Johnny Kling, one of the Cubs most essential players during the glory days, was also declining, and Chance decided to let him go for a younger player as well. Meanwhile, Johnny Evers suffered a series of personal mishaps that had begun with his broken ankle. The leg took longer to heal than expected, and on top of that he caught pneumonia. In December, he had lost his life savings when his business partner invested in two shoe stores that went bankrupt.

These setbacks were not the worst of it. In May 1911, Evers was the driver in an auto accident that killed one of his best friends, newspaperman George McDonald of the *Chicago Daily Journal*. Evers blamed himself even though police said it wasn't his fault. "I had been talking to him but a moment before, and the next instant he was lying on the ground, fatally injured," Evers recollected a couple of years later. "The shock of that sudden death was more than I could stand." He went into a "nervous prostration" and played only one more inning that summer until returning to the lineup at the end of the season.

Adding to their collective misfortunes, Chance collapsed on the field in Cincinnati on July 1. He had a blood clot on his brain—caused, no one doubted, by the multiple beanballs he had taken over his career, stretching all the way back to the one that nearly killed him as a teenager in California. He had been suffering through severe and constant headaches that were especially crippling on hot, sunny days. This time he was hospitalized for almost a month but still refused to call it quits even though doctors told him another blow to the head might be fatal. "They can't make me quit by hitting me on the head," he told Hugh Fullerton.

Despite their recent travails, the Cubs led the National League for fifty-three days in 1911 behind the hitting of Schulte and Jimmy Sheckard. Their mainstay pitcher again was Miner Brown, who won twenty-one games as a starter and racked up another thirteen saved games in relief. The heavy workload would prove Brown's undoing, however; he was never a dominant pitcher again.

Having given way to the Giants in the pennant race, the Cubs experienced a final indignity in October, in the City Series against the White Sox. A crowd of 36,308, purported to be the largest ever to see a baseball game in Chicago up to that point, watched the Sox defeat the Cubs, 4–2, in game 3 at Comiskey Park, on their way to a four-game sweep.

The next spring, Joe Tinker, Johnny Evers, and Frank Chance played their last game together on April 12, 1912, as the Cubs lost to Cincinnati, 3–2, in ten innings. After the game, Chance announced his retirement as a player. "He quit only when he knew that his playing had hurt the team," Fullerton remarked. "Death for himself didn't concern him." Johnny Evers had the best season of his career in 1912, with a .341 batting average and a stunning .431 on-base percentage. Joe Tinker excelled, too, finishing with a .282 batting average and seventy-seven runs batted in, earning him fourth place in the voting for the league's most valuable player award. Manager-only Chance finally took some real time off in September to undergo surgery to relieve the pressure from the blood clot.

In Chance's absence, the Evers-Tinker feud had lost its referee. On September 19, during a desultory loss in Brooklyn, the pair got into a fistfight on the bench after Tinker, as acting manager, accused Evers of loafing on the bases. A police officer had to pull them apart. The headline in the *Brooklyn Eagle* the next day read: "Chafing Cubs: Lack of Harmony in Team Publicly Displayed."

Meanwhile, owner C. W. Murphy was getting impatient with his team's lackluster performance. But Murphy was also losing face among fans, sportswriters, and fellow magnates on account of his blatantly self-serving rants and antics. As the Cubs faded out of contention and Chance continued to recuperate, Murphy publicly accused the team of sloppy play and even drunkenness. Chance fired back in the press, calling Murphy a liar and announcing that he had sold his one-tenth interest in the club (for $150,000). Chance also refused to comply with Murphy's demand that players sign a temperance vow for the 1913 season.

Chance had promised the buyer of his stake that he would not leave the team, so he returned for the City Series against the White Sox. But when the Cubs lost the decisive seventh game by a humiliating 16–0 score, a fuming Murphy stormed down to the bench and summarily fired his Peerless Leader.

Murphy asked Johnny Evers to take over as manager for the 1913 season. Evers was reluctant to take the job but convinced himself that doing so had nothing to do with Chance's ouster. Predictably, Evers was the last person Joe Tinker wanted to play for, and Murphy soon engineered a trade to the Reds, where Tinker wound up as player-manager and enjoyed one of the best seasons of his career.

Ten full seasons after master theorist Frank Selee had brought the trio together, the firm of Tinker-Evers-Chance was officially dissolved.

EPILOGUE

Hall of Fame

Baseball is the most serious pleasure ever invented.
HUGH S. FULLERTON, *American Magazine*, 1912

In the heart of Cooperstown, a burg in upstate New York where native son Abner Doubleday did not invent the game of baseball, sits the great shrine to America's national pastime. The National Baseball Hall of Fame and Museum, founded in 1936, dominates the east end of Main Street, where it serves as official memory keeper of the game's players, records, artifacts, and lore.

The building's three stories and fifty thousand square feet of exhibit and storage space contain some forty thousand relics of the game's storied past—the hickory bat Babe Ruth used to swat three home runs in a 1926 World Series game; the No. 44 uniform Hank Aaron wore as he circled the bases on April 8, 1974, having broken Ruth's career home-run record; plus all manner of officially validated balls, mitts, ticket stubs, scorecards, photographs, newspaper clips, films, and videotapes from great baseball moments.

These hagiographic testaments sit side by side respectful bows to its admittedly contentious social history: to women in baseball (the "Ladies"); to the game's unique appeal in destitute pockets of Latin America; and, of course, to the pride and the stain of Jim Crow–era Negro Leagues, to which African American players were shamefully relegated for more than half a century on account of organized base-ball's racist "color line."

On the ground floor, visitors step into a modern Parthenon for baseball's most revered luminaries. Here are monuments to the play-ers, managers, pioneers, and officials who have shaped the game's identity and character. All were "elected" under carefully crafted, if not always consistent, rules. Commemorative tablets, with their faces and text etched in bas-relief, honor Ruth and Ty Cobb, Mike "King" Kelly and Adrian "Cap" Anson, as well as Reggie Jackson, Nolan Ryan, Ken Griffey Jr., and hundreds more. Fans of the Chicago Cubs can pay homage to Ernie Banks, Billy Williams, Ferguson Jenkins, Ryne Sand-berg, Andre Dawson, and (at long last) Ron Santo.

Here, too, are the official baseball memorials for Joe Tinker, Johnny Evers, and Frank Chance, as well as Mordecai Brown and Frank Selee—star players and creators of the great Cubs dynasty of 1906–10.

Tinker, Evers, and Chance were inducted together in 1946. For many observers, their election—by a specially appointed, seven-member committee of baseball executives who voted to include them in a group of eleven veterans from the early days of the game—righted a long-standing oversight of the game's deadball era. This enshrinement is a fitting tribute to their brilliant teamwork, their remarkable longev-ity as a unit, and the club's unrivaled success on the field during their tenure.

The developing historical consensus, however, has been less gen-erous. While Chance has always been considered a natural choice, that's as much for his success as a manager as for his performance on the field. He barely missed being elected on his own the year before. Johnny Evers was one of the best second basemen of his day, and after his great Cubs career, he went on to star for the "miracle" Boston Braves in their come-from-behind race for the 1914 NL pennant and subse-quent World Series sweep. But scratch-hitting second basemen have never garnered much respect from baseball mavens and Hall of Fame purists, who consider Evers a borderline choice at best. And Joe Tin-ker? Well, hardly anyone today thinks he belongs in the Hall of Fame, mainly on account of his spotty record as a hitter. Tinker may have confounded Christy Mathewson, but hardly anyone else feared him at the plate. Even in his day, the wildly popular, slick-fielding Tinker always performed in the shadow of Honus Wagner.

Hence the sarcastic estimation that this threesome owes their Hall of Fame stations more to F. P. Adams's joking play on their names than to their knack for turning two.

Such modern-day second guesses are the stuff of arguments in bleachers, bars, gyms, and social media. Yet both sides miss an important point. Tinker and Evers and Chance may or may not belong in the Hall of Fame on the basis of their career records. Yet they do belong there, and they belong together. More compelling reasons than statistics merit them seats among baseball's immortals.

One reason is purely quantitative: Tinker, Evers, and Chance were the indisputable leaders of a great team that won a huge number of games. In fact, their Cubs won more games over any period of years than any other great team in history, from their single season record of 116, to their five-season record of 530, to their ten-season record of 986. That's more victories than the Yankees of Ruth and Gehrig, or the Yankees of Gehrig and DiMaggio; more than the Dodgers of Robinson and Campanella; more than the Yankees of Mantle and Berra, the Yankees of Jackson and Hunter, or the Yankees of Jeter and Rivera; more than the Reds of Bench, Morgan, Rose, and Pérez; and more than the Braves of Maddux, Glavine, and Smoltz. "The definition of a great ballplayer is a ballplayer who helps his team to win a lot of games," baseball historian Bill James has said. "If you're going to say these guys don't belong in the Hall of Fame, . . . you have to deal somehow with the phenomenal success of their team."

Baseball sabermetricians will continue to argue over their merits— even Bill James hedges his final verdict. But it is harder to dispute another, more qualitative justification for the high standing baseball has accorded to Tinker, Evers, and Chance. As this book has sought to show, baseball might not exist today—certainly no mythmaking Baseball Hall of Fame would exist—if not for this trio's rise to prominence, domination, and glory at a pivotal point in America's embrace of the game.

THE DOUBLEDAY MYTH

On December 30, 1907, less than three months after the Chicago Cubs of Tinker, Evers, and Chance won their first World's Championship, a blue-ribbon "commission" stacked with American jingoists "resolved" the question of baseball's origins by trotting out the tale of Abner Doubleday in Cooperstown and declaring him, a Civil War general of some renown, to be baseball's true-blue American inventor.

Doubleday, as any schoolchild's story book told us through the 1980s—and as many people still vaguely assume to this day—was the man who, on one fine day in May 1839, purportedly laid out four bases in the shape of a diamond in a Cooperstown cow pasture and then showed his mates how to play a bat-and-ball game he called "base ball." At least, this was the tale a panel of politicians and sports executives—no historians or baseball old-timers among them—put forth to a public then eager to celebrate the game as a piece of American pie.

The so-called Mills Commission, named after its chairman, businessman and former National League President Abraham G. Mills, had spent two years collecting evidence and taking testimony from aging former ballplayers and citizens. The panel arrived at its final conclusion, however, on the thin reed of a letter written by a seventy-one-year-old retired engineer in Colorado named Abner Graves. Graves said he had grown up in Cooperstown, and he described seeing a man he knew as Doubleday demonstrate this "pure American game" that morning in 1839. (Graves would have been five years old at the time.)

Graves's story fit neatly into the predilections of Mills and his benefactor, Albert G. Spalding, the former owner of the Chicago White Stockings. Though Spalding had given up the team five years earlier, he remained active in baseball as owner of a national chain of sporting-goods stores. He had also masterminded a worldwide publicity tour for baseball at the turn of the century. Both Spalding and Mills had long maintained that baseball was an American original, not an outgrowth of the English game of rounders, as Henry Chadwick had been insisting for years. It was hard even for the formidable Spalding to bigfoot the "Father of Baseball," however, so he devised the commission with Chadwick's blessing, then made sure Chadwick was not on it.

Doubleday proved a popular choice for canonization. Americans' patriotic fervor was escalating in the new century, and Major General Doubleday's long military career—he fired the first Union shot at Fort Sumter and commanded a division in the Battle of Gettysburg—added heroic luster to his brainchild. Doubleday had also conveniently passed away in 1893, so he could neither confirm nor deny his place in American history even though, as a prolific memoirist and letter-writer in later life, he had never even mentioned the game. No matter. The National Game now had an official American fountainhead.

Spalding and Mills were seeking to do something that kings and queens, governments large and small, institutions public and private, and other agents of "official culture" have tried to do in every era and corner of human civilization: they wanted to create a "public memory" for baseball. Governments do this to help preserve a country's social touchstones and foment national identity. Their public memory displays come in the form of monuments, heroic statues, commemorative holidays, national anthems, ritualistic state funerals, and other sacred public events.

Families and social groups also find ways to create public memories. Clans preserve stories of their immigrant ancestors' early struggles and key turning points. Universities, public charities, and social clubs give commemorative awards and put eminent names on buildings. For its part, organized baseball now creates its public memory through the Cooperstown Hall of Fame. But, at first, it tried to do so with the Mills Commission.

The commission sought to root the game in a purely American past rather than baseball's actual European heritage. They went in search of a story that each generation of baseball enthusiasts could hand down to the next—fathers to sons, old-timers to rookies—with a sense of patriotic pride. They felt that baseball, this common "American" invention, could unite disparate regions of the nation, and even serve as a public rallying point for an American century. So the Mills Commission misappropriated an old man's childhood reminiscence and pock-

eted a military hero in the bargain, manufacturing a patriotic figure-
head to help cement baseball's public memory.

They had (partially) good motives for doing so. Both Spalding and
Mills were products of baseball's first golden age of the 1870s and
1880s, when the likes of King Kelly were dazzling crowds with their
acrobatic skills and entertaining hijinks. As the game's elder statesmen
in the 1890s, however, Spalding and his fellow magnates watched (not
altogether helplessly) as baseball degenerated into a thug's game. Even
while a growing American middle class was opening up to outdoor
activities designed to enhance the quality of their new urban life—
bicycling, pedestrianism, golf, swimming, nature conservation—
organized baseball was spurning more men and women than it could
attract with its penchant for hoodlumism and billingsgate.

Spalding and Mills made a case for a public memory in a way that
is typical, scholars say, of those who promulgate official culture in almost every age and context: promote a nationalistic, patriotic past that
reinterprets and overrides the seeds of modern discontent. "Official
culture relies on . . . the restatement of reality in ideal rather than complex and ambiguous terms," writes cultural historian John Bodnar in
Remaking America, his influential work on public memory. "It presents
the past on an abstract basis of timelessness and sacredness." As an antidote to "dirty" ball, the Doubleday-in-Cooperstown myth hearkened
a bucolic image of a more innocent day, when boys could gather in a
pasture to play a game of fun and fair play.

Little did these self-assigned arbiters of baseball's public memory
realize that they had the perfect corrective to baseball's dark age already within their midst. Spalding, for one, could have looked in his
own backyard.

The yin of official culture's yang in the creation of public memory is
the vantage point of people who actually live through a milestone experience or event. Cultural historians call it "vernacular," as opposed
to official, culture. Vernacular cultures are diverse and often shifting
combinations of individuals and special interest groups like soldiers,
students, ordinary citizens, immigrants—and let's add ballplayers.
They are more inclined to express their values and interpret reality

based on personal reminiscences than on any imagined national mythology. They evoke the past by tapping into their own experiences—and what those experiences feel like—rather than what others tell them to feel.

Baseball's purest expressions of vernacular culture in the 1890s and early 1900s are the coming-of-age stories of Johnny Evers, Joe Tinker, and Frank Chance—and those of Harry Steinfeldt, Mordecai Brown, and Frank Selee, too. As boys, they grew up in different regions of a nation that was still coming to grips with its size and complexity. They each inherited an ethnic, class, or regional legacy that didn't always mesh well with those of their teammates or rivals. And none of them had the same notion of what he wanted to accomplish in life, or what he expected to get from the intensely competitive baseball enterprise that they were creating together.

Johnny Evers carried within him the ethnic pride of his Irish-immigrant grandfather, who arrived on American shores without an occupation or a dime. He encountered a new world that accepted his backbreaking labor even while it relegated him and his kind to the bottom rungs of the social pecking order. Michael Evers's descendants, led by his eldest, John J. Evers Sr., parlayed their clannish survival instincts and political wiles into a tenuous form of middle-class respectability. John Sr. became a midlevel political power to be reckoned with, even as his South Troy enclave still reeked of a bitterness cloaked in Roman Catholic sanctity. Not until a contingent of strutting Sons of Eire showed up as part of a "Gaelic Invasion" of America did the Irish-immigrant class receive any license to celebrate their ethnic pride outside the boundaries of their own tribe. Not until Little Johnny Evers stepped away from the tight bonds of familial obligation—even if just for the summer months—would their contribution to the popular culture find its ultimate platform and tribute: baseball's world's championship.

Joe Tinker had no such family history to fall back on. He was the son of an unwed mother and stepson of an itinerant laborer. But Joe happened to grow up in a time and place where boys, at least, were given leave to find their calling in athletic endeavors. Kansas City leaders realized early on that they had let their boomtown grow too fast and that it was too unwieldy to sustain real growth—that is, to attract and keep middle-class families. Political authorities on one hand and Protestant reformers on the other combined to give boys like Joe green spaces to play in and a moral construct, "muscular Christianity," within which to pursue their adolescent dreams.

The California culture that shaped the worldview of Frank Chance was unique to America. The impulses of his parents, grandparents, and next of kin had brought hundreds of thousands of settlers into a near-empty land with uncharted possibilities. Unlike the Irish or other European immigrants who crossed the Atlantic, unlike the forced passage of African slaves, or the subsequent African American migration from South to North, the California and Oregon settlers' experience had nothing to do with assimilation into—or resistance against—a preexisting, dominant culture. The inimitable Oregon Trail pioneers created their social ethos out of whole cloth, developing an entrepreneurial code of behavior that rested on little more than bravery and force of will.

When these three young scions met in Chicago in late 1902, forming their famous unit the following season, they entered a helter-skelter urban experience that was as far from pastoral Cooperstown as Earth is from Mars. Every social reality they had encountered, and conquered, in their formative youth now had to be reconciled with the near-anarchy of a city of two million people. One by one they were joined by Mordecai Brown, Johnny Kling, Harry Steinfeldt, Jimmy Sheckard, Ed Reulbach, and others, who each threw their own personal experiences and expectations into the mix.

With the help of the unflappable Frank Selee, his spirited wife May, and a visionary executive across town, Ban Johnson, who challenged everyone in organized baseball to recognize the opportunities that lay waiting for them, this hodge-podge collection of ballplayers transformed the game of baseball. They did it by remaining true to their own legacies, by standing up to the reality of each difficult situation, and by working in concert.

And they did it all with peerless distinction. Theirs was the vernacular culture that ultimately took hold of a discredited sport and carried it forward into the new century. The Chicago Cubs played "clean," if still fiercely competitive baseball. They built a great machine which, while it lasted, was invincible. Their new ethos caught fire with legions upon legions of new baseball "fans" young and old, both men and women, who now found a way to celebrate their own American experience by voluntarily—for a couple of hours, at least—immersing themselves in baseball's daily cauldron of joy and sorrow.

The Cooperstown myth—created and fostered by baseball's official culture—was a sham from the beginning, but it would remain powerful until revisionist historians unmasked it a century later. From its inception, however, the official myth was incapable of encompassing or controlling or explaining the innumerable, diverse, wholly unpredictable crosscurrents of experience that baseball players have always impressed upon their eager followers.

Joe Tinker, Johnny Evers, and Frank Chance can't take sole or even three-way credit for baseball's transformation in the early twentieth century. Yet their life stories, separately and together, elevate and extol the real popular memory of baseball as it exists today. They were living men of actual, great, not-quite-otherworldly accomplishment, and they belong in the Baseball Hall of Fame for this reason alone. "The one great reason why men are famous is that in one way or another they have come to symbolize traits of an ideal life," observed sociologist Charles Horton Cooley, an early twentieth-century adherent to the pragmatism of William James. "Their names are charged with daring, hope, love, power, devotion, duty, or truth, and we cherish them because human nature is ever striving after these things."

And yet, until 2016, when the Chicago Cubs won the World Series for the first time in 108 years, breaking the longest championship drought in American sports history, few baseball fans knew all that much about Tinker and Evers and Chance, the cornerstone of the franchise's only prior trophies. Those who have come across their names probably did so through of a piece of throwaway verse—eight lines of barely intelligible rhyme. The new assemblage of talented young bear cubs have finally reanimated the real cultural narrative of baseball—let's call it the Tinker to Evers to Chance narrative—to reveal the nature of team loyalty, fanaticism, and, yes, public memory.

It's been a long time coming, this new Cubs victory machine. Fans waited through some hundred years of hope, expectation, and near misses—always ending, it seemed, in despair, defeat, and agony. And yet they (we) remained true to this team for some strange reason too mysterious to comprehend.

Now, thanks to Tinker and Evers and Chance, we know why: We care because they cared. They cared because their very lives and triumphs seemed to depend on a childhood game they each felt compelled to play.

We can all see ourselves in them, in some small but not insignificant way. We cheer, we cry, we tremble, we exult. We carry their hearts on our sleeves. We can no more stop rooting for our favorite team and players than we can halt the complicated but ever-forward thrust of life. It is as if professional sport exists—and now thrives—for one absurdly simple reason: kids who play games must see and believe they can grow up to become adults who play games.

ACKNOWLEDGMENTS

I'm grateful for the help of many remarkable people in the making of this book, some of whom I've known for years, some I met along the way, and others I'll never get to meet—the faceless but essential compositors of American historical documents. A project such as this, which relies heavily on contemporaneous newspaper and magazine accounts, as well as local histories written at the turn of the twentieth century, would have been a fearsome effort only a decade ago, before the introduction of digital technology. Thanks to libraries and other volunteers, historical researchers now have direct access via our keyboards to thousands of period documents—most of them searchable by keywords. My thanks and appreciation go out to the good folks at Fulton County Postcards in New York, the LA '84 Foundation, state university libraries in California, Colorado, Oregon, and Texas, and the indispensable Society for American Baseball Research. Genealogical services such as Ancestry.com and Genealogybank.com have also made hundreds of newspapers available online. The digital reproduction projects of the HathiTrust partnership, the Internet Archive, and Google Books have put essential resources at everyone's reach. Special mention must go to the remarkable research of Gil Bogen, whose *Tinker, Evers and Chance* was my first stop in this project; while the sourcing here is my own, I've gained inspiration and invaluable pointers from his pathfinding work.

Special thanks to staff (and volunteers) of the Rensselaer County

Historical Society, led by Kathy T. Sheehan, who led me on a fascinating baseball history tour of Troy; the Fresno County Historical Society; the Library of Congress Reading Rooms; and the National Baseball Hall of Fame Library in Cooperstown, where Cassidy Lent and John Horne were responsive and always helpful. I've also been fortunate to have very supportive friends and family who gave me honest feedback on early drafts of the manuscript: my brother John Rapp and his wife Anita Andrew, brother Jim Rapp, sister Susie Heerdink; old friends George Linzer, Bob Benenson, Neil Skene, Larry Thompson, and Arline Riley; and new friends Jack Bales, Tim Wiles, and Robert Pruter. Longtime colleague (and fellow Cubs fan) Alan Ehrenhalt, as always, offered wise counsel and gentle suggestions. And most of all, I bow to my dear friend and book-writing mentor Nadine Cohodas, who kept me focused and energized from start to finish. (That said, any errors made along the way are my own.) I have great appreciation for my editor, Timothy Mennel of the University of Chicago Press. He saw the possibilities in my rough proposal and helped me shape the core ideas, then brought his deft editing skill to bear on the final product. He is a true collaborator.

My eternal devotion goes to my wife, Lee Anne George, who encouraged me to undertake this labor of love. And to my late father, who first taught me how to throw a baseball and catch it, then showed me how to explore a library in search of knowledge and truth. God bless him.

APPENDIX
Diaspora

BAN JOHNSON

The autocratic style and stubbornness that enabled Johnson to turn a backwater minor league into the robust American League were the personality traits that also served to bring him down. In the 1910s, a series of rulings on player contracts that favored the American League pushed NL owners to the brink. Then Johnson turned his old friend Charlie Comiskey into a lifetime enemy. When the Black Sox scandal rocked baseball in 1919–20, both leagues' owners turned to Judge Kennesaw Mountain Landis to restore public trust, effectively shunting Johnson out of the picture. He finally resigned in 1927, a sick and sullen man, and died four years later.

JOHN MCGRAW

The Giants won another pennant in 1911, the first of three in a row, although they lost the World Series each time. After their defeat by the Athletics in 1913, even Christy Mathewson criticized his overbearing manager in a ghostwritten article, which called the Giants a "team of puppets being manipulated from the bench on a string." McGraw went on to win six more NL flags, winning back-to-back World Series in 1921 and 1922. He resigned in 1932 and died two years later at the age of sixty.

The cause of death was listed as prostate cancer and uremia, though one reporter insisted it was because he was no longer top dog.

FRED MERKLE

The goat of the 1908 season had a long and fairly distinguished big league career, including a turn with the Cubs, though he could never manage to live down his rookie mistake. He became McGraw's regular first baseman in 1910, and the following year had his best season, with twelve home runs, eighty-four RBIs, and forty-nine stolen bases. He hung around professional baseball until 1929, when, managing in the minor leagues, a young player referred to him as a "bonehead." Merkle walked off the diamond and never returned.

C. W. MURPHY

The firing of Frank Chance raised eyebrows among his fellow magnates, but when Murphy then replaced manager Johnny Evers after one year, NL owners decided they'd had enough of their impetuous colleague. They enlisted Charles P. Taft to make Murphy an offer for his share of the franchise stock, by that time worth a reported $500,000. Murphy took the cash and returned to Wilmington, Ohio, where he built an ornate local playhouse on Main Street that is still in operation as the historic Murphy Theatre.

MR. AND MRS. FRANK SELEE

In 1999, ninety years after Frank Selee's death, the eleven-member Veterans Committee voted to install Selee in the Hall of Fame. Baseball historian Richard Johnson wrote a speech for Selee's great nephew to deliver at the induction ceremony, though it was never delivered. "Selee's teams were nothing less than true champions who conducted themselves in a manner which elevated the game both on and off the diamond," Johnson wrote.

After May Selee brought Frank's body back to New England in 1909, she moved back to New Mexico. She filed a homestead claim in 1911 for a plot of land near Silver City. At this point Bridget "May" Grant Selee, not yet forty years old, disappears from history.

HARRY STEINFELDT

The Cubs' showstopping third baseman made a half-hearted attempt at a comeback in 1911 in St. Paul and then Boston, but in mid-July he came down with a mysterious illness, thought to be typhoid fever. Then in August he was hospitalized with a "complete nervous breakdown." Over his wife's objections, he tried another comeback but was eventually cut loose. He went home brokenhearted to Bellevue, Kentucky, and soon came down with an extended illness that turned out to be fatal. Steinfeldt died on August 17, 1914, of a cerebral hemorrhage. He was thirty-seven.

FRANK CHANCE

The surgery to remove the blood clot in Chance's brain in September 1912 was a success. Dr. W. G. Frolich pronounced him "completely cured" of the nervous trouble that had forced him to give up baseball, though Chance would remain deaf in one ear for the rest of his life. Having washed his hands of Murphy and the Cubs, Chance quickly accepted a lucrative offer from the New York Highlanders' owner, casino operator Frank Farrell, to manage his newly renamed "Yankees."

The Yankees were a hapless ball club even with the Peerless Leader at the helm. The team had one true star, first baseman Hal Chase, a cocky, wisecracking Californian who today is best known as the most corrupt player in baseball history. He gambled on games with impunity and threw many of them. Chance and Chase locked horns from the start.

Knowing Chance could not hear out of his left ear, Chase would sit on his deaf side and mock his manager's throaty commands and facial expressions. Chance finally traded "Prince Hal" to the White Sox for two lackluster roster fillers.

After a seventh-place finish in 1913, and headed for a similar fate in 1914, Chance resigned at midseason. He returned to his home in Glendora, California, which he called Cub Ranch, and where he operated an orange grove and ran a construction business. Soon he took an ownership stake in the Los Angeles team of the Pacific Coast League and became its vice president and manager, winning a pennant in 1921. His health continued to betray him, but Chance ventured back east in 1923 for a short stint as manager of the Boston Red Sox. The club was still reeling after trading away Babe Ruth and its other stars, and finished dead last in the American League that year.

Charles Comiskey then offered him a job as manager of the White Sox. But during the off-season Chance was struck down by influenza, which left him with severe bouts of bronchial asthma and heart trouble. Johnny Evers became acting manager for the Sox in the interim, but except for a brief appearance on Opening Day, Chance never made it back to the Windy City. Chance reached out to both his old pals, and Tinker and Evers came west for a short and final reunion. Not long after, Chance died suddenly on September 15, 1924, six days after his forty-eighth birthday, the cause listed as lung and kidney failure.

Word of Frank Chance's passing spread rapidly, making headlines in every large- and small-city newspaper in the country. Even John McGraw was moved to offer tribute. "I am losing an old and bitter battler but a warm friend," Muggsy said. "He was a great player—I think one of the best first basemen ever in the game—but in addition he was a great leader because he asked no man to take any chance that he would not take."

Years later, when the Hall of Fame came knocking, his reputation had only grown. "Chance was a great fighting field manager," Grantland Rice remembered. "He was a fine first baseman, a dangerous hitter. But above all a game, scrappy battler, fearing nothing, not even a flock of bean-balls."

JOE TINKER

After a year as player-manager for the Cincinnati Reds, Tinker became one of the first big-name players to jump to the upstart Federal League in 1914. He played and managed for the Chicago Whales for two years in a modern brick and steel-reinforced ballpark that owner Charles Weeghman had constructed on the North Side, at the corner of Addison and Clark streets. The Whales finished a close second in 1914 and won the Federal League pennant the following year, outdrawing the Cubs in both seasons.

Tinker only added to his reputation as a straight shooter by lambasting NL owners over their nefarious labor practices. When the "outlaw league" folded at the end of 1915, Weeghman purchased the Cubs from the Taft family and brought Tinker along as manager as the NL team moved into the new park. That arrangement for Tinker lasted only one forgettable season.

Tinker then launched a second career as a businessman, first in baseball's minor leagues, eventually moving to Florida, where he became a wealthy man speculating in real estate in the Sunshine State. His wife, Ruby Rose, was having medical problems, however, most likely caused by severe depression. On Christmas Day in 1923, Ruby Tinker killed herself with a bullet to the head.

Joe eventually remarried, but the Florida land boom was going bust and the Depression would bring about his financial ruin. He scratched his way back with new ventures, including a bar and billiard parlor, and did some scouting for baseball clubs.

Several years later, while in Chicago to watch the Cubs clinch the 1938 NL pennant, Joe accepted a request to serve as a radio commentator for a championship boxing match. He was surprised to discover that Johnny Evers had answered a similar invitation. The startled old men, who supposedly had never reconciled after thirty wordless years, embraced each other in tears.

Tinker's business dealings and health turned sour again in the 1940s. But he recovered enough to celebrate the trio's induction to the Hall of

Fame in 1946. A spreading infection in his foot led to the amputation of his left leg a year later. Practically destitute, Tinker held on for a few more months before his death on July 27, 1948. "Today is my birthday," said the sixty-eight-year old. "It's a good day to go."

JOHNNY EVERS

The Crab sealed his reputation as a battler and clubhouse leader in 1914, when he captained the "Miracle" Boston Braves, going from a 25–40 record on July 4 to the NL pennant and then a World's Championship sweep. Evers was awarded the Chalmers' Award that year as the league's most valuable player. He was also the highest-paid player in baseball at the time.

That was his last good season, however. After Boston he spent some time with the Phillies before retiring in 1917. He went back to Troy and his shoe store and worked with the minor league Trojans, hobnobbing with players, old-timers, and visiting big leaguers. Evers briefly returned to the Cubs as manager in 1921, then to the White Sox three years later, both with meager results.

During the 1930s Evers ran a sporting-goods store in Albany, in partnership with his brother Joe. In 1942 he suffered a stroke that debilitated him for the rest of his life.

The Evers shoe store remained in family hands until it closed in the 1990s. John T. Evers, Joe's grandson, was cleaning out the storeroom when he found a shoebox filled with his great uncle's mementos. One of them was a tattered old baseball labeled as the one Evers held aloft on second base in the Merkle episode on September 23, 1908. The family sold the ball at auction, where actor Charlie Sheen bought it for $30,250. He sold it to another collector in 1999, who in turn put it up for auction in 2010, when it sold for $75,000 to sportscaster Keith Olbermann. It has since changed hands again to an anonymous collector.

John J. Evers Jr. died at sixty-five on March 28, 1947, one year after his induction into the Hall of Fame. In his last days, Evers took pleasure in the fact that the famous infield had entered the Hall of Fame at the same time. "I'm glad we made it all together," he said. "Chance should have been elected long ago. I wish he were alive to feel as happy about it as I do."

Then he added: "I'm glad for Tinker, too."

ABBREVIATIONS USED IN NOTES

Abbreviation	Name	Digital source (where applicable)
Newspapers:		
AB	*Albuquerque (NM) Citizen*	Newspapers.com
AR	*Arizona Republican*	Newspapers.com
AS	*Anaconda (MT) Standard*	Newspapers.com
BE	*Brooklyn (NY) Daily Eagle*	Newspapers.com
BG	*Boston Globe*	ProQuest Historical Newspapers, Chronicling America (LOC)
BH	*Boston Herald*	
CCT	*Cincinnati Commercial Tribune*	
CDJ	*Chicago Daily Journal*	
CDN	*Chicago Daily News*	
CE	*Cincinnati Enquirer*	Newspapers.com
CEP	*Chicago Evening Post*	
CI-O	*Chicago Inter-Ocean* (also: *Chicago Inter Ocean*)	Newspapers.com
CRH	*Chicago Record Herald*	
CTr	*Chicago Tribune*	Tribune Digital Archives
DFP	*Detroit Free Press*	Newspapers.com
DH	*Decatur (IL) Herald*	Newspapers.com
DP	*Denver Post*	Genealogybank.com
EP	*Evansville (IN) Press*	Newspapers.com
EPH	*El Paso (TX) Herald*	Portal of Texas History
FBR	*Fresno (CA) Bee Republican*	Newspapers.com
FEx	*Fresno Expositor*	
FMR	*Fresno Morning Republican*	Newpapers.com
FWG	*Fort Worth (TX) Daily Gazette*	Newspapers.com

FWR	*Fresno Weekly Republican*	Newspapers.com
GN	*Galveston Daily News*	
HI	*Helena (MT) Independent*	genealogybank.com
IN	*Indianapolis News*	Newspapers.com
ISJ	*Illinois State Journal*	Newspaperarchives.com
KCJ	*Kansas City (KS) Journal*	Newspapers.com
LAH	*Los Angeles Herald*	California Digital Newspaper Collection
LAT	*Los Angeles Times*	LA Times digital archives
LHD	*Leadville Herald Democrat*	Colorado Historic Newspaper Collection
MN	*Mansfield (OH) News*	Newspaperarchives.com
NYA	*New York American*	
NYC	*New York Clipper*	University of Illinois Library digital collection
NYEJ	*New York Evening Journal*	
NYEM	*New York Evening Mail*	
NYET	*New York Evening Telegram*	
NYEW	*New York Evening World*	Newspapers.com
NYG	*New York Globe*	
NYH	*New York Herald*	
NYS	*New York Sun*	Chronicling America (LOC)
NYT	*New York Times*	TimesMachine
NYTr	*New York Tribune*	
OB	*Omaha (NE) Daily Bee*	Newspaperarchives.com
Ore	*Oregonian (Portland, OR)*	Historic Oregon Newspapers
Osh	*Oshkosh (WI) Daily Northwestern*	Newspapers.com
PGT	*Pittsburgh Gazette Times*	Newspapers.com
PPo	*Pittsburgh Post*	Newspapers.com
PPr	*Pittsburgh Press*	
RDC	*Rochester (NY) Democrat & Chronicle*	Newspapers.com
RMN	*Rocky Mountain News*	genealogybank.com
SDT	*Seattle Daily Times*	Genealogybank.com
SFCa	*San Francisco Call*	Newspapers.com
SFChr	*San Francisco Chronicle*	
SL	*Sporting Life*	LA '84 Foundation Digital Collections
SN	*Sporting News*	Paper of Record (via SABR)
SPr	*Sheboygan (WI) Daily Press*	Newspaperarchives.com
SPS	*Syracuse (NY) Post Standard*	Newspaperarchives.com
STr	*Scranton (PA) Truth*	Newspapers.com
TDT	*Troy Daily Times*	Fulton County Postcards

TDW	*Troy Daily Whig*	Fulton County Postcards
TET	*Trenton (NJ) Evening Times*	Genealogybank.com
TR	*Troy (NY) Record*	Fulton County Postcards
TT	*Troy Telegram*	
TTR	*Troy Times Record*	Newspapers.com
WE	*Wichita (KS) Eagle*	Newspapers.com
WES	*Washington Evening Star*	Genealogybank.com, Chronicling America (LOC)
WNR	*Washington National Republican*	Chronicling America (LOC)
WP	*Washington Post*	ProQuest Historical Newspapers
WT	*Washington Times*	

Periodicals:

TAM	*The American Magazine*	University of Michigan, HathiTrust
BB	*Base Ball*	
BM	*Baseball Magazine*	LA '84 Foundation Digital Collections
BRJ	*Baseball Research Journal*	Society of American Baseball Research
JSH	*Journal of Sport History*	LA '84 Foundation Digital Collections
LD	*Literary Digest*	
Ou	*Outing Magazine*	LA '84 Foundation Digital Collections
PM	*Pearson's Magazine*	HathiTrust
SEP	*Saturday Evening Post*	

Websites:

BHOF	Baseball Hall of Fame and Museum
BRef	Baseball-Reference.com
EC	Encyclopedia of Chicago
LOC	Library of Congress
RS	Retrosheet.org
SABR	Society for American Baseball Research

NOTES

PREFACE

Having shipped off: Sally Ashley, *F.P.A.: The Life and Times of Franklin Pierce Adams* (New York: Beaufort Books, 1986), 65.

A man of "biting, brilliant wit": Charles Fountain, *Sportswriter: The Life and Times of Grantland Rice* (New York: Oxford University Press, 1993), 113.

rabid baseball fan: Ashley, *F.P.A.*

deep in the box score: "Chance's Crew Still on Top," SPS, July 12, 1910, 10.

They sent their rebuttals: Fountain, *Sportswriter*, 114.

This merry-go-round: Peter Armenti, "Tinker to Evers to Chance," *From the Catbird Seat* (blog), Library of Congress, April 2, 2012, https://blogs.loc.gov/catbird/2012/04/tinker-to-evers-to-chance.

Frank may write: Grantland Rice, *The Tumult and the Shouting: My Life in Sport* (New York: A. S. Barnes and Co., 1954), 316.

Its little known verse: Andy Strasberg, Bob Thompson, and Tim Wiles, *Baseball's Greatest Hit: The Story of "Take Me Out to the Ballgame"* (New York: Hal Leonard Books, 2008), 1.

They won 530: Bill James, *The New Bill James Historical Baseball Abstract* (New York: Free Press, 2001), 81.

CHAPTER ONE

Baseball bards: Robert Miller Smith, *Baseball: A Historical Narrative of the Game, the Men Who Played It, and Its Place in American Life* (New York: Simon and Schuster, 1947), 90.

"Slide, Kelly, Slide": For the lyrics to the song "Slide, Kelly, Slide," see Baseball Almanac, http://www.baseball-almanac.com/poetry/slide_kelly_slide.shtml; for the painting, see Digital Commonwealth, Massachusetts Collections Online, https://www.digitalcommonwealth.org/search/commonwealth:sf2687821.

How the country adored: Ban Johnson, as told to George Creel, "Slide, Kelly, Slide," SEP, April 30, 1930, 17.

If I could afford: Mike "King" Kelly, *Play Ball: Stories of the Ball Field* (Boston: Emery & Hughes, 1888). Chapter 15, issued digitally in 2008, is available at http://www .baseballchronology.com/Baseball/Books/Classic/Play-Ball_By-King-Kelly/Page -2.asp.

American children: David I. Macleod, *The Age of the Child: Children in America, 1890– 1920* (New York: Twayne Publishers, 1998).

To play at cricket: Clifford Putney, *Muscular Christianity: Manhood and Sports in Protestant America, 1880–1920* (Cambridge, MA: Harvard University Press, 2001), 26.

In the last decades: Macleod, *Age of the Child*, 1.

Their favorites: Kathryn Grover, ed., *Hard at Play: Leisure in America, 1840–1940* (Amherst: University of Massachusetts Press, 1992).

Soldiers took: Richard Hershberger, "The Antebellum Growth and Spread of the New York Game," BB, October 1, 2014.

Baseball was one: David Lamoreaux, "Baseball in the Late Nineteenth Century: The Source of Its Appeal," *Journal of Popular Culture*, Winter 1977, 597.

Player-driven outfit: David Quentin Voigt, *Baseball: An Illustrated History* (University Park: Pennsylvania State University Press, 1987), 13–39.

This erratic climate changed: Ibid.

Paying young men: *Young Men's Era*, October 8, 1891, cited in William J. Baker, "Disputed Diamonds: The YMCA Debate over Baseball in the Late 19th Century," JSH, Winter 1992, 257.

boys again: Albert G. Spalding, *America's National Game* (New York: American Sports Publishing, 1911), 60.

One day: "How Quick Wit Won a Game," RDC, March 6, 1904, 22.

Whole-souled: Adrian C. Anson, *A Ball Player's Career* (Chicago: Era Publishing, 1900), 119 (Google Books).

What no one had noticed: Weidman's full quote is "He hurdled—that's what the athletes call it—Bennett and Kelly lying on the ground, and crossed the plate with the winning run." RDC, March 6, 1904.

Players took: Charles DeMotte, *Bat, Ball & Bible: Baseball and Sunday Observance in New York* (Washington, DC: Potomac Books, 2013), xii.

Owners even tried: John Thorn, *Baseball in the Garden of Eden: The Secret History of the Early Game* (New York: Simon and Schuster, 2011), 178.

No one combined: Smith, *Baseball*, 91; Daniel Okrent and Steve Wulf, *Baseball Anecdotes* (New York: Diversion Books, 1989).

Weidman's vivid depiction: Retrosheet's database of games between Chicago and Detroit from 1880 through 1886 shows no games of this nature. See the website's Directory of Major League Years, at http://www.retrosheet.org/boxesetc/index .html.

these tall tales: The earliest source for the home plate stunt appears to be in Al Spink, *One Thousand Sports Stories* (Chicago: Martin, 1921), 2:144. Spink attributed his account to a childhood memory of William O'Brien, president of the Chicago City League. The tale was subsequently retold without reference to the original in the following works: Ira L. Smith and H. Allen Smith, *Low and Inside: A Book of Baseball Anecdotes, Oddities, and Curiosities* (Garden City, NY: Doubleday, 1949), 36; Jay Robert Nash, *People to See: An Anecdotal History of Chicago's Makers and Breakers* (New York: Rowman & Littlefield, 1981), 110; Peter Golenbock, *Wrigleyville: A Magical History Tour of the Chicago Cubs* (New York: St. Martin's Press, 1996), 33; Marty Appel, *Slide, Kelly, Slide: The Wild Life and Times of Mike "King" Kelly, Baseball's First Superstar* (Lanham, MD: Scarecrow Press, 1999), 72; and Kevin Moran, "Before Babe Ruth, Troy Native Michael 'King' Kelly Filled Stadiums across the Country," TR, November 10, 2010.

Kelly's feats: Golenbock, *Wrigleyville*, 34.

If anything: Howard W. Rosenberg, *Cap Anson 3: Muggsy John McGraw and the Tricksters: Baseball's Fun Age of Rule Bending* (Arlington, VA: Tile Books, 2005).

An increasingly urban society: Matthew Algeo, *Pedestrianism: When Watching People Walk Was America's Favorite Sport* (Chicago: Chicago Review Press, 2014).

but one drawback: Henry Chadwick, ed., *Spalding's Baseball Guide and Official League Book of 1895* (New York: American Sports Publishing, 1895), 10.

McGraw believed: *Cincinnati Times Star*, June 4, 1897, cited in Rosenberg, *Cap Anson 3*, 122.

The press began: Henry Chadwick, SN, October 9, 1897.

A milk and water: BG, January 13, 1894, cited in David Quentin Voigt, *American Baseball: From Gentleman's Sport to the Commissioner System* (State College: Pennsylvania State University Press, 2010), 245.

Chadwick insisted: Smith, *Baseball*, 22.

In August 1897: "Danger Signals: Straws Showing Which Way the Wind Blows," SL, August 6, 1897, 10.

New York Sun: "Baseball Endangered," NYS, August 8, 11, 15, 1897, 6.

Chicago Tribune: CTr, quoted in "A Warning to Baseball Managers," NYS, September 1, 1897, 6.

It was one thing: SL, July 24, 1897, cited in Bill Felber, *A Game of Brawl: The Orioles, the Beaneaters & the Battle for the 1897 Pennant* (Lincoln: University of Nebraska Press, 2007), 156.

The 5,200 people: PPo, May 26, 1897, cited in Felber, *Game of Brawl*, 109.

One Baltimore apologist: NYC, November 8, 1897.

so-called hoodlumism: "It's Only Exuberance," WP, reprinted in SL, February 27, 1897, 12.

such vile language: SL, August 8, 1895, 2.

Profanity belongs: SL, October 1, 1892, 3.

remarkably explicit: "Special Instructions to Players," issued in March 1898 by the National League of Professional Baseball Clubs, original copy posted online by Robert Lifson, Robert Edward Auctions, December 2, 2007, http://www.robertedwardauctions.com/auction/2008/spring/1182/1898-special

-instructions-players-regarding-obscene-language-baltimore-orioles-game
-ticket/.

Brush resolution: David Quentin Voigt, *American Baseball: From Gentleman's Sport to the Commissioner System* (University Park: Penn State University Press, 2010), 230.

outright bigotry: Robert Peterson, *Only the Ball Was White: A History of Legendary Black Players and the All-Black Professional Teams* (Oxford: Oxford University Press, 1992), 29.

Adrian "Cap" Anson: David Fleitz, "Cap Anson," SABR, http://sabr.org/bioproj /person/9b42f875.

Moses Fleetwood Walker: John R. Husman, "Cap vs. Fleet Walker," SABR, https://sabr .org/gamesproj/game/august-10-1883-cap-anson-vs-fleet-walker.

gentlemen's agreement: Jules Tygiel, *Baseball's Great Experiment: Jackie Robinson and His Legacy* (New York: Oxford University Press, 2008), 30–46.

Annual attendance: "1890–1899 Ballpark Attendance," Ballparks of Baseball, http:// www.ballparksofbaseball.com/1890-1899-mlb-attendance.

moribund, or "dead rabbit," towns: "Letter from a Fan," WE, January 23, 1898, 6; "Mad Westerners," SL, April 11, 1896, 1; "Reds Play Today," CE, April 10, 1898, 22; "Brewers Are Third," DFP, July 23, 1898, 6.

magnates at first: David Quentin Voigt, *The League That Failed* (Lanham, MD: Scarecrow Press, 1998), 204.

American Association: Edward Achorn, *The Summer of Beer and Whiskey: How Brewers, Barkeeps, Rowdies, Immigrants, and a Wild Pennant Fight Made Baseball America's Game* (New York: Public Affairs, 2013).

The reserve clause: Voigt, *League That Failed*.

Players League: Voigt, *Baseball*, 69–73.

Cleveland drew: Voigt, *American Baseball*, 75.

CHAPTER TWO

At 11:30 p.m.: Thanks to Douglas Rubin, a member of the Society of American Baseball Research (SABR) and an expert on nineteenth-century train travel by baseball teams, for his guidance in identifying Evers's travel itinerary. W. F. Allen, ed., *Official Guide of the Railways and Steam Navigation Lines of the United States* (New York: National Railway Publication, 1902), 207; Hugh S. Fullerton, WP, January 7, 1906; John J. Evers, "Some Baseball Confessions by Johnny Evers, of the Braves," NYTr, January 24, 1915.

The Irish Catholic funeral: TDT, August 22, 1902; TR, August 25, 1902.

He had a following: "News and Gossip," SL, June 21, 1902, 21.

The waves of families: Ralph Wilcox, "Irish Americans in Sports: The Nineteenth Century," in *Making the Irish American: History and Heritage of the Irish in the United States*, ed. J. J. Lee and Marion R. Casey (New York: New York University Press, 2006); Patrick R. Redmond, *The Irish and the Making of American Sport, 1835–1920* (Jefferson, NC: McFarland, 2014).

Many people: Bill James, *The New Bill James Historical Baseball Abstract* (New York: Free Press, 2001), 55.

If Irish American veins: "Major League Players from Troy," in *Troy's Baseball Heritage*, ed. Richard A. Puff (Troy, NY: Walter Snyder Printer, 1992), 48; Jim Overmyer, "City of Diamond Heroes," in *Troy's Baseball Heritage*, 21–28. Uncle Tom Evers played two years in the 1880s, and younger brother Joe played one game in 1913; BRef, http://www.baseball-reference.com/players.

Since the late 1880s: BRef, http://www.baseball-reference.com/teams/CHC.

The telegram: John T. Evers, "Johnny Evers 'The Crab,'" in *Troy's Baseball Heritage*, 29–32.

fabled "Haymakers": Richard A. Puff, "Haymakers and Daisycutters," in *Troy's Baseball Heritage*, 6–18.

By the 1890s: "Left at the Post," NYS, April 17, 1891, 4; "Again We Break Even," NYS, April 18, 1891, 4.

child wonder: "The Craftiest of the Cubs," NYH, January 22, 1911.

Johnny's grandfather: Passenger Lists of Vessels Arriving at New York, New York, 1820–97, roll M237, 1820–97, roll 041, U.S. Customs Service, National Archives records, Ancestry.com; 1850 U.S. Census: Troy Ward 6, Rensselaer, NY (Ancestry.com).

Pre-Famine Ireland: Kerby A. Miller, *Emigrants and Exiles: Ireland and the Irish Exodus to North America* (Oxford: Oxford University Press, 1988).

Michael Evers: *Troy City Directory, 1840–42* (Boston: Adams & Sampson, 1842); 1850 U.S. Census; 1880 U.S. Federal Census, Troy, Rensselaer, NY (Ancestry.com).

The local diocese: Samuel H. Williamson, "Seven Ways to Compute the Relative Value of a U.S. Dollar Amount, 1774 to present," MeasuringWorth, 2016, https://www .measuringworth.com/uscompare/relativevalue.php; Joan Lowe, "St. Joseph's Parish, Troy, NY," Troy Irish Genealogy Society, http://www.rootsweb.ancestry .com/~nytigs/StJosephsChurchHistory-J.Howe.htm.

Evers joined: TDT, August 22, 1902; Kathryn T. Sheehan, registrar and county historian, Rensselaer County Historical Society, Troy, New York, interview with author, April 15, 2015.

South Troy against the world: Ibid.

The roots of this tension: Rutherford Haynor, *Troy and Rensselaer County, New York* (New York: Lewis Historical Publishing, 1925).

Llamas have carried: Arthur James Weise, *Troy's One Hundred Years, 1789–1899* (Troy, NY: Wm. H. Young, 1891).

The national movement: H. E. Hoagland, "The Rise of the Iron Molders' International Union," in *American Economic Review*, June 1913, 296, http://www.jstor.org /stable/1827955.

Troy became: Don Rittner, *Remembering Troy: Heritage on the Hudson* (Charleston, SC: History Press, 2008).

"detachable" starched shirt collars: Weise, *One Hundred Years*.

Collar City: Jack Casey, *The Trial of Bat Shay* (Troy, NY: Diamond Rock Publishing,

2011); Fred DeMay, "Home Sweet Home on the Rensselaer Plateau," *New York State Conservationist*, October 2011, http://www.dec.ny.gov/docs/administration _pdf/1011hikerensselaerplat.pdf.

John started work: Tammis K. Groft, *Cast with Style: Nineteenth Century Cast-Iron Stoves from the Albany Area* (Albany, NY: SUNY Press, 1984); "Fuller, Warren & Co. Stoves," Hoxsie! Little Bits of History and Ephemera from Albany, Schenectady and Troy, http://hoxsie.org/2012/04/25/fuller_warren_co_stoves/; "Charter Election Yesterday," TDW, March 2, 1870; *Troy City Directory, 1874* (Boston: Sampson & Davenport, 1874).

He operated a brewery: "Edward Murphy Jr.," *Illustrated State Manual: The Red Book, 1895* (Albany: New York State, 1895); "Edward Murphy, Jr., Ex-Senator, Dead," NYT, August 4, 1911.

Under his watch: "Still in Murphy's Grasp," NYT, March 7, 1894.

In late 1875: *Troy City Directory, 1875* (Boston: Sampson & Davenport, 1875); Kerby Miller, *Ireland and Irish America: Culture, Class, and Transatlantic Migration* (Dublin: Field Day Publications, 2008).

Christian name: Evers, NYTr.

They were touted: Edward H. Lisk, *Representative Young Irish-Americans of Troy, N.Y.* (Troy, NY: Troy Book Makers, 2012), 1:19; "A Protracted Siege," TDT, June 5, 1888; Williamson, "Seven Ways."

The S.S. *Wisconsin*: "Welcome, Erin's Brawn," BG, September 26, 1888, 2; "Weather Today," NYTr, September 25, 1888, 5; [James Whelan], "Gaelic Invasion of America," *Sport* (Dublin), November 3, 1888.

Their sticks: "Young Irish Athletes," NYT, September 26, 1888.

these star athletes: Whelan, *Sport*; "GAA," Gaelic Athletic Association, https://www .gaa.ie; Paul Darby, *Gaelic Games, Nationalism and the Irish Diaspora in the United States* (Dublin: University College Dublin Press, 2009).

The GAA codified: Mike Cronin, "The Gaelic Athletic Association's Invasion of America, 1888," *Sport in History*, June 2007, 190.

The GAA hoped: Whelan, *Sport*, September 1, 1888.

They had placed advertisements: TT, October 13, 1888. The original set the last sentence in boldface.

What really caught: "The Irish Giants in Troy," TT, October 13, 1888.

Irish American boys: Wilcox, "Irish Americans in Sports"; Robert T. Walsh, "The Sports of an Irish Fair," Ou, March 1891, 432.

Hurling competitions: Séamus J. King, "A History of Hurling: Our National Game," http://www.seamusjking.com/history-of-hurling.html; Wilcox, "Irish Americans in Sports."

The ball, or *sliotar*: King, "History of Hurling."

Fastest game on grass: Eamonn, "Hurling: The Fastest Game on Grass," YouTube video, 5:21, https://www.youtube.com/watch?v=TmzivRetelE; Shea Shannon, "Hurling Trickshots," YouTube video, 1:23, May 27, 2013, https://www.youtube .com/watch?v=uRbYQNxcl3w&t=9s.

Their purpose: Peter Morris, *A Game of Inches: The Game on the Field* (Chicago: Ivan R. Dee, 2006), 419.

Another fielding skill: C.R.'s Video Vaults, "D. J. Carey—Hurling Skills," YouTube video, 17:01, April 5, 2013, https://www.youtube.com/watch?v=7fNg9hclfoA.

McGraw learned: Undated clipping from John McGraw file, BHOF.

Irish kids: Jerrold Casway, *Ed Delahanty in the Emerald Age of Baseball* (Notre Dame, IN: University of Notre Dame Press, 2004).

All outdoor games: James S. Mitchel, "The Celt as a Baseball Player," *The Gael*, May 1902, 151.

Ethnic and national identity: Lawrence J. McCaffrey, *The Irish Catholic Diaspora in America* (Washington, DC: Catholic University Press, 1997).

To the Gaelic invaders: Cronin, *Sport in History*.

Several hundred people: TT, October 15, 1888.

Some Victorian-era Protestants: Rev. Jonathan Townley Crane, *Popular Amusements* (Cincinnati, OH: Hitchcock and Walden, 1870) (Making of America Books Collection, University of Michigan Library).

Picnics called for: Cited in Lorett Treese, "A Very Civilized Affair," LAT, July 18, 1991.

The city streets: TDT, November 1, 1870; "Baseball Illegal in Albany," TTR, July 3, 1973; "Famous Captain of the Braves," BM, February 1915, 71.

Jack was hooked: John Evers, "When I Sat on the Bleachers," BM, September 1911, 17.

The Haymakers: "The Craftiest of the Cubs," NYH, January 22, 1911.

"Tom" Evers: "The Nationals' Opening," WNR, March 28, 1885.

The Union Association: "Tom Evers," BRef, http://www.baseball-reference.com /players/e/everst001.shtml; "Amateur Baseball," WP, June 5, 1890, 6; WES, January 20, 1909.

Although Kelly's parents: Overmyer, *Troy's Baseball Heritage.*

Like his father: "Craftiest of the Cubs," NYH; Evers, BM.

Jack graduated: John N. Wheeler, "The Keystone King's Start in Big Baseball," NYS, November 22, 1914, 16; C. P. Stack, "A Day with John Evers," BM, February 1915, 71; *Troy City Directory, 1901* (Boston: Sampson & Murdock, 1901).

Why wouldn't it: Evers, NYTr.

The Cheerups won: One of the minor league players Evers probably played against was an itinerant catcher named John J. "Jack" Evers. It's not clear whether they were related. This other Jack Evers also grew up in South Troy and at one point appeared to have a promising future in organized baseball, getting a tryout in the spring of 1902 with the Giants. "How Evers Got His Start," NYET, reprinted in LD, May 31, 1913, 1242; TDT, September 26, 1902; "Promising Young Catcher Who Is Practicing with the Giants," NYET, April 15, 1902; Jack Evers, BRef, http://www.baseball-reference.com/minors/player.cgi?id=evers-001joh.

Something happened: Wheeler, NYS.

Baker signed Evers: Frank Keetz, "Johnny Evers, the Find of the 1902 Season," Research Journals Archive (SABR), 1983.

At first it was: Newspaper citations in ibid.

a consistent hitter: "Johnny Evers," BRef, http://www.baseball-reference.com/minors /player.cgi?id=evers-002joh; "How Evers Got His Start," LD; "News and Gossip," SL, June 21, 1902.

his occupation: *Troy City Directory, 1902* (Boston: Sampson & Murdoch, 1902); "The State League," TDT, August 16, 1902.

By this time John Sr.: Evers, NYTr.

John Sr.'s health: Obituary, TDT, August 22, 1902; TR, August 25, 1902.

St. Joseph's Church: Funeral, TDT, August 25, 1902.

Johnny took solace: Evers, NYTr.

Johnny rejoined: Ibid., emphasis added.

He played his last game: "Troy Defeated Albany Yesterday," TR, September 1, 1902; Evers, NYTr; Peter Morris, *Catcher: How the Man Behind the Plate Became an American Folk Hero* (Chicago: Ivan R. Dee, 2009), 94.

Hungry, exhausted: Evers, NYTr.

Chicago Tribune: CTr, quoted in "The Baseball Players," TDT, September 26, 1902.

CHAPTER THREE

The sun was warm: "Ideal Decoration Day Weather," KCJ, May 31, 1899; "Yellow Fever in Cuba during the Spanish American War," University of Virginia Historical Collections, http://exhibits.hsl.virginia.edu/yellowfever/cuba.

Decoration Day: "God Save America" and "Blues Break Even," KCJ, May 31, 1899, 3 and 5.

At the sprawling Fairmount Park: Mrs. M. W. Ellsworth, *Queen of the Household* (Detroit: Ellsworth & Brey, 1900), 566, http://www.foodtimeline.org/foodpicnics .html#picnicmenus; "Christian Endeavorers," KCJ, May 31, 1899, 12; "C.E. at Fairmount," KCJ, May 30, 1899; "Missouri's Dead," KCJ, May 11, 1899, 7.

He undressed you: Dan Daniel, "Daniel's Dope," NYET, July 29, 1943.

a threesome: 928 Flora Ave., later moving to 1015 E. Sixteenth St., *Kansas City Directories, 1894–1899* (Kansas City: Hoye Directory Co., 1894–99) (Ancestry.com).

Ruby Rose: "Pioneer Merchant's Death," KCJ, February 28, 1898; W. A. Phelon Jr., "Chicago Gleanings," SL, October 31, 1903, 4.

Early Kansas City: Theodore A. Brown and Lyle W. Dorsett, *K.C.: A History of Kansas City* (Boulder, CO: Pruett, 1978), 42.

The wooden sidewalks: John Edward Hicks, *Adventures of a Tramp Printer, 1880–1890* (Kansas City, MO: Indian Creek Books, 1950), 27.

Local historians: Brown and Dorsett, *K.C.*

still an ugly city: Sherry Lamb Schirmer, *A City Divided: The Racial Landscape of Kansas City, 1900–1960* (Columbia: University of Missouri Press, 2002), 15; see also Joel Arthur Tarr, *The Search for the Ultimate Sink: Urban Pollution in Historical Perspective* (Akron, OH: University of Akron Press, 1996).

This community stopped: Henry Schott, "A City's Fight for Beauty," *The World's Work*, February 1906, 7191 (digital collection of University of Michigan, http://hdl .handle.net/2027/mdp.39015010799289).

in a word, planning: William H. Wilson, *The City Beautiful Movement in Kansas City* (Columbia: University of Missouri Press, 1964), 43–47.

Kessler and Meyer: *Report of the Board of Park and Boulevard Commissioners of Kansas City, Mo.* (Kansas City, MO: Hudson-Kimberly, 1893), 12.

Kessler's vision: "Beautiful Dreamer," *KC History: Missouri Valley Special Collections* (blog), Kansas City Public Library, http://www.kclibrary.org/blog/week-kansas -city-history/beautiful-dreamer.

Within a decade: Howard E. Huselton, "Kansas City's Parks and Boulevards," *Art and Progress*, November 1, 1911, http://www.jstor.org/stable/10.2307/20560515.

ten-minute walk: *Polk's Official Arrow Street Guide of Greater Kansas City* (Kansas City, MO: Gate's City Directory, 1900); *Kansas City Directories, 1894–1899.*

brief coexistence: F. C. Lane, "Joe Tinker the Shortstop Manager and His Remarkable Career," BM, July 1913, 42.

Elizabeth Williams: *1870 U.S. Federal Census*, Grasshopper, Atchison, KS (Ancestry.com); *1875 Kansas Territory Census*, Kansas State Historical Society (Ancestry.com).

Resident Tom Wilson: Gil Bogen, *Tinker, Evers and Chance: A Triple Biography* (Jefferson, NC: McFarland, 2003); Dan Johnson, "Chancing upon Tinker," Kansas City *Kansan*, August 6, 2000; undated newspaper article cited by Kevin Smith in Bogen, *Tinker, Evers and Chance*, 14.

He lived in Oquawka: 1880 U.S. Federal Census, Oquawka, Henderson, IL (Ancestry.com).

In early 1900: The family at 1015 E. Sixteenth St. was recorded as Decker— William W., wife Elizabeth, and nineteen-year-old son Joseph P. [*sic*], whose occupation is recorded as "ball player"—1900 U.S. Federal Census, Kansas City, MO (Ancestry.com); *Kansas City Directories, 1894–1899.*

Lacking companionship: Lane, "Joe Tinker," BM, 46.

Kling "bought" Tinker: Joe Tinker, "How I Became a Ball Player," NYET, August 27, 1913.

He tried out: *Kansas City Directories, 1894–1899.*

Tinker joined: Henry B. F. MacFarland, "The Christian Endeavor Movement," *North American Review* 182, no. 591 (February 1906), 194–203, http://www.jstor.org /stable/25105522 (digital collection of University of Northern Iowa).

Clark created: Sydney E. Ahlstrom, *A Religious History of the American People* (New Haven, CT: Yale University Press, 1974), 858.

object of life: Anderson and Anderson, *Physical Training.*

gospel of work: Steven J. Overman, *The Protestant Ethic and the Spirit of Sport: How Calvinism and Capitalism Shaped America's Games* (Macon, GA: Mercer University Press, 2011), 119.

Roosevelt: Theodore Roosevelt, *The Strenuous Life: Essays and Addresses* (New York: Century Co., 1901), 155 (HathiTrust).

Social Gospellers: Clifford Putney, *Muscular Christianity: Manhood and Sports in Protestant America, 1880–1920* (Cambridge, MA: Harvard University Press, 2001), 26.

At the forefront: Ibid., 118.

Opening Day: "One Great Day for Fans," DP, May 6, 1900, 20.

blackface tune: "Mr. Johnson, Don't Get Gay," *National Jukebox*, Library of Congress, http://www.loc.gov/jukebox/recordings/detail/id/5817.

A very fast player: Otto C. Floto, "Sports of the Day," DP, March 11, 1900, 16.

Practically every town: Duane Smith and Mark Foster, *They Came to Play: A Photographic History of Colorado Baseball* (Nowise: University Press of Colorado, 1997), 4.

Tebeau: "George Tebeau," BRef, http://www.baseball-reference.com/players/t /tebeage01.shtml; DP, April 20, 1900.

Tinker is one: Floto, "Sports of the Day," DP, May 31, 1900, 7.

All the youngsters: RMN, May 20, 1900, 28.

Tinker was a good boy: Floto, "Sports of the Day," DP, June 11, 1900, 12; Tinker, "How I Became a Ballplayer."

The four-club circuit: Skylar Browning and Jeremy Watterson, *Montana Baseball History* (Charleston, SC: History Press, 2015).

Baseball was not new: Ibid.

his fortunes turned: *Great Falls Tribune*, cited in Browning, *Montana Baseball*.

Tinker . . . made a hit: "Strikes Her Old Gait," AS, July 1, 1900, 22.

The good reviews: "Helena Defeated," AS, July 9, 1900, 4; "Anaconda Win," AS, July 13, 1900, 4; "It Was a Great Game," AS, July 16, 1900, 4; "Can't Lose the Hoodoo," AS, July 18, 1900, 4.

The club couldn't: F. C. Lane, "Joe Tinker," BM; "Gossip of the Diamond," AS, August 4, 1900, 4; "At the Hotels," HI, August 14, 1900, 7.

The best part: Browning, *Montana Baseball*; "Avenged Their Defeat," AS, September 20, 1900, 17.

Only one problem: James A. Scott, *Montana: The Magazine of Western History*, cited in Browning, *Montana Baseball*.

in Portland: Jim Price, "A Tale of Four Cities," in *Rain Check: Baseball in the Pacific Northwest*, ed. Mark Armour (Cleveland, OH: SABR, 2006); "Portland Baseball," PdxHistory.com, http://www.pdxhistory.com/html/portland_baseball.html.

Tinker got a raise: Chicago Federal Club memo on Tinker's salary history, player file, BHOF.

He joined a group: "Baseball of a Year," SDT, October 12, 1901, 18.

The following season: "Joe Tinker," BRef, http://www.baseball-reference.com/register /player.cgi?id=tinker001jos; "Portland Loses Both," Ore, October 14, 1901, 3.

Lucas declared: "Ball Season Is Over," Ore, October 14, 1901, 3.

Like a deer: "Developed Baseball Stars," WP, December 27, 1908, M6.

The pact was: David Quentin Voigt, *Baseball: An Illustrated History* (University Park: Pennsylvania State University Press, 1994), 96.

Chicanery is the ozone: John Saccoman, "John Brush," SABR, http://sabr.org/bioproj /person/a46ef165.

Brush applied: "Recruiting for the Reds," WES, November 11, 1901.

Tinker refuses: WES, November 26, 1901; SL, November 16, 1901, in "In the Baseball World," Ore, November 25, 1901.

If they want me: WES, November 26, 1901.

The back-and-forth: "One Loyal Ball Player," TET, November 29, 1901, 7.

That December: "Joe Tinker Goes to Chicago," Ore, December 11, 1901; Tinker, "How I Became a Ballplayer"; Tinker player file, BHOF.

C.A. Whitmore: "Joe Tinker 'Makes Good,'" Ore, May 16, 1902, 5.

In Joe Tinker: "Three Old Favorites," SDT, June 27, 1902.

CHAPTER FOUR

They relished the idea: Kevin Starr, *Americans and the California Dream, 1850–1915* (New York: Oxford University Press, 1973).

William Chance and: 1880 U.S. Census, Fresno, California (Ancestry.com).

Fresno: *1850–2010 Historical US Census Populations of Counties and Incorporated Cities/ Towns in California*, California State Data Center, California Department of Finance, http://www.dof.ca.gov/research/demographic/state_census_data_center /historical_census_1850-2010/documents/2010-1850_stco_inccities-final.xls; *Imperial Fresno: Resources, Industry and Scenery* (Fresno, CA: Fresno Republican, 1897); Paul E. Vandoor, *History of Fresno County, California, with Biographical Sketches* (Los Angeles: Historic Record Co., 1919).

Known in and around: Myron Angel, *A Memorial and Biographical History of the Counties of Fresno, Tulare and Kern, California* (Chicago: Lewis Publishing Co., 1892), 385 (Internet Archive).

One of his contemporaries: C. B. Glasscock, *Lucky Baldwin: The Story of an Unconventional Success* (Indianapolis, IN: Bobbs-Merrill, 1933); Sandra Lee Snider, *Elias Jackson "Lucky" Baldwin: California Visionary* (Los Angeles: Stairwell Group, 1987).

They chugged over: FWR, June 13, 1890; *Transcontinental Railroads and Land Grants 1850–1900*, State Library of Arizona, https://s-media-cache-ako.pinimg.com /originals/de/49/4c/de494c26594d720eeb331e42a5e88902.jpg; American-rails .com, http://www.american-rails.com/new-york-central-system.html#gallery [pageGallery]/7/.

The comely mare: "Los Angeles Beats Kingston," NYEW, July 29, 1890; "Los Angeles," *Pedigree Online*, http://www.pedigreequery.com/los+angeles; "Kingston," *Pedigree Online*, http://www.pedigreequery.com/kingston2.

the "Great Pathfinder": John C. Frémont, *The Expeditions of John Charles Frémont*, ed. Donald Jackson and Mary Lee Spence (Urbana: University of Illinois Press, 1970) (Internet Archive).

The Joneses' relatives: Recollections of Mary Anne Jones, Contra Costa County, California, filed by N. G. Paden, March 1941, BANC MSS C-D 5090, Bancroft Library, University of California, Berkeley.

Other family connections: *Missouri Marriages, 1766–1983* (Provo: Ancestry.com Operations, 2004) (Ancestry.com); Susan Badger Doyle, "Cornelius Gilliam (1798–

1848)," *The Oregon Encyclopedia*, https://oregonencyclopedia.org/articles/gilliam
_cornelius/#.WNwCdxLytQY.

Working a farm: William Smith Bryan, *A History of Pioneer Families of Missouri* (St. Louis: Bryan Brand, 1876), 161 (Google Books); Will Bagley, *So Rugged and Mountainous: Blazing the Trails to Oregon and California, 1812-1848* (Norman: University of Oklahoma Press); Doyce B. Nunis Jr., ed., *The Bidwell-Bartleson Party, 1841 California Emigrant Adventure* (Santa Cruz, CA: Western Tanager Press, 1991), cited in Bagley, *So Rugged*.

We sold our home: Recollections of Mary Anne Jones.

The year 1846: Bernard DeVoto, *The Year of Decision 1846* (New York: St. Martin's Griffin, 2014); Robert W. Merry, *A Country of Vast Designs: James K. Polk, the Mexican War and the Conquest of the American Continent* (New York: Simon & Schuster, 2009); John Bicknell, *America 1844: Religious Fervor, Westward Expansion, and the Presidential Election That Transformed the Nation* (Chicago: Chicago Review Press, 2014).

Nothing about the trip: Mary Elizabeth Munkers Estes, *Crossing the Plains in 1846* (Rootsweb, Ancestry.com), http://freepages.history.rootsweb.ancestry.com /~cchous/oregon_trail/crossing/munkers.htm; Elizabeth Lord, *Reminiscences of Eastern Oregon* (Portland, OR: Irwin-Hudson, 1903), excerpted at http:// freepages.history.rootsweb.ancestry.com/~cchouk/oregon_trail/crossing /munkers.htm.

The first half of the journey: Will Bagley, "South Pass," Wyoming State Historical Society, http://www.wyohistory.org/essays/south-pass; Lord, *Reminiscences*.

Boys like William: "Reminiscences of A. H. Garrison, His Early Life Across the Plains and of Oregon from 1846 to 1903," manuscript 874, Oregon Historical Society, Internet Archive.

The Applegate cutoff: Ross A. Smith, *Oregon Overland: Three Roads of Adversity* (self-published, 2000), http://oregonoverland.co.

Which trail: Dennis Chance showed up in Sonoma County, California, as early as 1847, according to the account in Angel, *Memorial and Biographical History*, 385.

When the Chance clan: David L. Durham, *California's Geographic Names: A Gazetteer of Historic and Modern Names of the State* (Clovis, CA: Word Dancer Press, 1998), 490; Wilber Fisk Draper biographical entry, in James Miller Guinn, *History of the State of California and Biographical Record of the San Joaquin Valley* (Chicago: Chapman Publishing, 1905), 880 (Internet Archive).

Dennis Chance died: Angel, *Memorial and Biographical History*, 385.

William worked: Ibid.; 1880 U.S. Census.

Fresno at that time: Paul E. Vandoor, *History of Fresno County, California, Vol. 1* (Fresno, CA: Historic Record Co., 1919), 357; Robert de Roos, *The Thirsty Land: The Story of the Central Valley Project* (Stanford, CA: Stanford University Press, 1948), 21, cited in Todd A. Shallat, *Water and The Rise of Public Ownership on the Fresno Plain, 1850-1978* (Fresno, CA: City of Fresno Public Works Department, October 1978), 4.

Ready for Business: FMR, November 13, 1880.

"Cow town wonder": John Panter, "Central California Colony," *Fresno Past and Present* 6, no. 2 (Summer 1994), 2–11, http://www.valleyhistory.org/poandp.pdf.

The combination of: FMR, May 10, 1884, 3; Vandoor, *Fresno County*, 344.

The Chances moved: Angel, *Memorial and Biographical History*, 95; FWR, January 3, 1890.

Baldwin had come: C. B. Glasscock, *Lucky Baldwin: The Story of an Unconventional Success* (Indianapolis, IN: Bobbs-Merrill, 1933), 49; Alvaro Parro, "Elias 'Lucky' Baldwin: Land Baron of Southern California," KCET, http://www.kcet.org /socal/departures/leimert-park/elias-lucky-baldwin-land-baron-of-southern -california.html.

By the summer of 1890: "Flyers Going East," SFChr, April 14, 1890, 3; "Turf Notes," SFCa, June 23, 1890, 3; "A Mud Runner," LAH, June 22, 1890.

The reports back: "Turf Notes," SFCa, August 25, 1890, 3.

Whatever else California was: Starr, *California Dream*, 68.

Say, Mr. Daniels: "Some Battling Young Ballplayers," FEx, November 27, 1889, cited in Gil Bogen, *Tinker, Evers and Chance: A Triple Biography* (Jefferson, NC: McFarland, 2003), 7.

In a nearby photography studio: 1889 Fresno Expositor Youth Team photo, Fresno Historical Society Archives.

Baseball in California: David Vaught, *The Farmers' Game: Baseball in Rural America* (Baltimore: Johns Hopkins University Press, 2013), 38.

Frank played pitcher: Harvey T. Woodruff, "Stubborn Scotch Strain Made Frank Chance the Peerless Leader," RMN, May 18, 1913, 8.

He met a girl: "Frank Burdick's Birthday," FWR, April 4, 1890, 6.

In April 1892: "Personals," FMR, April 28, 1892, 3.

When word reached: "W. H. Chance, Dying," FMR, July 27, 1892, 3; Grant Marshall, "History of Central California Conference," Central California Conference of Seventh-Day Adventists, http://ccc.adventist.org/about-us; "W. H. Chance," FMR, July 29, 1892, 7.

Washington College: John Steven McGroarty, *Los Angeles from the Mountains to the Sea, Vol. III* (Chicago: American Historical Society, 1921), 766 (Google Books); *Catalogue*, Washington College (Irvington, CA), January 1, 1873, 134, 138 (Google Books).

Frank appears: Philip Holmes and Jill M. Singleton, *Irvington Fremont: Images of America* (Charleston, SC: Arcadia Publishing, 2005), 23–27. The uncertain paper trail of Chance's education is also covered in Bogen, *Tinker, Evers and Chance*, 6–7.

His heart couldn't: FMR, December 16 and 19, 1893, and January 24, 1894; FWR, June 22, 1894, 6.

He was knocked senseless: "A Serious Accident," FMR, April 24, 1894.

The frightening episode: FMR, May 1, 1894, 3.

hale and hearty: FWR, June 22, 1894, 6; "Back from the Yosemite," FWR, August 10, 1994, 10.

The ball struck: "An Exciting Game," FWR, October 26, 1894, 8.

The California League: John E. Spalding, *Always on Sunday: The California Baseball League, 1886 to 1915* (Manhattan, KS: Ag Press, 1992), 14.

Californians showed: Ibid., 27–31

Baseball here: *Sporting Life*, undated issue, cited in Spalding, *Always on Sunday*, 141.

Despite the ups: "Porterville's Challenge," FMR, January 11, 1896, 3.

Chance had appeared: "Boxing Tournament," FWR, January 10, 1896, 5.

Prizefighting was illegal: Leo N. Miletich, *Dan Stuart's Fistic Carnival* (College Station: Texas A&M University Press, 1994), 4; "1890s: The Reigns of Corbett & Fitzsimmons," ProBoxing-fans.com, http://www.proboxing-fans.com/boxing -101/history/1890s-the-reigns-of-corbett-fitzsimmons.

Amateur athletic clubs: "Boxing Tournament," FWR, April 2, 1897.

In May 1896: "Boxing at the Barton," FWR, May 22, 1896.

Frank continued to box: "Athletes Entertain," FMR, April 14, 1897, 2; "Shea Will Be Umpire," FMR, June 20, 1897, 3.

A former classmate: "Chance Has Had Busy Career in the Majors," Providence *Evenings News*, December 18, 1912; FMR, May 19, 1896, 2; DH, October 30, 1896, 6; e-mail correspondence with family descendent Robert Eden Martin, November 17, 2015, http://www.edenmartin.com; DH, October 30, 1896, 6.

He did well enough: FMR, May 19, 1896, 2; "Moultrie County," DH, October 16, 1896, 6; "Colts to Leave Today," CTr, March 10, 1897, 8; Hot Springs became a baseball mecca for big league spring training well into the next century. See "Baseball's Golden Days in Hot Springs," May 3, 2013, Hot Springs Historic Baseball Trail, http://www.hotspringsbaseballtrail.com/untold-stories/baseballs-golden-days -in-hot-springs.

Back in Fresno: "The Home Team Won," FMR, January 26, 1897, 2.

Word of his fine play: "On the Diamond," FMR, April 1, 1897, 3.

Fresno manager Russ Woldenburg: "Some Baseball News," FMR, September 22, 1897.

By October: Spalding, *Always on Sunday*, 66–68; FMR, September 22, 1897, September 29, 1897; "They Were Not in It," FWR, October 8, 1897, 2; "On the Diamond," LAH, December 10, 1897.

Hart would later dispute: Frank C. Gilruth, "Chance of the Chicago Champs," BM, December 1908, 24.

Before Frank's last season: Frank Selee, "Selee's Satisfaction," SL, January 1, 1898, 7.

My ability to lick: Uncredited news clipping, October 31, 1929, Frank Chance file, BHOF.

CHAPTER FIVE

Freezing Weather Due: "Seasons from 1900 to 2099," Holocenes.com, http://www .holoscenes.com/special/seasons.html; "12 Below Today, No Relief Near," CTr, February 18, 1903; "Freezing Weather Due Here Today," CI-O, March 20, 1903.

A coal miners' strike: Jonathan Grossman, "The Coal Strike of 1902 — Turning Point in U.S. Policy," U.S. Department of Labor, http://www.dol.gov/dol/aboutdol

/history/coalstrike.htm; "Deaths Charged to Coal Famine," CTr, January 12, 1903, 2; "The Coal Famine of 1903," *Connecting the Windy City* (blog), January 7, 2014, http://www.connectingthewindycity.com/2014/01/the-coal-famine-of -1903.html.

Anyone who knew: "Cubs Ready to Start," CDN, March 24, 1902; "Orphans Begin Work," CRH, March 12, 1903; "Cubs in Action," SL, March 28, 1903, 4.

This has been a great day: "Colts Have a Lively Day," CI-O, March 20, 1903.

No trophy had fallen: "Chicago Cubs Team History and Encyclopedia," BRef, http:// www.baseball-reference.com/teams/CHC/.

James A. Hart: SL, May 31, 1902; "May Take His Team to Coast," CTr, December 16, 1902, 6; "Orphans to Train at Los Angeles," CI-O, February 14, 1903, 4; "Decides to Make West Coast Trip," CTr, February 14, 1903.

Frank G. Selee: "Frank Selee Is the Man, Signs to Manage Chicago National League Team," CTr, October 27, 1901, 20; SL, May 16, 1903.

Selee had played: Frank Selee, BRef, http://www.baseball-reference.com/managers /seleefr99.shtml; SL, August 6, 1904; "Cubs in Los Angeles," CDN, March 11, 1903.

The Chicago Nationals: Art Ahrens, "How the Cubs Got Their Name," *Chicago History*, Spring 1976, 39; "Notes of the Diamond," WT, March 30, 1903.

In 1900, Johnson and: Eugene C. Murdock, *Ban Johnson: Czar of Baseball* (Westport, CT: Greenwood Press, 1982), 59.

Ban Johnson stepped in: Murdock, *Ban Johnson*, 44; Ban Johnson, as told to Irving Vaughan, "Thirty-Four Years in Baseball," CTr, February 24, 1929, sec. 2, 1; "Chicago White Sox Attendance Data," Baseball Almanac, http://www.baseball -almanac.com/teams/wsoxatte.shtml; "1900–1909 Attendance," Ballparks of Baseball, http://www.ballparksofbaseball.com/1900-09attendance.htm.

Johnson went right after: Michael J. Haupert, "The Economic History of Major League Baseball," Economic History Association, https://eh.net/encyclopedia /the-economic-history-of-major-league-baseball; G. Edward White, *Creating the National Pastime: Baseball Transforms Itself, 1903–1953* (Princeton, NJ: Princeton University Press, 1996); Murdock, *Ban Johnson*.

Knowledgeable observers: Joe Vila, "In Position to Dictate," CTr, January 4, 1903, 10.

That person was: John Saccoman, "Garry Hermann," SABR, http://sabr.org/bioproj /person/d72a4b39; SN, November 24, 1927, cited in Murdoch, *Ban Johnson*, 67.

The fever spread: Robert Pruter, "Youth Baseball in Chicago, 1868–1890: Not Always Sandlot Ball," JSH (Spring 1999), 8, 12.

Lincoln Steffens captured: Lincoln Steffens, *The Shame of the Cities* (New York: McClure, Phillips, 1904), https://archive.org/details/shameofcitiesoostefuoft (digital collection of University of Toronto).

crush of new arrivals: *Centennial History of the City of Chicago* (Chicago: Inter Ocean, 1905), available at https://archive.org/details/centennialhistoryoointe#page/28 /mode/up.

The newcomers piled: Jane Addams, "The Housing Problem in Chicago," *Annals of the American Academy of Political and Social Sciences*, July 1901, 99–103.

An honest government: Harry Pratt Judson, "The Municipal Situation in Chicago," *American Monthly,* January 1903, 434; "Iroquois Theater Fire," *Chicagology* (blog), https://chicagology.com/notorious-chicago/iroquoistheatre/.

Ubiquitous—there were: Royal Melendy, "The Saloon in Chicago," *American Journal of Sociology* 6, no. 3 (November 1900), 289–306, https://doi.org/10.1086/210977.

Chicago saloons reflected: Perry R. Duis, *The Saloon: Public Drinking in Chicago and Boston, 1880–1920* (Urbana: University of Illinois Press, 1999), 250.

Working both ends: James L. Merriner, *Grafters and Goo Goos: Corruption and Reform in Chicago, 1833–2003* (Carbondale: Southern Illinois University Press, 200), 69.

Other commercial forces: Gunther Barth, *City People: The Rise of Modern City Culture in Nineteenth-Century America* (Oxford: Oxford University Press, 1980), 25.

In the ball park: Ibid., 187.

Johnson and Comiskey: Robin F. Bachin, "Baseball Palace of the World: Commercial Recreation and the Building of Comiskey Park," in *Sports in Chicago*, ed. Elliot J. Gorn (Urbana: University of Illinois Press, 2008), 79.

I had the wit: Ban Johnson, as told to George Creel, "Making the American League," SEP, March 22, 1930, 12.

As American League: Ibid.

National League owners: Bill Lamberty, "Harry Pulliam," SABR, http://sabr.org /bioproj/person/6e05b19c; "National League," SL, April 18, 1903, 7.

Henry Chadwick: Andrew J. Schiff, *"The Father of Baseball": A Biography of Henry Chad- wick* (Jefferson, NC: McFarland, 1908), Henry Chadwick, "Chadwick's Chat," SL, May 2, 1903, 12.

Frank Selee's reputation: Baseball Hall of Fame and Museum, http://baseballhall.org /hof/selee-frank; Edward Lewis, "Public Opinion," SL, July 31, 1909, 4.

a master practitioner: Major Leagues, Baseball-Reference.com, http://www.baseball -reference.com/leagues/; Bill Felber, *A Game of Brawl: The Orioles, the Beaneaters & the Battle for the 1897 Pennant* (Lincoln: University of Nebraska Press, 2007).

The fact that: Elwood Andrews Roff, *Base Ball and Base Ball Players: A History of the National Game of America* (Chicago: E. A. Roff, 1912), https://archive.org/details /baseballbaseba11ooroff (Internet Archive).

Selee was forever: T. H. Murnane, "Passing Up the Bunt," WP, March 25, 1906, 8.

Frank Gibson Selee: Willis Alonzo Dewey, ed., "News Item," in *Medical Century: The National Journal of Homeopathic Medicine and Surgery*, 17 (New York: Medical Center Publishing, 1910), 347; W. Rothstein, *Physicians in the Nineteenth Century* (Baltimore: Johns Hopkins University Press, 1972), cited by Dana Ullman, "The Case for Homeopathic Medicine," *Huffington Post*, April 12, 2010, http://www .huffingtonpost.com/dana-ullman/the-case-for-homeopathic_b_451187.html; Charles E. Bruce, "Melrose," *Directory of the City of Malden for 1885* (Boston: Press of Rockwell and Churchill, 1885), 227; "Nathan Pierce Selee," *Amherst College Bulletin* 3, no. 6 (1914), 135.

He joined the: "Lodge #1031," Elks USA Local Lodges Online, http://www.elks.org /lodges/home.cfm?LodgeNumber=1031.

With some help: Frank G. Selee, "Twenty-One Years in Baseball," BM, May 1908, 23; "Seven Ways to Compute the Relative Value of a U.S. Dollar Amount—1774 to the Present," MeasuringWorth, http://www.measuringworth.com/uscompare /result.php?year_source=1884&amount=1000&year_result=2015#.

helped along by a lawyer friend: Moody went on to become navy secretary and attorney general—and ultimately a Supreme Court justice—during the presidency of Theodore Roosevelt. Merrill Edward Gates, "William H. Moody," *Men of Mark in America, Volume 1* (Washington, DC: Men of Mark Publishing, 1905), available at https://en.wikisource.org/wiki/Index:Men_of_Mark_in_America_vol_1.djvu.

faraway Oshkosh: "Oshkosh: A Brief History," Oshkosh Convention and Visitors Bureau, http://www.visitoshkosh.com/about-us/oshkosh-a-brief-history.

Selee's baseball fever: Selee, BM.

Milwaukee never beat: "1887 Northwestern League," BRef, http://www.baseball -reference.com/minors/league.cgi?id=2a57e4d7.

To the amazement: "Selee's Start in Oshkosh," Osh, October 29, 1901, 3.

At Hart's instigation: Atlanta Braves, BRef, http://www.baseball-reference.com /teams/ATL.

Selee was happy: Selee, BM.

The new manager: "Frank Selee Is the Man: Signs to Manage Chicago National League Team," CTr, October 27, 1901, 20.

Though widely respected: "National League News," SL, June 25, 1904, 7.

Wife of the Colts' manager: "Wife of the Colts' Manager Is an Enthusiastic Fan," CTr, August 31, 1902, 11.

Sporting Life reported: "St. Louis Siftings . . . a Lady Correspondent," SL, April 18, 1903, 3.

Those scribes: "Colts Frisk at Los Angeles," CTr, March 20, 1903.

The former Bridget: Two newspaper articles establish that Mrs. Frank Selee was Bridget Grant. A 1904 news account of lineman John Grant's death by electrocution states that his only relative was a sister, "Mrs. Frank Selee, wife of the manager of the Chicago Nationals" ("Touched Live Wire," BG, April 21, 1904). A 1909 wedding announcement of Michael Grant states that he is "a brother-in-law of the late Frank Selee, the well-known baseball manager" ("Pueblo Fireman Weds Daughter of Former Chief," DP, September 27, 1909, 9); *New York Passenger Lists, 1820–1957* (Ancestry.com); Margaret Lynch-Brennan, *The Irish Bridget: Irish Immigrant Women in Domestic Service in America, 1840–1930* (Syracuse, NY: Syracuse University Press, 2014).

She eventually settled: Catherine Eagan's brother, John Eagan, emigrated to America and settled in St. Louis in the 1850s: Missouri Marriage Records, 1805–2002, 41 (Ancestry.com).

The wedding was: "Wife of Colts' Manager," CTr, August 31, 1902.

Selee fell ill: "Manager Frank Selee Sick," CTr, October 13, 1902, 15.

Faywood was known: Robert Hixson Julyan, *The Place Names of New Mexico* (Albuquerque: University of New Mexico Press, 1996), 130; AB, March 24, 1903, 5.

A meandering train: "Cubs to Leave Los Angeles," CDN, March 25, 1903; "Orphans Play at Tuscon, Ariz.," CRH, March 27, 1903.

Bacon had sent: Frank Keetz, "Johnny Evers, the Find of the 1902 Season," Research Journals Archive (SABR), 1983.

That $200: Johnny Evers, "More Baseball Confessions by Johnny Evers, of the Braves," NYTr, January 31, 1915, sec. 2, 3.

At each stop: Ibid.

All Johnny Evers did: "Colts Lose 3–2, in the Eleventh," CTr, May 4, 1903.

Evers was soon: "Bobby Lowe, Bref, http://www.baseball-reference.com/players/1 /loweboo1.shtml; Evers, NYTr.

Tinker had arrived: Joe Tinker, "How I Became a Ball Player," NYET, August 27, 1913.

Later that summer: "Pirates Land on Taylor," August 29, 1902, 4; "Colts Beat the Pirates," CTr, August 30, 1902, 6; "Wife of Colts' Manager," CTr, August 31, 1902.

He "fought the ball": James C. Gilruth, "Chance of the Chicago Champs," BM, December 1908; John J. Evers and Hugh S. Fullerton, *Touching Second* (Chicago: Reilly & Britton, 1910), 90 (New York Public Library, Internet Archive).

I signed as: William Patten and J. Walker McSpadden, eds., *The Book of Baseball* (New York: P. F. Collier, 1911), 28; Evers, NYTr.

It didn't matter: Bill James, *The Politics of Glory: How Baseball's Hall of Fame Really Works* (New York: Macmillan, 1994); Evers, NYTr; Patten and McSpadden, *Book of Baseball*, 28.

By early June: "1903 Chicago Cubs," BRef, http://www.baseball-reference.com/teams /CHC/1903.shtml.

Then the New York Giants: Ibid.; John Snyder, *Cubs Journal: Year by Year and Day by Day with the Chicago Cubs since 1976* (Cincinnati: Clerisy Press, 2008), 117.

Selee's democratic deference: "Cubs to Leave Los Angeles," CDN, March 25, 190; Evers and Fullerton, *Touching Second*, 65; "Chance Elected Colts' Captain," CTr, July 10, 1903, 8.

A more telling statistic: 1900–1909 Ballpark Attendance, *Ballparks of Baseball*, http:// www.ballparksofbaseball.com/1900-1909-mlb-attendance/.

Also a product of: Snyder, *Cubs Journal*, 120.

A little bet: Ira Smith and H. Allen Smith, *Low and Inside* (New York: Doubleday, 1949), 155.

On the way back east: "In the Sporting World," Osh, April 7, 1904, 6.

When he was five: Cindy Thompson and Scott Brown, *Three Finger: The Mordecai Brown Story* (Lincoln: University of Nebraska Press, 2006), 11.

The local physician: Ibid.

Brown was left with: *Denver Express*, September 17, 1909, cited in Thompson and Brown, *Three Finger*, 11–12.

In New York in June: "Colts Shut Out the Gotham Giants," CI-O, June 12, 1904, 17; "Selee's Men Win Great Battle," CTr, June 12, 1904, sec. 2, 1.

Gloom unutterable: CTr, June 12, 1904.

If that day: Snyder, *Cubs Journal*, 121; Murdock, *Ban Johnson*, 55.

Chicago's strong run: "Tempest in a Teapot," SL, August 6, 1904; *The Baseball Encyclo-pedia* (Toronto: Macmillan Co., 1969); "1904 Major League Baseball Attendance," BRef, http://www.baseball-reference.com/leagues/MLB/1904-misc.shtml.
The sporting press: Francis Richter, ed., *Reach's Official American League Baseball Guide for 1905* (Philadelphia: A. J. Reach, 1905).
They took the men: "Work, Ocean Baths, Sleep Putting Cubs in Fine Trim," CI-O, March 7, 1905, 4.
Expectations were high: Harry W. Ford, "Fans Glad the Baseball Season Is Approaching," CI-O, April 9, 1905, 43.

CHAPTER SIX
On a quiet Saturday: Royal Feltner, "Early American Automobiles, 1906," http://www.earlyamericanautomobiles.com/1906.htm.
This peculiar weekend: Newspaper game accounts include: SY (I. E. Sanborn), "Spuds Stem Tide and Beat Giants," CTr, August 19, 1906; "Giant Killers Wallop Matty and Win Opener," CI-O, August 19, 1906; CEP, August 20, 1906, cited in Richard Chabowski, *Windy City World Series I* (Bloomington, IL: iUniverse, 2012); LHD, August 19, 1906; "Had Fun with McGraw," BE, August 19, 1906, 30.
The Rooters were: "Nearly Everyone Is Crazy about Baseball," CTr, September 9, 1906, pt. 7, 1; West Side Grounds Historical Marker, Illinois State Historical Society, http://www.historyillinois.org/FindAMarker/MarkerDetails.aspx?MarkerID=56; *Rand, McNally and Co.'s Street Number Guide* (Chicago: Rand McNally, 1902), digital collection of the University of Chicago, https://catalog.lib.uchicago.edu/vufind/Record/1585058); "Present State of the Commercial Automobile Movement throughout the Country: Chicago," *The Horseless Age: The Automobile Trade Magazine*, July 5, 1905, 19–22.
The Rooters' exuberant ringleader: New York *Commercial*, undated issue, cited in "Edward G. Heeman," *The Commercial West*, January 20, 1903, 38 (Google Books).
As earnest as he seemed: "How They Dress on the Board of Trade," CTr, November 4, 1906, 2.
generalissimo extraordinary: Ibid.
This was a bold assertion: Frank Deford, *The Old Ball Game: How John McGraw, Christy Mathewson and the New York Giants Created Modern Baseball* (New York: Grove Press, 2005).
The Giants had won: In 1904, McGraw had defiantly refused to play the AL pennant-winning Boston Americans in a snub to Ban Johnson; hence no world's championship that year. See Benton Stark, *The Year They Called Off the World Series: A True Story* (Garden City Park, NY: Avery, 1991); "The Referee," CTr, April 29, 1906, pt. 2, 1.
in a June rematch: "The 1906 Chicago Cubs Regular Season Game Log," RS, http://www.retrosheet.org/boxesetc/1906/VCHN01906.htm.
Board of Trade employees: "Commodities Markets," EC, http://www.encyclopedia.chicagohistory.org/pages/317.html.

Typically regal New York: Walter Lord, *The Good Years: From 1900 to the First World War* (New Brunswick, NJ: Transaction Publishers, 2011).

When the 1906 season: Mark Okkonen, *Baseball Uniforms of the 20th Century: The Official Major League Baseball Guide* (New York: Sterling Publishing, 1991), 101.

The crowd had swelled: "Games Played Saturday, August 18," SL, August 25, 1906, 5.

Photographs show: "Photograph of Yesterday's Huge Crowd at the West Side Ball Park," CI-O, August 19, 1906, 29.

One hundred and fifty: CTr and CI-O, August 19.

They had painted: "Had Fun with McGraw," BE, August 19, 1906, 30.

He had come to town: "M'Graw's Punishment," SL, September 1, 1906, 10.

From the time the bell: SY (I. E. Sanborn), CTr, August 19.

The contest didn't disappoint: 1906 game logs, RE; CTr and CI-O, August 19.

another paroxysm of glee: I. E. Sanborn, CTr, August 19.

The roar which followed: Ibid.

The first sign: "Colts Can't Escape Rain," CTr, March 15, 1905, 1; "Selee's Cubs on Journey East to Open Season," CI-O, March 29, 1905, 4.

Then Selee came down: W. A. Phelon, "Chicago Gleanings," SL, July 15, 1905, 9.

Selee applied to Hart: "National League News," SL, July 8, 1905, 5; "Selee out of It," SL, August 5, 1905, 7.

Hart quickly named: "Chance May Displace Selee as Colts' Keeper," PPr, July 17, 1905.

Or, more likely: "John R. Walsh Dies, Free Only Nine Days," NYT, October 24, 1911; "The Story of John R. Walsh," *Commoner*, November 12, 1907, 7, http://nebnewspapers.unl.edu/lccn/46032385/1907-11-22/ed-1/seq-7.pdf ((Nebraska Newspapers).

Selee had asked: Frank Selee, "Twenty-One Years in Baseball," BM, May 1908, 23; David Finoli, *The Pittsburgh Pirates Encyclopedia* (New York: Sports Publishing, 2003).

Once back in Chicago Selee: Ibid.

To help him: "Everybody Will Join in This," SL, August 12, 1905, 2, citing CTr; "$4,000 for Selee; Cubs Win from Boston, 7 to 4," CI-O, September 20, 1905, 4; "Selee's Managerial Record," SN, September 23, 1905, 2.

Chance began his: Hugh Fullerton, "How Ball Players Hit," CTr, April 29, 1906, 2.

The hurler known as: Jake Weimer, BRef, http://www.baseball-reference.com/players/w/weimeja01.shtml.

Chance, meanwhile: "Chance Steals Game in Ninth," CTr, April 29, 1906, 1; "Reds Defeated by Chance's Daring," CI-O, April 29, 1906, 9.

There's no way: C. T. Rankin, "Charles Murphy, a Growing Power in Organized Baseball," BM, June 1912, 43; Charles W. Murphy, "Big Year for Baseball," CTr, December 31, 1905, 2.

Murphy's companion: Edward Mott Wooley, "The Business of Baseball," *McClure's Magazine*, July 1912, 245.

Taft called Chance: Charles B. Cleveland, *The Great Baseball Managers* (New York:

Thomas Y. Crowell, 1950), 84; Edwin Pope, *Baseball's Greatest Managers* (New York: Doubleday, 1960), 26; "Manager Chance Is Magnate," ISJ, September 6, 1906, 2.

After consummating: "Murphy Takes Up Hart's Burden," CTr, July 16, 1905, 1; "C. W. Murphy in Chicago Club," NYTr, July 16, 1905, 6; "Charles W. Murphy Becomes President of Champion Cubs," CI-O, November 2, 1905, 4; "National League Meeting," OB, December 14, 1905, 5.

The flamboyant Tinker: 1905 Fielding Leaders, BRef, http://www.baseball-reference .com:8080/leagues/NL/1905-fielding-leaders.shtml.

Perhaps Evers: George Rice, untitled newspaper clipping (probably Chicago *Journal*), December 12, 1912, BHOF.

Tinker and myself: Johnny Evers, "More Baseball Confessions by Johnny Evers, of the Braves," NYTr, February 7, 1915, sec. 2, 2.

When Tinker finally: Hugh S. Fullerton, "Battles of the Ball Field," CTr, July 22, 1906, 2; "Chicago Wins One-Sided Game," CTr, September 14, 1905, 6; "Tinker and Evers Fight," IN, September 14, 1905, 10.

Just before game time: "Tinker and Evers Fight," IN.

It was a real hard ball: "Johnny Evers Speaks," uncredited newspaper clip, December 26, 1936, BHOF.

We never spoke: Jerome Holtzman and George Vass, *Baseball, Chicago Style: A Tale of Two Teams, One City* (Chicago: Bonus Books, 2001), 50.

We were fighting: Frank Graham, "Setting the Pace," uncredited news clipping, February 6, 1940, 24, BHOF.

You simply did not: Ray Joyce, "Front 'n' Center," *Italian Sentinel*, undated news clipping, BHOF.

Tinker closed the matter: F. C. Lane, "Joe Tinker the Shortstop Manager and His Remarkable Career," BM, July 1913, 42.

We need pitchers: John J. Evers and Hugh S. Fullerton, *Touching Second: The Science of Baseball* (Chicago: Reilly & Britton, 1910), 69 (Internet Archive).

What followed was: Evers, *Touching Second*, 70.

"Tri-Sigma" outfield: "Fielders Shine in This Victory," CTr, April 27, 1906, 10.

Wildfire Schulte, from: Scott Turner, "Frank Schulte," SABR, http://sabr.org/bioproj /person/66b47e26; Sean D. Hamill, "Now They Know: Jimmy Slagle Played Here," NYT, November 6, 2007; Don Jensen, "Jimmy Sheckard," SABR, http:// sabr.org/bioproj/person/08c48a23.

Again, inside gossip: Evers and Fullerton, *Touching Second*, 70–71.

Harry M. Steinfeldt: "Steinfeldt Still with Team," CTr, January 23, 1906, 8; "Murphy Signs Steinfeldt," CI-O, January 25, 1906, 4.

But Murphy's investment: Harry Steinfeldt, BRef, http://www.baseball-reference .com/players/s/steinha01.shtml; "How Infielders Throw the Ball," Sheboygan (WI) *Daily Press*, May 18, 1909, 8.

Born in St. Louis: 1880 U.S. Federal Census, Dallas, Texas, Roll 1299, 94B, District 057

(Ancestry.com); FWG, June 11, 1891; "The Finest Beer on Earth," advertisement, FWG, January 1, 1895, 8; *General Directory of the City of Fort Worth City, 1894–95* (Galveston, TX: Morrison & Fourmy, 1894), 83.

At sixteen, Harry: "After League Transgressions," NYT, September 14, 1894, 3; "New Recruits for Class B," NYT, September 21, 1894, 3; Evan Friss, *The Cycling City: Bicycles and Urban America in the 1890s* (Chicago: University of Chicago Press, 2015), 49.

The League of American Wheelmen: "Some Road Problems," *Good Roads*, August 1894, http://www.oldbike.eu/museum/history/early-roads-usa/safer-roads -campaign; Friss, *Cycling City*; Irving A. Leonard, *When Bikehood Was in Flower: Sketches of Early Cycling* (Tuscon, AZ: Seven Palms Press, 1983).

The LAW refused: "New Recruits for Class B," NYT; "The Roundup Column," MN, May 23, 1903, 10.

Blackface minstrelsy: John Strausbaugh, *Black Like You: Blackface, Whiteface, Insult & Intimidation in American Popular Culture* (New York: Penguin, 2006), 102.

Minstrel legacies trace a path: Brander Matthews, "The Rise and Fall of Negro Minstrelsy," *Scribner's Magazine*, June 1915, 754–759; "The Cakewalk, 1897–1915," *Basin Street*, http://www.basinstreet.com/cakewalk.htm; Strausbaugh, *Black Like You*.

The proprietor and star: Edward Le Roy Rice, *Monarchs of Minstrelsy, from "Daddy" Rice to Date* (New York: Kenny Publishing, 1911), 214 (Google Books).

Field intermixed: "Original Ragtimers," EP, December 1, 1906, 3; "Fields' Minstrels," FWG, October 23, 1892, 10.

Steinfeldt was probably: "Al Field's Minstrels Tonight," GN, January 15, 1892, 5; advertisement, Gainesville *Daily Hesperian*, December 29, 1891, 3; advertisement, Oklahoma *Times-Journal*, March 25, 1892.

At almost every stop: GN, June 8, 1895, 2.

Manager Buck Ewing: "Harry Steinfeldt," undated newspaper clipping, c. 1899, BHOF.

Frank Chance remembered: "Sports and Sportsmen," EPH, March 16, 1901, 3; "Murphy Back in Chicago," CTr, January 27, 1906, 10; "Comiskey Back; Has Signed Isbell," CI-O, February 22, 1906, 4.

The Giant Killers: "Dumont's Gossip," CI-O, May 20, 1906, 13.

The Sunday game: CI-O game accounts, May 20–24, 1906; CRH, May 20, 1906, 1, cited in Chabowski, *Windy City*.

The outcasts refused to leave: "Giant Killers Defeat Giants; 28,000 Applaud," CI-O, May 21, 1906, 8.

We were pointed: Evers, "More Baseball Confessions."

It is a game of: Evers and Fullerton, *Touching Second*, 196.

Not that they didn't: "Mordecai Brown," BRef, http://www.baseball-reference.com /players/b/brownmo01.shtml.

The Cubs' other reliable: Cappy Gagnon, "Ed Reulbach Remembered," *Baseball Research Journal* (1982), SABR, http://research.sabr.org/journals/online/45-brj-1982 /375-ed-reulbach-remembered.

He sent Huff: Evers and Fullerton, *Touching Second*, 71.

Chance also tapped: Ibid.; Orval Overall, BRef, http://www.baseball-reference.com
/players/o/overaor01.shtml.

On August 21: CEP, August 21, 1906, and *Chicago Chronicle*, August 22, 1906, cited in
Chabowski, *Windy City*; SY (I. E. Sanborn), "Spuds Winners in Hot Battle," CTr,
August 22, 1906.

Their .763 winning percentage: The Seattle Mariners in 2001 are the only other team
to record 116 wins in a season, against 46 losses, for a .716 winning percentage.
BRef, http://www.baseball-reference.com/leagues/AL/2001.shtml.

The team drew a record: 1906 Major League Attendance, BRef, http://www.baseball
-reference.com/leagues/MLB/1906-misc.shtml; Chicago Cubs attendance data,
Baseball Almanac, http://www.baseball-almanac.com/teams/cubsatte.shtml.

The *Trib* also took: "Nearly Everybody in Chicago Is Crazy about Baseball," CTr,
September 9, 1906, pt. 7, 1.

No one, even: 1906 Chicago White Sox Game Log, RS, http://www.retrosheet.org
/boxesetc/1906/TCHA01906.htm; BRef, http://www.baseball-reference.com
/teams/CHW/1906.shtml; "Standing of the Clubs," CTr, August 2, 1906, 6.

Fielder Jones, Comiskey's: David Larson, "Fielder Jones," SABR, http://sabr.org
/bioproj/person/41a3501e; Bruce A. Rubenstein, *Chicago in the World Series,
1903–2005: The Cubs and White Sox in Championship Play* (Jefferson, NC: McFarland, 2006), 5; "1906 Chicago White Sox," BRef, http://www.baseball-reference
.com/teams/CHW/1906.shtml.

The *Tribune*'s acerbic: Dryden's first use of the memorable phrase "Hitless Wonders"
was applied to the Cubs after they won game 2 of the World Series to even things
up to 1–1: "In the course of one night the west side crew switched from hitless
wonders to demon sluggers." "Sad Slaughter of Sox: Dryden," CTr, October 11,
1906; W. A. Phelon, "Chicago Gleanings," SL, June 11, 1904, 9.

Only three starters: "1906 Chicago White Sox," BRef.

luckiest bunch of ball players: "Baseball Notes," STr, July 9, 1906, 3.

They proceeded to win: Chicago White Sox 1906 game log, RS.

Nobody can talk: CDJ, October 4, 1906, cited in Chabowski, *Windy City*, 340.

I don't know of: Ibid.

The City Council passed: "Council Declares Holiday in Baseball Champions' Honor,"
CI-O, October 9, 1906, 1.

The *Tribune* ran: CTr, October 14, 1906, 5.

All through the weary: "And the Spell Continues," CI-O, October 10, 1914, 6.

The Cubs and Sox: John Snyder, *Cubs Journal: Year by Year and Day by Day with the
Chicago Cubs since 1876* (Cincinnati: Clerisy Press, 2008), 120.

The Cubs are top-heavy: "Wide World of Sport," WP, October 9, 1906, 8.

Years later: Gene Carney, "Uncovering the Fix of the 1919 World Series: the Role of
Hugh Fullerton," *Nine*, Fall 2004, 39.

Fullerton typed out: A contrite city editor eventually published Fullerton's forecast,
as written, after the series had concluded: Hugh S. Fullerton, "Series Verifies

Fullerton's Dope," CTr, October 15, 1906, 4; Frederick G. Lieb, *The Story of the World Series* (New York: G. P. Putnam's, 1949), 44.

Baseball is talked about: "Nearly Everyone in Chicago Is Crazy about Baseball," CTr, September 9, 1906, sec. 7, 1.

More people than: "Horse Blanket Series: Dryden," CTr, October 9, 1906, 2.

Here's how the cross-town series: Joseph J. Kreuger, *Baseball's Greatest Drama* (Milwaukee, WI: Husting, 1942); Lieb, *Story of the World Series*; Snyder, *Cubs Journal*; Holtzman and Vass, *Baseball, Chicago Style*; and Chabowski, *Windy City.*

The air in the ball park: Charles Dryden, "Dryden's Story of Sox Triumph," CTr, October 10, 1906, 3.

Hotel managers: "Arrest of Ticket Peddlers," CTr, October 10, 1906, 3.

The *Chicago Tribune* hosted: "Fans Guest of 'Tribune,'" CTr, October 12, 1906, 2.

Cubs rooters sent: CTr, October 12, 1906, cited in Chabowski, *Windy City*, 371.

Cap Anson: CTr, October 12, 1906.

An African American fan: CI-O, October 15, 1906, 9.

The moment the Sox: "Ovation for Winner," SL, October 20, 1906, 7.

Baseball officialdom: "The Final Result," SL, October 20, 1906.

glorious uncertainty of baseball: CI-O, October 14, 1906, 6.

CHAPTER SEVEN

Just after sunset: I. E. Sanborn, "Champion Cubs Feast with Fans," CTr, October 18, 1907, 10; Frank B. Hutchinson Jr., "World's Champion Cubs Are Given a Great Reception," CI-O, October 18, 1907, 4.

The printed programs: Banquet Program, October 17, 1907, BHOF, Banquet Programs Collection, Series II, Team Banquets, folder 15, Chicago Cubs, Baseball Hall of Fame, Cooperstown, NY.

The Auditorium Annex: The building is now called the Congress Plaza Hotel; Joseph M. Siri, *The Chicago Auditorium Annex: Adler and Sullivan's Architecture and the City* (Chicago: University of Chicago Press, 2004).

ornate banquet hall: William R. Host and Brooke Anne Portman, *Early Chicago Hotels* (Chicago: Arcadia Publishing, 2006), 65 (Google Books); Leslie A. Hudson, *Chicago Skyscrapers in Vintage Postcards* (Chicago: Arcadia Publishing, 2004), 15–18 (Google Books).

Gentleman, the City: J. Hamilton Lewis, "Call of America" (audio recording), Senate speech advocating U.S. entry into World War I, in "American Leaders Speak: Recordings from World War I and the 1920 Election, 1918–1920," Library of Congress, http://www.loc.gov/teachers/classroommaterials/connections/american -leaders/thinking.html.

J. Hamilton Lewis: Ray Hill, "The Senate's Dandy: James Hamilton Lewis of Illinois," Knoxville (TN) *Focus*, December 16, 2012, http://knoxfocus.com/2012/12/the -senates-dandy-james-hamilton-lewis-of-illinois; *Biographical Directory of the United States Congress*, http://bioguide.congress.gov/scripts/biodisplay.pl?index =L000284; "J. Hamilton Lewis Is Dead," CTr, April 10, 1939, 1; E. D. Cowen,

"James Hamilton Lewis, a Political Paradox," *Ainslee's Magazine*, February 1900, 309–317, Google Books; Sanborn, CTr.

Mid-Atlantic-trained accent: James Fallows, "American Announcer-Speak: The Origin Story," *The Atlantic*, June 9, 2015, http://www.theatlantic.com/national /archive/2015/06/american-announcer-speak-the-origin-story/395492/.

Six months earlier: Frank B. Hutchinson Sr., "Chicago to Begin Fight for Baseball Honors Thursday," CI-O, April 7, 1907, 13.

By early spring: Dumont, "Dumont's Gossip of Events in the World of Sport," CI-O, April 7, 1907, 13.

Bring me your lumber: Norman Dent, "The Romance of Chicago," *Munsey's Magazine*, April 1907.

I do not see: Frank B. Hutchinson Jr., "To Arrange Dates for the American Association Today," CI-O, March 1, 1907, 4.

It would be a long: I. E. Sanborn, "Cubs Beaten by a Muff," CTr, April 19, 1907, 10.

They were bolstered: The 1906 Cubs had a run differential of +323 (704 – 381) while the 1908 Cubs were at +164 (625 – 461); the 1905 New York Giants were at +273 (778 – 505) and the 1909 Pittsburgh Pirates were at +253 (701 – 448). BRef, http:// www.baseball-reference.com/leagues/NL/.

John McGraw's Giants: 1907 Chicago Cubs game log, RS, http://www.retrosheet.org /boxesetc/1907/TCHN01907.htm; John Snyder, *Cubs Journal: Year by Year and Day by Day with the Chicago Cubs since 1976* (Cincinnati: Clerisy Press, 2008), 137–142.

In the second of: Charles Dryden, "Cubs Beat Matty; Fans Start Riot," CTr, May 22, 1907, 10.

The magnates had decided: "Talk on Ball Rules," CRH, April 4, 1903, 4.

Less compliant in: "Bingham Bluff," SL, June 1, 1907, 4; Steven Riess, "The Baseball Magnates and Urban Politics in the Progressive Era: 1895–1920," JSH (January 1974), 58–59.

Having won Chicago's: "McGraw Says It Was Bad Judgment," uncredited clipping, October 15, 1906, Frank Chance player file, BHOF; *Scrapps Tobacco Die-Cuts, 1888: Scrapbook, 1888–1929*, BHOF.

New York and Chicago reporters: Charles Dryden, "Manager Chance Hurls Bottles at Brooklyn Crowd," CTr, July 9, 1907, 11; "Brooklyn Game Finishes in a Riot," NYEW, July 8, 1907, 1; Robert Edgren, "Dodgers Have Adopted a New Coat of Arms," NYEW, July 9, 1907, 8.

For an instant: Dryden, CTr.

Bottles flew at: Edgren, NYEW.

That Chance was provoked: John B. Foster, "Brooklyn Budget," SL, July 20, 1907, 3.

a disgrace to Brooklyn: Edgren, NYEW.

Real athletes in real: Charles Dryden, "Cubs Wrinkle Bostons' New Uniforms," CTr, June 18, 1907, 12.

Some of his epigrams: Richard Orodenker, *The Writer's Game* (New York: Twayne Publishers, 1996), 35.

with readership numbers: *Rowell's American Newspaper Directory* (New York: Printer's Ink, 1909), 168–171 (Internet Archive).

a core audience for sports: Bill Burgess, "The Sporting Life," June 25, 2009, *Baseball Fever*, http://www.baseball-fever.com/showthread.php?91319-The-Sporting -Life; Steve Gietscheir, "The Sporting News," SABR, http://sabr.org/bioproj /topic/sporting-news.

In Chicago, where: Alfred Lawrence Lorenz, "The Whitechapel Club: Defining Chicago's Newspapers in the 1890s," *American Journalism* 15, no. 1 (Winter 1998), 83– 102, http://www.loyno.edu/~lorenz/Whitechapel.html (digital version, Loyola University of New Orleans).

Aside from Lardner: Richard A. Schwarzlose, "Newspapers," *Encyclopedia of Chicago*, Chicago Historical Society, http://www.encyclopedia.chicagohistory.org /pages/889.html; "Chicago Newspapers," Chicago Public Library, http://www .chipublib.org/chicago-newspapers-on-microfilm; Hugh S. Fullerton, "The Men Who Made the Game," SEP, April 21, 1928.

Fullerton and other scribes: Jack Bales, "Baseball's First Bill Veeck," BRJ, Fall 2013, http://sabr.org/research/baseball-s-first-bill-veeck; Orodenker, *Writer's Game*.

Hugh Stuart Fullerton: *Contemporary Authors Online*, Gale Literature Collections, reprinted by Bill Burgess in "Meet the Sportswriters" forum, *Baseball Fever*, http:// www.baseball-fever.com/showthread.php?57538-Meet-The-Sports-Writers /page3.

Unlike Dryden: Hugh S. Fullerton, "Tricks That Win Ballgames," CTr, April 15, 1906, 2; Grantland Rice, "The Greatest Baseball Reporter in the World," *American Magazine*, August 1912, reprinted at Baseball Chronology, http://www .baseballchronology.com/baseball/People/Writers/F/Hugh_Fullerton.asp.

The Tigers had led: BRef, http://www.baseball-reference.com/teams/DET/1907 .shtml.

Game hero Slagle: John Thorn, "The Oldest Trick in the Book," *Our Game* (blog), https://ourgame.mlblogs.com/the-oldest-trick-in-the-book-75680352dc9a.

Five special trains: "Two Thousand Local Fans off for Detroit Contests," CTr, October 11, 1907, 2; Snyder, *Cubs Journal*, 142.

Sportswriters before the game: Bruce A. Rubenstein, *Chicago in the World Series: The Cubs and White Sox in Championship Play* (Jefferson, NC: McFarland, 2006), 28.

Chicago's most rabid: "Streets Blocked by Cheering Fans," CTr, October 13, 1907, 2.

At 2:30 p.m.: "Huge Crowd in Dearborn Street," photo, CTr, October 13, 1907, 2.

The object of: See Rob Edelman, "Electric Scoreboards, Bulletin Boards, and Mimic Diamonds," *Base Ball* 3, no. 2 (Fall 2009), 76–87; Robert Pohl, "Lost Capitol Hill: Meader's Electric Scoreboard," *The Hill Is Home*, http://thehillishome.com/2012 /01/lost-capitol-hill-meaders-electric-scoreboard; "Playograph at Old News and Observer Building," *Photojournalism NC*, http://www.sometimesimakethings .com/inls740/items/show/259; Dale Alison, "Painting of Playograph at the Burlington Gazette in Iowa," *Twitpic*, http://twitpic.com/sy27i; Irving E. Sanborn,

"How the World's Series Is Flashed to Fifty Million People," BM, November 1920, 572.

This was, in a way: "First Pirates Radio Game," MLB.com, http://m.mlb.com/video /topic/6479266/v4940549/kdka-radio-station-broadcast-the-first-baseball -game.

Everybody saw: "Thousands See Game," WES, October 9, 1907, 6.

Back in Chicago: "Streets Blocked by Cheering Fans, CTr, October 13, 1907, 2.

Passersby and pedestrians: Ibid.

The electric bulletin boards: "Feminine Fans Favor Cubs," CTr, October 11, 1907, 2.

Newspapers, which had: CDN, September 12, 1887, cited in Lawrence Pernot, *Before the Ivy: The Cubs' Golden Age in Pre-Wrigley Chicago* (Urbana: University of Illinois Press, 2015), 177.

Skeptical baseball owners: Quoted in A. R. Gratty, "Pittsburgh Points," SL, June 30, 1906, 10.

Western Union: David Hochfelder, *The Telegraph in America, 1832–1920* (Baltimore: Johns Hopkins University Press, 2012), 109. Hochfelder also gave a presentation titled "How the Telegraph Made Baseball the National Pastime," at the SABR Symposium on Nineteenth-Century Baseball, November 10, 2014, New York, NY.

The company leased: Hochfelder, *Telegraph in America*, 110.

Baseball and the telegraph: Western Union Telegraph Company Records, boxes 450–452, Archives Center, National Museum of American History, Smithsonian Institution.

As a result: "The Baseball Season," NYT, September 15, 1907, 8.

In November 1907: H. R. Hempel and Jos. Techen, "Cubs on Parade. Monographic. Notated Music," Library of Congress, https://www.loc.gov/item/ihas .200033368; H. R. Hempel, composer, "Cubs on Parade: March Two-Step" (Chicago: Tomaz F. Deuther Music Publisher, 1907), Lester S. Levy Collection of Sheet Music, Johns Hopkins University Sheridan Libraries Special Collections, https://jscholarship.library.jhu.edu/handle/1774.2/12066.

It wasn't the first: "Baseball Sheet Music," Library of Congress, https://www.loc.gov /collections/baseball-sheet-music/about-this-collection.

U.S. piano manufacturers: U.S. Piano Sales History, 1900–2007, *Bluebook of Pianos*, 1912, http://www.bluebookofpianos.com/uspiano.htm; "Selling for a Song," *From the Stacks* (blog), New York Historical Society, December 16, 2011, http:// blog.nyhistory.org/selling-for-a-song.

Print publishers: Patricia Bradley, *Making American Culture: A Social History, 1900– 1920* (New York: Palgrave Macmillan, 2009), 32.

One of the leading: "Music Publishing," *Encyclopedia of Chicago*, Chicago Historical Society, http://www.encyclopedia.chicagohistory.org/pages/862.html; "Will Rossiter," IMSLP Petrucci Music Library, http://imslp.org/wiki/Will_Rossiter; Gil Bogen, *Tinker, Evers, and Chance: A Triple Biography* (Jefferson, NC: McFarland, 2003), 86; "Rare 1908 Sheet Music Featuring Johnny Evers and Joe Tinker, Composers," lot 268, *Collectible Classics*, http://www.auctionscc.com/?showpage =/archive/20140626/chicago-cubs/268/&i=264&p=3.

Deuther house issued: The White Sox March, Notated Music Collection, Library of Congress, https://www.loc.gov/item/ihas.200033457.

it was only: Andy Strasberg, Bob Thompson, and Tim Wiles, *Baseball's Greatest Hit: The Story of Take Me Out to the Ball Game* (New York: Hal Leonard, 2008), 111.

Think about it: Dave Headman, professor of music theory at Eastman School of Music, University of Rochester, quoted in ibid., 86.

By October 1908: Strasberg, Thompson, and Wiles, *Baseball's Greatest Hit*, 110–114.

Ironically, the song: Ibid., 26–27.

since been featured: Ibid., 22.

celebratory banquets and toasts: Sanborn, CTr; Hutchinson, CI-O.

No one wanted: Banquet Program, BHOF.

You start out young: Sanborn, CTr.

CHAPTER EIGHT

In July 1866: Henry Chadwick, *The Base Ball Book of Reference: The Revised Rules of the Game for 1867* (New York: J. C. Haney & Co., 1867; Bedford, MA: Applewood Books, n.d.).

Earlier versions of baseball: Peter Morris, *A Game of Inches: The Game on the Field* (Chicago: Ivan R. Dee, 2006), 40.

It should be distinctly: Chadwick, *Base Ball Book*, 18–19.

In Section 22: Ibid., 21–22.

If two hands: Ibid., 24 (emphasis in original).

Father Henry Chadwick: "Henry Chadwick Is Dead," CTr, April 21, 1908, 13.

The afternoon festivities: Charles Dryden, "Home Opening of Cubs Is at Hand," April 22, 1908, 12; "Cubs Take Game by Clever Work," April 23, 1908, CTr; Richard G. Tobin, "World's Champions Start the Season at Home Today," CI-O, April 22, 1908; Frank B. Hutchison Jr., "Cubs Raise League Pennant and Defeat Cincinnati, 7–3," CI-O, April 23, 1908. 4.

Murphy had commissioned: George R. Matthews, *When the Cubs Won It All: The 1908 Championship Season* (Jefferson, NC: McFarland, 2009), 30; "Death Notices," CTr, January 11, 1971.

More evidence of Murphy's: Dryden accounts, CTr, April 22–23.

One newspaper photograph: "Incidents Which Marked Opening Game," photos, CTr, April 23, 1908, 8.

Ladies' Day policy: "Ladies' Day for West Side," CTr, March 28, 1908, 10.

That Spring in New York: Christina Stewart, "The Merry Widow Hat (1907–1914)," *Pretty Clever Films*, April 9, 2014, http://prettycleverfilms.com/costume-design -film-fashion/merry-widow-hat-1907-1914/#.WBTQReErJQY; "The Rise and Neatness of the 'Merry Widow' Hat," CI-O, May 3, 1908, 30.

A girl with a white dress: CDJ, August 28, 1908, cited in G. H. Fleming, *The Unforget-*

table Season (Lincoln: University of Nebraska Press, 1981), 191; Sid Mercer, NYG, April 23, 1908, in Fleming, *Unforgettable Season*, 50.

At a ball game: Jack Ryder, CE, May 18, 1908, 3.

The Cubs found out: 1908 Chicago Cubs Game Log, RS, http://www.retrosheet.org /boxesetc/1908/VCHN01908.htm.

Chance had the same: 1908 Chicago Cubs, BRef, http://www.baseball-reference.com /teams/CHC/1908.shtml.

His name was Henry: David Jones, "Heinie Zimmerman," SABR, http://sabr.org /bioproj/person/e73e465a.

As Sheckard and Zimmerman: "Chaotic Cubs," SL, August 1, 1908, 7; undated New York *Globe* item, cited in Peter Golenbock, *Wrigleyville: A Magical History Tour of the Chicago Cubs* (New York: St. Martin's Press, 1996), 128; CTr, I. E. Sanborn, "Notes of the Cubs," June 2, 1908, 8.

A great pennant race: See Cait Murphy, *Crazy '08: How a Cast of Cranks, Rogues, Boneheads, and Magnates Created the Greatest Year in Baseball History* (New York: HarperCollins, 2007).

All there is to Evers: Hugh S. Fullerton, in *The Book of Baseball: The National Game from the Earliest Days to the Present Season*, ed. William Patten and J. Walker McSpadden (New York: P. F. Collier, 1911), 29.

He was an obsessive student: Johnny Evers and Hugh S. Fullerton, *Touching Second: The Science of Baseball* (Chicago: Reilly & Britton, 1910), 218; Bradley Woodrum, "What Is Sabermetrics," FanGraphs, February 9, 2012, http://www.fangraphs .com/blogs/what-is-sabermetrics-and-which-teams-use-it/.

Evers's bedside companions: Undated news clipping, Johnny Evers file, BHOF; Evers and Fullerton, *Touching Second*, 259.

The Cubs were at home: "Inquisitive Fans," CTr, July 19, 1908, sec. 3, 2.

One run shall be: Francis R. Richter, ed., *The Reach Official American League Base Ball Guide for 1908* (Philadelphia: A. J. Reach Co., 1908), 574, http://library.si.edu /digital-library/book/reachofficialame19081phil (Smithsonian Libraries).

Chicago had long passed: J. Weintraub, "Why They Call It the Second City," Chicago *Reader*, July 29, 1993, http://www.chicagoreader.com/chicago/why-they-call-it -the-second-city/Content?oid=882456.

Young as she is: Norman Dent, "The Romance of Chicago," *Munsey's Magazine*, April 1907, 5.

If you didn't honestly: Joe Tinker, as told to Francis J. Powers, *My Greatest Day in Baseball*, ed. John Carmichael (Lincoln: University of Nebraska Press, 1996), 135.

New York was educated: Cindy Thompson, "Who's to Blame?" *The Inside Game: Official Newsletter of SABR's Deadball Era Committee*, SABR, September 23, 2008, 5.

Muggsy wasn't around: I. E. Sanborn, "Cubs Win Weird Game Which Goes 10 Innings," CTr, May 26, 1908, 8.

The Cubs have never been: "McGraw Predicts Downfall of the 'Cubs,'" SL, June 6, 1908, 1.

On Tuesday, August 11: "Cubs Play in Form Back of Pfiester and Blank Giants," CI-O, August 12, 1908, 4; I. E. Sanborn, "Rift in Clouds for the Champs," CTr, August 12, 1908.

Muggsy shouted at: Sanborn, "Rift in Clouds for the Champs."

The victory left: 1908 Standings, August 11, 1908, RS, http://www.retrosheet.org /boxesetc/1908/08111908.htm; 1908 Chicago Cubs Game Log, RS, http://www .retrosheet.org/boxesetc/1908/VCHN01908.htm.

Umpiring that afternoon: David W. Anderson, "Hank O'Day," SABR, http://sabr.org /bioproj/person/94b47a84.

corker of a pitching matchup: "Pirates Beat the Cubs in Ten Long Innings," PGT, September 5, 1908, 7.

Clarke trotted home: Ibid.; I. E. Sanborn, "Cubs Will File Protest," CTr, September 5, 1908, 10.

Cut it out, Johnny: News clipping, Evers file, BHOF.

Murphy got wind: PPo, September 6, 1908, in Fleming, Unforgettable Season, 209.

After calling O'Day: Lowell Reidenbaugh, Baseball's 25 Greatest Pennant Races (St. Louis: Sporting News, 1987), 22.

Even O'Day half admitted: Bill Corum, "Sports," New York Journal American, c. 1947, Evers File, BHOF; Joe Tinker, "Tinker's Story of Fateful Game," SN, April 9, 1947, 16.

By mid-September: Events of Thursday, September 18, 1908, RS, http://www .retrosheet.org/boxesetc/1908/09171908.htm

Tinker broke the silence: Johnny Evers, CRH, October 14, 1910, 10, cited in Thom Karmik, "Chance versus Mack," Baseball History Daily, October 31, 2016, https:// baseballhistorydaily.com/2016/10/31/chance-versus-mack.

The "Napoleon of baseball": NYEW and CDN, September 23, 1908, in Fleming, Unforgettable Season, 241–243.

Tonight the walls: Charles Dryden, "Cubs Twice Defeat Giants and Crowd Them for First Place," CTr, September 23, 1908.

The Cubs had inched: "The Baseball Fight Waxes Warmer," NYTr, September 23, 1908, 5; "Benefit Tribune Hospital Fund," advertisement, CTr, September 23, 1908, 8.

Chance had used up: 1908 Chicago Cubs Game Log, RS, http://www.retrosheet .org/boxesetc/1908/VCHN01908.htm; Christy Mathewson, BRef, http://www .baseball-reference.com/players/m/mathech01.shtml.

Four innings breezed by: NYH, September 24, 1908, in Fleming, Unforgettable Season, 246.

Tinker did not like: "Game Ends in a Row," WP, September 24, 1908, 8.

Born in Watertown: Trey Strecker, "Fred Merkle," in Deadball Stars of the National League, ed. Tom Simon (Dulles, VA: Brassey's, 2004), 64.

Then came the bone-headed: Charles Dryden, "Game Ends in Tie, May Go to Cubs," CTr, September 24, 1908, 12.

The ball fell somewhere: John Evers, letter to the editor, Time, May 12, 1929.

Kroh "solved the problem": Johnny Evers, *My Greatest Day in Baseball*; BE, April 14, 1943.

But Emslie, who was: Strecker, *Deadball Stars*, 64.

Those within reach: NYH, September 24 1908, in Fleming, *Unforgettable Season*, 245.

He had to run: "The Craftiest of the Cubs," NYH, January 22, 1911, 7.

Suspended games: "Rule 7.02(a), Suspended, Postponed, and Tie Games," *Official Baseball Rules, 2016 Edition* (New York: Office of the Commissioner of Baseball, 2016), 86, http://mlb.mlb.com/mlb/downloads/y2016/official_baseball _rules.pdf.

The first newspaper accounts: "Bridwell's Hit Wins for Giants; Riot Follows at Polo Grounds," NYEW, September 23, 1908, 1; Charles Dryden, "Game Ends in Tie," CTr, September 24, 1908, 12; "Chicago and Giants Mix Up in the Ninth," PP, September 24, 1908, 1. "The Verge of a Riot," AR, September 24, 1908, 1.

McGraw's flacks: NYG, Fleming, *Unforgettable Season*, 206; Sam Crane, NYEJ, September 24, 1908, in Fleming, *Unforgettable Season*, 250. NYH, September 24, 1908, in Fleming, ibid., 247.

Chicagoans, as one might: I. E. Sanborn, "Bluff of Giants Typical," CTr, September 27, 1908, sec. 3, 2.

The wheels of justice: NYTr, September 26, 1908, in Fleming, *Unforgettable Season*, 256; Bill Lamberty, "Harry C. Pulliam," SABR, https://sabr.org/bioproj/person /6e05b19c.

The umpires gave him: Photo of Henry O'Day memo to Pulliam, September 23, 1908, BHOF, in *Waiting4Cubs* (blog), September 23, 2016, http://www.chicagonow.com /waiting-4-cubs/files/2016/09/ODay-note002.jpg.

O'Day rarely discussed: "The Merkle Play," SL, October 1914, 19.

A hush fell upon: Cited in Jim Rasenberger, *America, 1908: The Dawn of Flight, the Race to the Pole, the Invention of the Model T and the Making of a Modern Nation* (New York: Scribner, 2006); "The Baseball Muddle," NYT, September 25, 1908, 6.

On Sunday, as Chicago: Hugh Fullerton, NYA, October 5, 1908, in Fleming, *Unforgettable Season*, 286.

Some 3,500 Giants fans: NYW, October 5, 1908, in Fleming, *Unforgettable Season*, 287.

A year later, Dovey: Dovey to Macbeth, quoted in Frank Deford, *The Old Ball Game: How John McGraw, Christy Mathewson, and the New York Giants Created Modern Baseball* (New York: Grove Press, 2005), 149.

As the train sped: "Fifteen Cubs Leave to Meet Giants in Battle for Pennant," CI-O, October 8, 1908, 4; "Cubs Rush on to Victory in the Battle of Today," CTr, October 8, 1908, 12.

If the Cubs don't win: "Fears Effects of 'Fanitis,'" CTr, October 8, 1908, 12; NYH, cited in *Waiting4Cubs* (blog), October 2016, http://www.chicagonow.com/waiting-4 -cubs/2016/10/250000-fans-surround-ballpark-shut-down-city-108-years-since -1908-part-xxxi.

Fans were lining up: "The Cubs Win the Pennant," NYT, October 9, 1908, 1; "Cubs Take Pennant by Beating Giants, 4–2, in Great Game," CI-O, October 9, 1908, 1.

And still they came: "The Cubs Win the Pennant," NYT, October 9, 1908, 1; NYET, in
Fleming, *Unforgettable Season*, 303; "Tries to See Game; Is Killed," CTr, October 9, 1908, 2; W. J. Lampton, NYT, in Fleming, *Unforgettable Season*, 312.

The Cubs players arrived: "Sidelights on the Combat," CTr, October 9, 1908, 3.

The fighting blood: Ibid.

What happened next: "Game Viewed by New York Eyes," NYS, October 8, in CTr,
October 9, 1908, 3.

But Chance had been: "Frank Chance Is Still Sore at Giants," SFChr, December 18,
1908, 11.

Mordecai Brown and: Mordecai Brown, *My Greatest Day in Baseball*, 176.

The game itself: CI-O, October 9, 1908, 1.

Unconscious of everything: Sanborn, CTr, October 9, 1908; Mordecai Brown, BRef,
www.baseball-reference.com/players/b/brownmo01.shtml.

After the relative calm: Brown, *My Greatest Day in Baseball*.

No doubt Mathewson: Christy Mathewson, *Pitching in a Pinch: or Baseball from the
Inside* (New York: Grosset and Dunlap, 1912), 1 (Project Gutenberg).

Then he had me: Arthur R. Ahrens, "Tinker vs. Matty: A Study in Rivalry," SABR,
http://research.sabr.org/journals/tinker-vs-matty; Mathewson, *Pitching in a
Pinch*.

No better illustration: Christy Mathewson, "Outguessing the Batter," PM, May
1911, 568.

The Cubs had "stolen": "New York Papers Praise Cubs," CTr, October 9, 1908, 2.

Chicago is proud: "The Great American Game," CTr, October 9, 1908, 10.

Even more significant: "New York Papers Praise Cubs," CTr; Tad, NYEJ, October 9,
1908, in Fleming, *Unforgettable Season*, 316.

Hearst's *New York American*: NYA, October 9, 1908, in Fleming, *Unforgettable Season*, 320.

CHAPTER NINE

They called him: "William Howard Taft," *Biography*, August 8, 2016, A&E Television
network, http://www.biography.com/people/william-howard-taft-9501184#us
-presidency.

An animated crowd: I. E. Sanborn, "Rooter Taft Sees Cubs Take Fall," CTr, September 17, 1909, 11; "Taft as Fan Sees Cubs Lose," CI-O, September 17, 1909, 3;
Edward B. Moss, "The 'Fan' and His Ways," *Harper's Weekly*, June 11, 1910, 13.

Once play was under way: Sanborn, CTr.

The Giants were up: Fred B. Hutchinson Jr., "Chance's Cubs Make It Three Straight
from Poor Giants," CI-O, June 9, 1907, 27; John Thorn, "The Lucky Seventh,"
Our Game (blog), MLB, October 3, 2016, https://ourgame.mlblogs.com/the
-lucky-seventh-9f16359c12f9#.mmod4djoz; Michael Aubrecht, "Seventh-Inning
Stretch," Baseball Almanac, http://www.baseball-almanac.com/articles/7th
_inning_stretch.shtml.

Unfortunately for the Cubs: Honus Wagner, BRef, http://www.baseball-reference
.com/players/w/wagneho01.shtml; 1909 Chicago Cubs Game Log, RS, http://
www.retrosheet.org/boxesetc/1909/VCHN01909.htm.

Business and professional men: Moss, "The 'Fan' and His Ways."

On July 5, 1909: "The Last Rites," SL, July 24, 1909, 13; "Baseball Praised at Selee Funeral," BH, July 12, 1909, 14.

A contingent of Elks brothers: "The Last Rites," SL.

Less than two weeks after: "Harry C. Pulliam Attempts Suicide," NYT, July 29, 1909, 1.

Although he had been: Bill Lamberty, "Harry Pulliam," Deadball Stars of the National
League (Washington, DC: Brassley's, 2004), 22–23 (SABR).

the dandified bachelor: Angelo J. Louisa and Floyd Sullivan, "The Strange Death of
Harry C. Pulliam," in Mysteries from Baseball's Past: Investigations of Nine Un-
settled Questions, ed. Angelo J. Louisa and David Cicotello (Jefferson, NC: McFarland, 2010), 44–75; "Pulliam Threatened Suicide," CTr, July 29, 1909, 1.

Perhaps it took a woman: Margaret Brown, "The Transformers of Baseball," PM,
May 1909, 523–526. At the time of this writing, the author seems to have shed
any memories of the previous year's bottle incident in Brooklyn or the October
riot that erupted at the Polo Grounds after the Merkle affair—the last gasps,
perhaps, of the baseball cranks.

Coming to McGraw's aid: Nie, "The Giant and the Giants," BM, November 1908, 7.

Joe Tinker and Johnny Evers: Joseph Wallace, ed., The Baseball Anthology: 125 Years of
Stories, Poems, Articles, Photographs, Drawings, Interviews, Cartoons, and Other
Memorabilia (New York: Henry N. Abrams, 2004), 108; Johnny Evers and Hugh S.
Fullerton, Touching Second: The Science of Baseball (Chicago: Reilly & Britton,
1910) (Internet Archive); Frank Chance, The Bride and the Pennant (Chicago:
Laird and Lee, 1910); Noel Schraufnagel, The Baseball Novel: A History and Anno-
tated Bibliography of Adult Fiction (Jefferson, NC: McFarland, 2008), 4.

Tinker took his rising: "Tinker Trapped by Stage's Lure," CTr, October 30, 1908, 10;
J. G. Davis, "Mr. Tinker Gets a Curtain Call," CTr, November 11, 1908, 10.

Strand wanted something: George S. Adelman, "Joe Tinker's Greatest Play in One Act:
A Prize Story," CTr, August 29, 1953, 1; "Tinker and Sherman Double," Variety,
January 1, 1910, 3, https://archive.org/details/variety17-1910-01.

Adelman came up with: Adelman, CTr.

"The Great Catch": Chicago Journal scrapbook item, Tom Tinker, cited in Gil Bogen,
Tinker, Evers, and Chance (Jefferson, NC: McFarland, 2003), 102; "Local The-
atrical Notes," Chicago Suburbanite Economist, February 19, 1909, 8; Percy M.
Cushing, "Playing for What There Is in It," Ou, September 1909.

During the season: John Snyder, Cubs Journal: Year by Year and Day by Day with the
Chicago Cubs since 1876 (Cincinnati: Clerisy Press, 2008), 161.

The Cubs had scored: R. W. Lardner, "Cubs in Batfest Whip Reds 9 to 6," CTr, October 2, 1910, sec. 3, 1; "Evers Breaks His Right Leg," CTr, October 2, 1910, sec. 3, p. 1.

The Cubs did win: Snyder, Cubs Journal, 162–63.

The first clue: Tom Simon, "Harry Steinfeldt," SABR, http://sabr.org/bioproj/person /c1dc8fd5; Gil Bogen and David Anderson, "Johnny Kling," SABR, http://sabr.org /bioproj/person/b647d3a9.

These setbacks: F. C. Lane, "The Gamest Player in Baseball," BM, September 1913, 53.

They can't make me: Hugh Fullerton, CCT, January 13, 1912, cited in Bogen, Tinker, Evers and Chance, 121–123.

The next spring: Fullerton, CCT.

In Chance's absence: Ibid.

Chance had promised: Ibid.

Murphy asked Johnny Evers: Bogen, Tinker, Evers and Chance, 127. Cincinnati Reds Team History and Encyclopedia, BRef, http://www.baseball-reference.com /teams/CIN.

EPILOGUE

On the ground floor: "Hall of Famers," BHOF, http://baseballhall.org/hall-of-famers.

Tinker, Evers, and Chance: "Frank Chance Named to the Hall of Fame," NYT, April 24, 1946, 34; Baseball Hall of Fame Explorer, http://baseballhall.org/explorer.

The developing historical: David Shiner, "Johnny Evers," in The Miracle Braves of 1914: Boston's Original Worst-to-First World Series Champions, ed. Bill Nowlin (SABR Digital Library, 2014); Bill James, The Politics of Glory: How Baseball's Hall of Fame Really Works (New York: Macmillan, 1994), 214.

He barely missed: Ed Orman, "Sport Think," FBR, February 4, 1945, 18.

One reason is purely: Team History and Encyclopedia pages, BRef; Hall of Fame Inductees, BRef, http://www.baseball-reference.com/awards/hof.shtml; Bill James, The New Bill James Historical Baseball Abstract (New York: Free Press, 2001), 81.

On December 30, 1907: Zev Chafets, Cooperstown Confidential: Heroes, Rogues, and the Inside Story of the Baseball Hall of Fame (New York: Bloomsbury, 2009), 27; John Thorn, "The Letters of Abner Graves," Our Game (blog), February 20, 2013, https://ourgame.mlblogs.com/the-letters-of-abner-graves-8fc6a4694419# .uaodaeia6.

Though Spalding had given up: Bill McMahon, "Albert Spalding," SABR, www.sabr .org/bioproj/person/b99355e0.

Both Spalding and Mills: Chafetz, Cooperstown Confidential, 24; John Thorn, Baseball in the Garden of Eden: The Secret History of the Early Game (New York: Simon and Schuster, 2011), 273.

Spalding and Mills: John E. Bodnar, Remaking America: Public Memory, Commemoration, and Patriotism in the Twentieth Century (Princeton, NJ: Princeton University Press, 1992), 13.

Official culture relies: Ibid.

The one great reason: Charles Horton Cooley, Social Process (New York: Charles Scribner's Sons, 1918), 113.

And yet, until 2016: Craig Keolanui, "Top 25 Longest Active Championship Droughts in Sports," *The Sportster*, December 16, 2014, http://www.thesportster.com /entertainment/top-25-longest-active-championship-droughts-in-sports.

APPENDIX

Ban Johnson: Eugene C. Murdock, *Ban Johnson, Czar of Baseball* (Westport, CT: Greenwood Press, 1982).

John McGraw: Don Jensen "John McGraw," SABR Biography project, http://sabr.org /bioproj/person/fef5035f.

C. W. Murphy: "C. W. Murphy, Cubs' Owner in 1906–1914, Dies," CTr, October 17, 1931, sec. 2, 1; Lenny Jacobsen, "Charles Murphy," *SABR Biography Project*, https://sabr.org/bioproj/person/e707728f.

In 1999: Richard Johnson, "Proposed Induction Speech for Frank Gibson Selee," June 29, 1999, Frank Selee file, BHOF Library; telephone conversation with Richard Johnson, April 15, 2015.

After May Selee: "Baseball Praised at Selee Funeral," BH, July 12, 1909; "The Last Rites," SL, July 24, 1909; "Land Office Notes," EPH, March 3, 1911, 9; Probate file papers, No. 82175, Commonwealth of Massachusetts Probate Court.

Harry Steinfeldt: Tom Simon, "Harry Steinfeldt," SABR Biography Project, http://sabr .org/bioproj/person/c1dc8fd5.

Frank Chance: Gil Bogen, *Tinker, Evers and Chance: A Triple Biography* (Jefferson, NC: McFarland, 2003); Grantland Rice, "Sportlight," Pentwater (MI) *News*, February 2, 1945, 3, Google News.

Joe Tinker: Bogen, *Tinker, Evers and Chance*, 232.

Johnny Evers: David Shiner, "Johnny Evers," *SABR Bio Project*, http://sabr.org/bioproj /person/efe76f7c; Rich Mueller, "1908 Merkle Ball Consigned to Auction," *Sports Collectors Daily*, January 6, 2010, http://www.sportscollectorsdaily .com/1908-merkle-ball-consigned-to-auction/; Tim Layden, "Tinker to Evers to Chance . . . to Me," *Sports Illustrated Vault*, December 3, 2012, http://www .sportscollectorsdaily.com/1908-merkle-ball-consigned-to-auction/; personal conversation with John T. Evers, February 13, 2015; Bogen, *Tinker, Evers and Chance*.

"I'm glad we made it": Undated news clipping, "Evers Thinks of Others as He Rejoices over Baseball's Hall of Fame Selection," cited in Bogen, *Tinker, Evers and Chance*, 222.

INDEX

Page numbers in italics refer to illustrations.